Praise for *Manipu*

T0276368

This is a brilliant book, written by one c. _____ _____ _____ _____ nal-
ists and coming at a time of profound crisis in twenty-first century journalism.
More than ever, Canadians are being exposed to disinformation. Countless
journalists are being laid off in newsrooms across the country. And this is
happening as thousands of public relations specialists are being hired to fill
the void. The self-serving "business model" of modern corporate journalism is
proving to be bankrupt. With impressive detail, Cecil Rosner helps us understand the scale of the challenge, and in the book's most stirring chapter —
titled "Fighting Back" — he outlines how we can grab back control.
— Tony Burman, former head, CBC News and Al Jazeera English

Manipulating the Message holds up the mirror to the faces of media who
have been knowingly, and at times unknowingly, complicit to the harms
caused by colonial biases against Indigenous people. This book serves as a
hard hitting reality check for journalists who wish to implement the Truth
and Reconciliation Commission Calls to Action for themselves as storytell-
ers. It will make you think, it will make you ask questions, and even answer
some of those questions. A must read.
— Sheila North, former Grand Chief,
Manitoba Keewatinowi Okimakanak

In *Manipulating the Message*, Cecil Rosner exposes the dirty little secret of the
mainstream media: that much of what passes for "news" in the United States
and Canada is planted by powerful interests pushing their own selfish agendas.
As Rosner demonstrates, "fake news" is not just insidious bot farms pushing
outlandish lies on social media; it is, perhaps more insidiously, the manipulation of the public's intellectual diet through respected news outlets by publicists
seeking to orchestrate politics and policy on their own behalf. Rosner explains
how this is secretly and systematically accomplished by spinmeisters on behalf of politicians, corporations, bureaucrats, scientists, pollsters, think tanks,
law enforcement, military and intelligence agencies, and online "influencers."
Enriched by his own first-person stories as a veteran journalist, Rosner explains
in clear and accessible prose that what's at stake is nothing less than truth itself.
— Mark Feldstein, professor, Richard Eaton chair of
broadcast journalism, University of Maryland

Manipulating the Message is a strong cup of coffee that journalists and their audiences need. Veteran investigative journalist Cecil Rosner confronts a long history of snake oil salesmen, political flaks, mercenary researchers, junket organizers, and internet influencers whose one goal is to shape the news we read. From seemingly mundane press releases to deceptively planted sources, *Manipulating the Message* uncovers sticky traps that await the careless and the hurried. Rosner turns a journalist's eye on his own profession, shedding light on failures and triumphs alike in information wars being waged behind the headlines. He also takes an unflinching look at how racial bias and gendered glass ceilings entangle newsroom decision-making. A must-read for anyone who follows the news. For journalists, a valuable wayfinder for getting out from under the influence.

— PATRICIA W. ELLIOTT, professor, investigative and community journalism, First Nations University of Canada

Cecil Rosner is one of the most incisive, ethical, knowledgeable, and engaged journalists I have ever met. He is a true humanitarian with nearly half a century of experience as a highly respected Canadian journalist. His wonderful book, *Manipulating the Message*, is a great gift to students, journalists, and all others who seek to advance their critical thinking about the truth and reliability of information in the news.

— LAWRENCE HILL, award-winning author

During his forty-five-year-long career as one of Canada's top journalists, Cecil Rosner has been lied to a lot — by politicians, police, and corporate giants. More importantly, he's caught and exposed them. His book *Manipulating the Message* is an important but also unexpectedly entertaining unveiling of the behind-the-scenes battle of the powerful and a free press in a war for the truth. It's the type of book everyone should care about.

— KARYN PUGLIESE, assistant professor, Toronto Metropolitan University, and editor in chief, Canadaland

Manipulating
the Message

MANIPULATING
the Message

How Powerful Forces Shape the News

CECIL ROSNER

DUNDURN
PRESS

Publisher: Kwame Scott Fraser | Acquiring editor: Kathryn Lane | Editor: Dominic Farrell
Cover designer: Laura Boyle
Cover image: Texture: istock.com/paseven; hand: istock.com/rudall30

Library and Archives Canada Cataloguing in Publication

Title: Manipulating the message : how powerful forces shape the news / Cecil Rosner.
Names: Rosner, Cecil, 1952- author.
Description: Includes bibliographical references and index.
Identifiers: Canadiana (print) 20230495281 | Canadiana (ebook) 20230495303 | ISBN 9781459751255 (softcover) | ISBN 9781459751279 (EPUB) | ISBN 9781459751262 (PDF)
Subjects: LCSH: Fake news. | LCSH: Journalism.
Classification: LCC PN4784.F27 R67 2023 | DDC 070.4/3—dc23

We acknowledge the support of the Canada Council for the Arts and the Ontario Arts Council for our publishing program. We also acknowledge the financial support of the Government of Ontario, through the Ontario Book Publishing Tax Credit and Ontario Creates, and the Government of Canada.

Dundurn Press
1382 Queen Street East
Toronto, Ontario, Canada M4L 1C9
dundurn.com, @dundurnpress 🐦 f 📷

For Alice, Georgia, Benjamin, Simone, and Mina.
The future.

Contents

Preface

"SAVE IT FOR THE BOOK."

That's the good-natured advice editors dispense whenever journalists complain about all the anecdotes and insights that don't make it into their daily reports. Colleagues and friends encouraged me to collect that material and write about my experiences. But there was a problem. I didn't want to catalogue a series of random events that might be meaningful to me and no one else. The more I reflected on it, the more I realized there was a common theme running through many of the stories I had reported on or supervised over the years: I was being manipulated. I was being used as a conveyor belt for other people's messages and agendas. If I were going to write about anything, it would be that.

In a career that has spanned more than forty-five years, I have worked as a reporter, a researcher, an editor, a television producer, a senior producer, an executive producer, a bureau chief, a managing editor, and a news director. Throughout this time, I have spoken to thousands of people and helped to create thousands of stories. The aim has always been to search out facts and report the truth. In investigative journalism, which I have focused on for much of my career, a further objective is to hold powerful interests to account. But those powerful interests have an interest in not being held accountable. Governments, corporations, large institutions, think tanks — they all have an agenda and all attempt to use the media to push their agenda. They have always succeeded to some degree.

Today, two trends are converging to ensure their continued success. The first is the growth of the public relations and communications industry. I don't believe there ever was a golden age of journalism, but there was a time when I could call the home of a cabinet minister for a comment. A time when a front-line worker in a company or government would answer a direct media question. Those times are over. Every major government department and every private and public institution now tightly controls its information flow. Communications specialists and spokespeople have proliferated. The global public relations industry today is worth more than US$100 billion.[1]

Alongside this growth is the decline in the number of people practising journalism. Newspapers, radio stations, and television networks have seen their business models upended in the digital age. The loss of advertising revenue to online giants like Google and Facebook has devastated conventional Canadian media. Dozens of newspapers and broadcast outlets have closed, while the survivors have cut back extensively on newsgathering. A handful of companies control most of Canada's media landscape, and they don't hesitate to lay off staff and cut costs to preserve their bottom line. While some digital start-ups have entered the news space, the erosion of journalistic capacity has continued. There are fewer than 12,000 reporters in Canada compared to nearly 160,000 employees in the advertising, public relations, and communications industry.[2] For every journalist trying to figure out the truth, thirteen people are influencing that journalist's perception of reality. It isn't a fair fight.

The mad scramble to fill space in newspapers, newscasts, and websites while employing fewer and fewer journalists has inevitably led to reduced fact-checking. The case of American Dan Nainan is especially revealing. He was a go-to source for major publications in the United States on everything from millennial voting patterns to social media tactics. But Daily Beast reporter Ben Collins noticed something strange in the news stories that used Nainan as a source. Nainan claimed to be thirty-six in a *Wall Street Journal* story but thirty-one in a *New York Times* piece the same year. Collins did some simple legwork and confirmed that Nainan was actually fifty-five years old.[3] It turned out Nainan was a comedian and wannabe millennial who spun any tale that sounded credible. But publications like the *New York*

Times, Forbes, Cosmopolitan, and AP published their reports of Nainan's fanciful stories and purported millennial status without checking.

"Journalism without checking is like a human body without an immune system," according to former *Guardian* reporter Nick Davies.[4] While writing a book about the newspaper industry, Davies commissioned Cardiff University researchers to analyze more than two thousand U.K. stories from five major dailies. They found that only 12 percent of the stories originated from ideas the reporters generated on their own. Much of what passes for news is created in the boardrooms of public relations professionals and communication strategists, then packaged and offered up to a willing media. Moreover, the researchers found that most of the factual claims in the news stories were completely uncorroborated.[5]

Journalism historian Mitchell Stephens says many modern practitioners use the concepts of balance and fairness as a measure of their objectivity, and this is often an excuse for not bothering to verify a fact. As long as an opinion is attributed and a competing view is included, they are content. "They attempt to chain opinions to their opposites, hoping, it seems, that these beasts will annihilate each other, leaving what passes in journalistic thinking for the truth."[6] This practice means that the media take much of what comes their way at face value, not bothering to verify or corroborate statements and claims. But when the initial messaging comes from people who are paid to obscure bad news, highlight the positive, and polish the image of their institution, the journalists are not being fair and balanced — they are being manipulated.

By now, many of my journalistic colleagues will be bristling, upset at the notion that they are doing someone else's bidding. And to be fair, there are outstanding journalists across many organizations who fight these pressures every day. It is possible to search for the truth and resist being captured by government or corporate interests. But the number of journalists with the time and resources to do so properly is small. For every bold journalist fighting to hold powerful institutions to account, there are many more who amplify their messages. Some simply repeat the assertions of press releases without doing any checking, often blaming a lack of time as the reason. Others forgo original digging and build their careers by translating into

3

stories the dependable stream of juicy scoops they get from the government, police, or the military — a stream that continues as long as the coverage remains positive. Still others, especially in the world of entertainment and travel reporting, seem content to tag along on all-expense-paid junkets as a reward for their compliance in spreading information that has been massaged to serve the interests of the sponsor. And there are media organizations that deliberately sidestep controversial stories for fear of retaliation or upsetting the status quo. The vast majority of journalists are honest, ethical, and hard-working, but the reality of their working environment and the forces trying to exert influence over them often overwhelms even the best of intentions.

Does that mean journalists are producing *fake news*? Journalists are justified in hating the term. It can be, and has been, brandished as a weapon by anyone who doesn't like how they are being portrayed in the media, whether that depiction is factual or not. But the reality is, with so much manipulation of messaging taking place, false narratives *can* be disseminated by the media. Powerful forces want their spin to be placed on everything, and their efforts to recruit the media to do their bidding are unending. The war in Ukraine has shown how forces on all sides of the conflict try to shape the narrative to serve their own military and political ends. The Covid-19 pandemic similarly demonstrated how one person's truth could be twisted into another person's propaganda. Social media platforms have given the purveyors of disinformation a powerful new way of deliberately distorting facts and spreading their messages. The public depends on journalists to serve up well-researched, unbiased, independent, and truthful accounts of all major issues, and not to be co-opted or misled by any spin doctors or special interests. It's an objective most journalists aspire to, but it's not always fulfilled.

What follows will be an analysis of all the ways journalists can be manipulated. In doing so, I'll recount some stories from my career that touch on this issue. I will also highlight some methods to combat this trend. Because if journalists are being misled, then the general public is being misled as well. It doesn't have to be this way.

Chapter 1

How Manipulation Works

WHEN A JOURNALIST COMES CALLING, COULD YOU MANIPU-late them into writing exactly what you want? That's what university profes-sor Stuart Ewen wondered when a reporter asked to visit his class at Hunter College in Manhattan. The reporter was researching a story about unique university courses across the city and was intrigued by Ewen's seminar, "The CULT(ure) of Publicity." Ewen agreed to the visit, on one condition. He told the reporter he wasn't going to inform his students she would be there. The class was big enough, and she could easily pass for a student, so he suggested she just try to blend in with the others to avoid disruption.

"An unusual opportunity had dropped into my lap," the professor of media studies wrote. Here was a chance to put some principles of PR into practice. Despite what he told the reporter, he let his students know she was coming. They brainstormed ways of stage-managing the class to ensure the journalist came away with a compelling story. One of the ideas was to stage a phony show of enthusiasm by having students frequently raise their hands, a stunt that would be accompanied by a secret signal indicating whether the professor should call on them to speak. They also all agreed to dress in black to project a bohemian image.

When the reporter's story came out, Ewen judged the experiment a suc-cess. She bought into the choreographed event, writing about urban hipsters who engaged in a coffee-house exchange of ideas. The reporter had no idea she had been the actual subject in class that day. She was thoroughly duped. "Gratified and amused, we congratulated ourselves on having mastered the Way of Spin," Ewen wrote.[1]

It may seem like an extreme example, but it also reveals an essential truth about daily journalism. Most reporting only skims the surface when covering a story, never delving beneath the shallow veneer to reveal what is really going on. It generally takes people's statements at face value. That's a risky practice when the objective is to find the truth. Politicians, corporations, and even ordinary people have a variety of motivations when speaking to the media. Sometimes they deliberately try to present a false or misleading narrative to suit their aims. In some cases, people who genuinely intend to provide honest information to the media don't, because they have faulty memories.

Journalist and media trainer Steve Buttry found that out when he tracked down members of a girls' basketball team that had won a state championship twenty-five years earlier. He interviewed many of the original players, who all shared vivid and heartfelt accounts of how the final game unfolded. Several described how one of their shortest teammates flustered the other team's star player by provoking several fouls. But Buttry discovered that story was greatly exaggerated when he watched a video of the game. "All those first-hand accounts I had heard were inaccurate, fuelled by the emotions (joy or anguish) [stirred up by] an important moment in their lives, and shaped by a legend that grew from the game." He learned a simple lesson about journalistic verification from the experience: "Don't trust even honest witnesses. Seek documentation."[2]

The problem for many reporters working on the front lines of daily journalism is that there is often little or no time for serious verification. At the beginning of my journalism career, I had a maximum of two deadlines on any given day, one for each edition of the newspaper. Across all media, deadlines have become more pressing and punishing every year. Editors expect news copy to flow rapidly and to be repurposed for multiple platforms. Many reporters are required to take their own pictures, edit their own radio and television packages, and create an endless flow of content for the ever-expanding range of social media sites. Every minute devoted to checking a fact or understanding some background context is a minute lost to the unforgiving objective of hitting the next deadline. Newsrooms with investigative reporters allow more time for fact-checking, but many daily reporters have no such luxury. Unless a reporter filing a breaking news story believes an interview or statement looks overtly suspicious or sketchy, it will often go directly into their report without any corroboration. But as Buttry found, even the most seemingly helpful statements from friendly sources can turn out to be false.

I often tell my students that the task of the journalist and the historian are broadly similar. Both seek to figure out what has happened in the past, whether the event occurred twenty years ago or five minutes before. Both seek clues in documents, records, physical evidence, and statements from eyewitnesses or knowledgeable sources. The Greek historian Thucydides, one of the founders of modern historiography, warned against the dangers of being misled when interviewing witnesses to an event. In writing about the history of the Peloponnesian War, he provided some insight into his method: "With regard to my factual reporting of the events of the war I have made it a principle not to write down the first story that came my way … different eyewitnesses give different accounts of the same events, speaking out of partiality for one side or the other or else from imperfect memories."[3]

Buttry discovered that when sources have imperfect memories, journalists can be led astray. For the same reason, many historians approach oral histories with a healthy degree of skepticism. But it's the warning by Thucydides that witnesses often speak with a partiality for one side or the other that points to the more dangerous pitfall for those seeking to relate the truth. The fact of the matter is that over the last century an entire industry has arisen to enhance the ability of those with a partiality for one side or another to disseminate their messages.

PR: PROFESSIONAL PERSUADERS

I will be elaborating on the history and practice of public relations extensively in this book, but at the outset, it's important to stress just how pervasive its influence on journalism is. It's not as if journalists are oblivious to the intentions and tactics of publicists. They routinely deride them as spinmeisters and propagandists. Reporters who take jobs with a PR agency are often called out for "going over to the dark side." Yet public relations and journalism often coexist in college and university faculties, and friendships exist across both camps. Despite their wariness, journalists nonetheless have grown to rely on PR practitioners for access and scraps of information. When time is short and a deadline looms, a PR person can suddenly be seen as more of a help than a hindrance.

Every few years, a new research report shows how easy it is for PR agencies to plant their messages in the media. As far back as 1980, the *Columbia Journalism Review* did a test. It focused on one issue of the *Wall Street Journal*, contacting all the companies referenced in more than one hundred stories spread throughout the paper. It asked each company if there had been an underlying news release that gave rise to the story. The findings were illustrative of a phenomenon that has persisted and gotten worse over time. Three of every four news stories were based solely on the original press releases. In nearly half the examples, the releases were incorporated either verbatim or with minor changes into the news stories. The magazine said the most troublesome finding was that 29 percent of the stories carried the byline "By a *Wall Street Journal* Reporter." Asked to comment on the results, the *Journal*'s executive editor said, "Ninety percent of daily coverage is started by a company making an announcement for the record. We're relaying this information to our readers."[4]

The Center for Media and Democracy in the United States conducted a similar experiment in 2006, documenting how seventy-seven television stations used thirty-six video news releases (VNRs) — PR statements from companies such as General Motors, Pfizer, and Intel that provide video that an ad agency had produced. In each case, these stations actively disguised the fact that they were airing supplied content, making it appear to be their own reporting. In almost all cases, stations failed to balance the clients' messages with independently gathered footage or basic journalistic research. More than one-third of the time, stations aired the prepackaged VNR in its entirety.[5]

Online news sites have an insatiable appetite for video as well. A decade after this analysis of video news release uptake, a U.S. communications firm found that 76 percent of producers and journalists working for the digital side of U.S. media outlets reported using outside video. "Significantly, 74% of them will post or link to the entire video," said the president of the firm that produced the report. "This provides an unequalled opportunity for direct communication of the entire PR or marketing message to consumers."[6]

Many PR practitioners are former journalists and are acutely aware of the pressures their former colleagues face. They design their messages accordingly. In a paper entitled "How to get journalists to open, click, and love your email pitch," one PR professional describes an ideal scenario: "Journalists are time-poor and sometimes, even if they're interested in your pitch, you won't hear anything back. Just as likely is that a story falls through 10 minutes before deadline, a space in the magazine crops up, and yours could be in line to fill it. If your email has everything they could possibly need to bash the story out in a rush, you're in luck." The unstated corollary is that in such situations there will be no critical questions posed or alternative viewpoints sought.[7]

The situation is no different in Canada. One executive I spoke to said his agency deliberately writes press releases in the form of typical news stories, making it easy for outlets to cut and paste. "The number of news releases I've written for clients that get printed word for word — I mean word for word — is ridiculous," according to the executive. "And they'll put the name of the newspaper on it. They don't even bother calling for an interview." While the problem is particularly pronounced at the local media level, where resources are thin, it is also increasingly evident in more prominent media outlets. Few PR agents are willing to discuss this issue publicly, but there is widespread acknowledgement of the practice, and someone's conscience occasionally compels them to speak out.

One such case arose in 2000 when former PR agent Eric Sparling wrote a piece for the *Toronto Star* entitled "Confessions of a Former Spin Doctor." He said he did the job for a year but became disgusted and quit. "I owe you an apology," the piece began. "I've lied, cheated and swindled. Yeah, I know, you've done that, too, but I did it professionally." His boss billed US$120 per hour for his services, even though he had just one year's experience under his belt. But Sparling said business was booming. He described his methodology in straightforward terms:

We write stories that our clients want us to write, send them to newspapers, magazines or TV stations, and journalists write their stories using our information. Often they'll get another perspective on the topic by contacting another source — that's called "balanced reporting." Sometimes they won't — we really liked it when that happened. It meant that our message wasn't diluted by an opposing opinion. If we were lucky, the journalists we contacted would be lazy or overworked. That way they wouldn't have the time or energy to come up with their own story angles, quotes or research, and they'd just use ours — our quotes, our research, our priorities.

When a press release triggers a news story, the PR industry refers to it as "earned media" — or a mention that did not come with a price tag. This kind of publicity is often more valuable than a paid advertisement, since it carries the authority and credibility of the news organization. Sparling noted that the news stories sometimes reused the exact headline from the press release. On other occasions, the entire statement was reproduced, with the only change being the addition of a reporter's name at the top.[8]

Sparling's candid confessions did not sit well with the PR industry. Sarah Jones, president of the Canadian Public Relations Society, didn't hold back: "Sparling's inaccurate and ill-chosen allegations of dishonest behaviour on the part of all public relations practitioners is [*sic*], at best, ignorant, and at worst, an offence to all of us who work in the public interest," she wrote in a letter to the editor. She pointed out that the society's 1,800 members adhere to a code of professional standards that requires them to practise the highest standards of honesty, accuracy, integrity, and truth and to never knowingly disseminate false or misleading information.[9]

Despite the attempt to portray Sparling as an outlier, a survey conducted a month earlier in the United States provided comprehensive data about the extent of lying and deception in the industry. The trade publication *PRWeek* asked 1,700 PR executives about ethics in their practice. One-quarter of respondents admitted to having lied on the job, and 39 percent reported that they had exaggerated the truth. Nearly two-thirds of those surveyed said they had felt compromised in their work because of a lack of candour on the part of their clients. The editor of *PRWeek* at the time, Adam Leyland, told the *New York Times* that some practitioners reacted to the survey by saying "they just wanted to resign from the industry and lie on a beach, examining their navel." But Leyland preferred to put a bright spin on the results: "If 25 percent told a lie, that means 75 percent did not."[10]

OFFICIAL SOURCES

To understand how manipulation works, it's important to know the value news organizations have historically placed on official sources. Early in my journalism career, I came across a solid political scoop. I discovered that Otto Lang, a former Liberal transportation minister in the government of Pierre Trudeau, was about to be appointed executive vice-president of Pioneer Grain Company in Winnipeg. Lang had also been the minister responsible for the Canadian Wheat Board and regularly dealt with policies concerning the production and export of grain. Within two months of losing his seat and cabinet portfolios, Lang was already in discussion with one of the country's major grain companies about a senior post. He was set to take the position the following month.

I checked into conflict-of-interest guidelines and discovered that three years earlier, Lang's Liberal government had stipulated a one-year "cooling-off period" before senior government officials could accept positions in private life relating to their former jobs. Pierre Trudeau himself had reiterated the guideline and made it clear that cabinet ministers who re-entered private life had to wait a year before giving counsel on commercial matters relating to their former department. Though this wasn't a law, I concluded that Lang was clearly in violation of his government's own guidelines. Just to make sure, I contacted an official with Pioneer Grain to find out the nature of Lang's future duties. He confirmed that they would include discussions with Ottawa. "I guess it's pretty inevitable that an executive of the company does get involved in negotiations with the government at various points in time," he told me.

I took all this information to my editors at the *Winnipeg Free Press* and told them I could file the story right away. Not so fast, they said. "You can't just accuse a cabinet minister of a conflict. You need to get someone to say that." In other words, a reliable source was required. My protests were fruitless, so I got on the phone with the objective of finding someone who would confirm something I already knew. I reached Stanley Knowles, the venerable NDP member of Parliament, and explained the situation. He hadn't heard about Lang's new job prospect. I reminded him about the guidelines. Knowles quickly and eloquently denounced his political opponent. "Knowles accuses Lang of conflict of interest," read the front-page headline in the next day's newspaper. "I certainly think this is a conflict of interest and it's one that ought not to be tolerated," he said in the story. "As a minister who was involved in things related to the grain trade he knows the score from the inside."[11]

The story is an example of the crucial role sources play in news production. Journalism academics have studied this issue for years and generally agree that the paradigms of objectivity and balance lead journalists to place primary importance on quoting what sources say, irrespective of whether the statements are corroborated or truthful. Here is how Matt Carlson, a U.S. journalism professor, explained it: "As a philosophy of news and a strategy guiding its production, objectivity precludes reporters not only from injecting opinion, but instils even a distrust of direct journalistic observation as acceptable proof of what happened. Instead, journalists construct stories through attribution, linking information directly to sources often through quotations. For objective journalism, sources do more than provide information; epistemologically, they serve as an essential form of evidence."[12] What's more, the reliance on sources "frees the journalist from the extra labour of adjudicating claims" and "indemnifies journalists from charges of bias while allowing for the inclusion of critical statements." Journalists quickly learn to identify the likely suspects who will provide reliable comments on a variety of story topics. Such sources are usually traditional and predictable ones, often representing official government and societal institutions.

Many media organizations have an established system of "beats" through which reporters gather news. These typically revolve around police, courts, city halls, legislatures, and, in some news organizations, fields like health care and business. Officialdom often predominates in these beats since they are available and considered authoritative. Historically, they have reinforced the dominance of white, male, Western, and heterosexual perspectives and prejudices. The reality is that continuous repetition of commentary from official sources usually serves to reinforce the status quo.

After studying decades of literature on the issue, Carlson summed the situation up this way: "These studies share an interest in how news routines sustain the status of elites by turning to them as sources and, therefore, presenting their interpretations as both factual and appropriate. This dynamic permits a restricted group of authorized sources to define the world while other voices are excluded."[13]

Former *Guardian* reporter Nick Davies also said reporters prefer to rely on official sources, partly because they are well organized, with press officers and websites and background material. But there's another reason — news organizations know they are less likely to be attacked if they go with official sources. "The official line is safe."[14] In the world of shrinking newsrooms, it's easier and more economical to run cheap stories that can be gathered quickly and without controversy. Independent investigation is costly and inherently risky. Davies also argues many news organizations prefer to sidestep the "electric fence" of libel suits, condemnation by lobby groups and official-dom, and other headaches by avoiding stories that stray too far from official narratives. Any journalist who has tried to file a report quoting sources with alternative viewpoints that veer away from conventional wisdom will recognize this principle.

Nothing illustrates this better than the inability of investigative reporter Seymour Hersh to find a mainstream publisher for his exposé of the My Lai massacre in Vietnam. Hersh was the first to reveal the mass slaughter of an entire village by U.S. soldiers during the Vietnam War, but official sources were denying it, and many news organizations deferred to them rather than looking at the facts Hersh had uncovered. He eventually distributed the story through a small, independent agency, and it became one of the most explosive stories about the conflict in Vietnam, one that affected the trajectory of the war.

The tendency to defer to official sources is nowhere more evident than in times of war. Stories that question or try to discount official government narratives are painted as disloyal, subversive, or even aiding the enemy. The few journalists who stand up to this kind of pressure know they can often pay a heavy price for doing so. This was evident during the run-up to the 2003 invasion of Iraq, when most mainstream U.S. journalists bought into the administration's assertion that Saddam Hussein had weapons of mass destruction. Those who suggested otherwise were often mocked or accused of treachery.

A more recent example is the idea that the only response possible to Russia's invasion of Ukraine is to send more and more arms to support Ukraine until it wins on the battlefield. Voices calling for negotiations and compromise are often left out of media commentaries and debate. U.S. journalist Jeremy Scahill says this amounts to dangerous groupthink. He is one of several writers in alternative and independent media challenging the conventions of official sources. "As the world was thrust into Cold War 2.0, the Western commentariat dusted off the wide brush wielded for decades by the cold warriors of old, labeling critics of the policy of massive weapons transfers to Ukraine or unquestioning support for the government of President Volodymyr Zelenskyy as Russian stooges or puppets," he wrote in The Intercept.[15]

Recognizing the devotion journalists pay to sources, corporations and public interest groups began to develop strategies to exploit this industry practice. This first became evident around the turn of the twentieth century in the United States, when investigative journalism in popular magazines exposed the excesses of rapidly expanding U.S. corporate interests. Ida Tarbell, for instance, wrote a nineteen-part series on Standard Oil Company showing how it was rigging prices and exploiting its monopoly status. Upton Sinclair revealed intolerable conditions in the country's largest meat-packing plants. Others, like Lincoln Steffens, aimed at municipal corruption and how politicians enriched themselves by serving corporate interests. Mass circulation magazines like *Colliers*, *McClure's*, and *Cosmopolitan* were only too eager to run these stories once they discovered the enormous public interest in learning about the excesses of modern capitalism.[16]

Responding to this negative publicity became critical for corporate America. One of the first people to take up the challenge was Ivy Lee, a journalist who made the early leap into a field that would eventually be known as public relations. Born in 1877, he worked as a reporter for New York newspapers before co-founding one of the first public relations firms in the United States in 1904. He is also widely credited with inventing the press release. One of his clients, the Pennsylvania Railroad, was in crisis after a crash in Atlantic City in 1906 that killed more than fifty people. He convinced the company it would be better to pre-empt newspaper questions and coverage by issuing a prompt statement that set out its version of events. The statement said the railroad's general manager was on the scene, hard at work supervising the cleanup and investigation. "The Pennsylvania Railroad Company is leaving nothing undone to get at the cause of the accident," the press release said. In what would become an all-too-common event in the future, the *New York Times* printed the statement in its pages verbatim.[17]

Lee proclaimed his public relations work to be fact-based. "Accuracy, Authenticity and Interest" was his motto, but the interests of his clients were always at the forefront. In 1914 he represented multi-millionaire businessman John D. Rockefeller when the Ludlow Massacre occurred. The United Mine Workers were striking for better pay and working conditions at the Rockefeller-controlled Colorado Fuel and Iron Company in Ludlow. The bitter dispute erupted into violence when company and state guards attacked a tent colony of miners and their families, killing about two dozen men, women, and children. Soon after the incident, Lee began issuing a series of bulletins every few days called "Facts Concerning the Strike in Colorado for Industrial Freedom." PR historian Stuart Ewen says they were "filled with calculated inaccuracies" meant to deflect blame from the company for what some historians have called the deadliest labour dispute in U.S. history. Lee tried to pin the violence on "well-paid agitators sent out by the union," even calling eighty-two-year-old U.S. labour leader Mother Jones "a prostitute and the keeper of a house of prostitution." Called on to testify the following year at a commission on industrial relations, he said the messages were the truth. "By the truth, Mr. Chairman, I mean the truth about the operators' case."[18]

If Lee was one of the founders of American public relations, Edward Bernays was its earliest theoretician. He drew on various writers to formulate his views, including his uncle, Sigmund Freud. Unlike some of his contemporaries, he didn't shy away from the term *propaganda*, even using that word as the title of his 1928 text on the topic. Bernays began crystallizing his theories about public relations after the First World War, when American authorities used propaganda to demonize the enemy and mobilize public support for the war effort. He worked directly for the wartime Committee on Public Information, even contributing to the Paris Peace Conference in 1919. "It was, of course, the astounding success of propaganda during the war that opened the eyes of the intelligent few in all departments of life to the possibilities of regimenting the public mind," he said.[19]

Bernays had an elitist view of who should lead society and how those leaders should go about ensuring there was a consensus for their agenda. Here is how he laid out his vision in the opening passage of his 1928 book, *Propaganda*:

> The conscious and intelligent manipulation of the organized habits and opinions of the masses is an important element in democratic society. Those who manipulate this unseen mechanism of society constitute an invisible government which is the true ruling power of our country.
>
> We are governed, our minds are molded, our tastes formed, our ideas suggested, largely by men we have never heard of. This is a logical result of the way in which our democratic society is organized. Vast numbers of human beings must coöperate in this manner if they are to live together as a smoothly functioning society.
>
> Our invisible governors are, in many cases, unaware of the identity of their fellow members in the inner cabinet.
>
> They govern us by their qualities of natural leadership, their ability to supply needed ideas and by their key position in the social structure. Whatever attitude one chooses to take toward this condition, it remains a fact that in almost every act of our daily lives, whether in the sphere of politics or business, in our social conduct or our ethical thinking, we are dominated by the relatively small number

of persons — a trifling fraction of our hundred and twenty million — who understand the mental processes and social patterns of the masses. It is they who pull the wires which control the public mind, who harness old social forces and contrive new ways to bind and guide the world.[20]

Bernays went on to a lengthy and successful career, representing corporate clients such as American Tobacco, Procter & Gamble, General Electric, CBS, and Dodge Motors. He also advised several presidents and foreign countries on how to influence people. One of his earliest and most celebrated PR coups involved recruiting a group of women to light up cigarettes and smoke in public at the New York Easter Parade in 1929. This was a practice frowned upon at the time, but Bernays got the women to proclaim the cigarettes as "torches of freedom" and a symbol of their liberation. The *New York Times* reported the event this way: "A group of young women, who said they were smashing a tradition and not favoring any particular brand, strolled along the lane between the tiered skyscrapers and puffed cigarettes."[21] The *Times* had been duped. The women *were* favouring a particular brand, Lucky Strikes, which had bought and paid for the entire affair.[22]

If the theory Bernays expounded is correct, that the unseen manipulators of society are the people who successfully influence the masses, it calls into question the role played by media to help audiences understand the world around them. Having spent my career in media, I am disturbed by the idea that powerful and often hidden forces have shaped the stories I have helped produce. But there is no denying the pervasive ability of government, corporations, and powerful institutions to push their messages. Bernays, picking up on a phrase used by journalist Walter Lippmann in his 1922 book, *Public Opinion*, spoke about this process as the manufacturing of consent. Edward Herman and Noam Chomsky famously elaborated on the concept and concluded: "Leaders of the media claim that their news choices rest on unbiased professional and objective criteria, and that they have support for this contention in the intellectual community. If, however, the powerful are able to fix the premises of discourse, to decide what the general populace is allowed to see, hear, and think about, and to 'manage' public opinion by regular propaganda campaigns, the standard view of how the system works is at serious odds with reality."[23]

Canadian public relations history may not be as colourful as its counterpart south of the border, but it's hard to know for sure, since few people have documented it. The Canadian government was arguably the first PR practitioner when it began a campaign at the end of the nineteenth century to attract new immigrants to the country. Hundreds of thousands of pamphlets extolling the virtues of the Canadian West were printed and distributed. The government raided the ranks of newspapers to hire agents who would help spread the word. It also arranged free tours of the West for British and American reporters and editors. In return, the journalists pledged to write about their impressions. Thus was born the Canadian press junket, a tool that has been used ever since to cajole the media into telling a favourable story.[24]

Big Canadian companies started getting into the act early in the twentieth century. Worried about potential government nationalization of telephones, Bell Telephone hired a *Toronto Star* reporter in 1905 and began ramping up its PR efforts among employees and the public. By 1914, it had a formal publicity department. Canadian Pacific Railway did the same, hiring a freelance writer in London and appointing him head of "European propaganda." One of his first assignments was to invite twelve leading British newspaper editors to tour Canada as guests of the president of CPR. Eventually, he came to Canada and worked full-time as the railway's publicity agent. Much of the railway's early PR focus was on encouraging people to tour Canada on the train.[25] Despite these early activities, PR growth in Canada was not as rapid as it was in the United States. In 1983 one researcher looked at one hundred Canadian corporations and found that just 22 percent had established a public relations department before 1950. Another 35 percent set them up between 1951 and 1970, and 43 percent only did so between 1971 and 1980.[26]

Today, public relations is one of the biggest growth industries. In 1991 Statistics Canada counted 23,780 people in public relations and communications.[27] Thirty years later there were 158,595. Lined up against this army of message-massagers were 11,360 reporters, down over those same thirty years from 13,470 despite the significant increase in Canada's population.[28] The gap will only continue to widen. Enrolment in journalism schools is rapidly declining, while the government projects more than 70,000 new public relations jobs will be available in the next decade.[29]

Modern PR agencies offer everything from corporate communications, reputation management, brand building, media training, and crisis management to government relations and lobbying. Corporate executives are coached on how to interact with media, especially on how to deflect difficult questions while bridging to pre-arranged message tracks. It is virtually impossible for any journalist to reach a decision-maker in a government department or organization without first passing through a phalanx of PR intermediaries who all have a role to play in shaping the ultimate message.

While many PR practitioners subscribe to a professional credo of telling the truth, the overriding concern must always be the interests of the client who pays the bills. Some PR firms will openly offer to use any means necessary to support their clients' aims. The Archimedes Group, for instance, was an Israeli company that proclaimed it would "use every tool and take every advantage available in order to change reality according to our client's wishes." That included setting up fake fact-checking pages, bogus accounts, and front organizations. Facebook finally banned the group, removing hundreds of its accounts for what it called "coordinated inauthentic behavior" in Nigeria, Senegal, Togo, Angola, Niger, Tunisia, Latin America, and Southeast Asia.[30]

Then there is Ryan Holiday, former marketing director for American Apparel, who has made a career out of duping the media. In the introduction to his 2012 book, *Trust Me, I'm Lying*, he gets right to the point: "If you were being kind, you'd say my job is in marketing and public relations, or online strategy and advertising. But that's a polite veneer to hide the harsh truth. I am, to put it bluntly, a media manipulator — I'm paid to deceive. My job is to lie to the media so they can lie to you. I cheat, bribe, and connive for bestselling authors and billion-dollar brands and abuse my understanding of the Internet to do it."[31]

Holiday proceeds to document all the ways he misled media outlets, big and small, to print stories that benefitted his clients. Just as a lark, he also would give interviews to media outlets on topics he knew nothing about, all to show how easy it is to mislead journalists. As a summary of his strategy, he offers the following:

> Usually, it is a simple hustle. Someone pays me, I manufacture a story for them, and we trade it up the chain — from a tiny blog to Gawker to a website of a local news network to the *Huffington Post* to the major newspapers to cable news and back again, until the unreal becomes real. Sometimes I start by planting a story. Sometimes I put out a press release or ask a friend to break a story on their blog. Sometimes I "leak" a document. Sometimes I fabricate a document and leak that. Really, it can be anything, from vandalizing a Wikipedia page to producing an expensive viral video. However the play starts, the end is the same: The economics of the Internet are exploited to change public perception — and sell product.[32]

It's hard to know how much of Holiday's account is true and how much is just puffery, designed to increase book sales. But he pinpoints some of the key ways online outlets can be recruited to amplify messages. Internet sites favour stories and headlines that will attract clicks, so Holiday packages messages in a way that exploits the need.

In later chapters, I will show how this same process manipulates media into covering sketchy stories based on studies, polls, think tank reports, so-called trends that circulate on social media, and other manufactured messages. A different kind of manipulation is directed at radio and TV talk shows, which need people to interview. Every time a guest is booked, there is an opportunity for unfiltered messages to emerge. The more slick and glib the talking head, the more often they will be booked. Hosts need to be thoroughly prepared and knowledgeable to be able to challenge exaggerated or misleading claims, especially when an interview is live. Every time there is a provincial or federal budget, for instance, the finance minister does the rounds of talk shows. Occasionally, they are held to account by a journalist who has had the time to research the subject in detail, but more frequently, they are just provided with a platform to reiterate pre-arranged talking points.

On a more sophisticated level, there are PR agencies such as the Washington-based Berman Group, which create entities that sound as if they are independent but, in reality, are backed by corporate interests. Its founder, Rick Berman, has been dubbed "Dr. Evil" by his critics, but he doesn't apologize for the tactics. The *Washington Post* says he has created a constellation of non-profit groups to carry corporate messages. Among them is the food industry–funded Center for Consumer Freedom, which opposes "food police" and "animal-rights misanthropes," and the Center for Union Facts to fight unions. One group has opposed Mothers Against Drunk Driving over its efforts to lower the legal alcohol limit, while another raises doubts about the dangers of mercury in fish.[33]

In 1991 Berman created the Employment Policies Institute (EPI), which has waged a relentless battle against raising the minimum wage in the United States. The institute said its 2013 media outreach resulted in more than 830 radio, TV, print, and online stories in that year alone.[34] Many of those stories did not mention that Berman also represented the restaurant industry or bother inquiring into who else supported the EPI. In essence, the media were misled into calling the EPI a "think tank" or an independent non-profit organization that had no connection to the very people who would profit from the policies it advocated. "The campaign illustrates how groups — conservative and liberal — are again working in opaque ways to shape hot-button political debates, like the one surrounding minimum wage, through organizations with benign-sounding names that can mask the intentions of their deep-pocketed patrons," said the *New York Times*.[35] As for Berman, he thinks it's all fair game in the world of public relations. As he told Morley Safer of CBS News, "The businesses themselves don't find it convenient to take on causes that might seem politically incorrect, and I'm not afraid to do that."[36]

None of this would surprise the founding practitioners and theoreticians of public relations. Bernays himself pioneered the technique of forming front groups to feed information to the media and public in deceptive ways. When he worked for electronics manufacturer Philco, it was the Radio

Institute of the Audible Arts. When he worked for Mack Trucks, it was the Trucking Information Service, the Trucking Service Bureau, and Better Living Through Increased Highway Transportation.[37]

In the 1940s and 1950s, Bernays represented the United Fruit Company. He helped the company wage a relentless war against Guatemala's socialist leader, Jacobo Arbenz, who was threatening the company's stranglehold on the banana industry. It eventually resulted in a 1954 CIA-backed coup that removed Arbenz and preserved Guatemala's banana-republic status. One of the strategies Bernays devised in his advocacy for United Fruit was creating a front group called the Middle America Information Bureau. It published brochures and sent out press releases under the guise of an independent-sounding institute. But Bernays was pulling the strings at the behest of the company. In a memo to bureau staff, he directed that "all material released by this office must be approved by responsible executives of the United Fruit Company," and that "in view of the widely known constructive activities of the company, mention of United Fruit will enhance the value of the story to editor and readers and should be made."[38]

While the early PR gurus proclaimed devotion to accuracy and truthfulness, their strategies caught the attention of fascist propagandists in Germany. The Nazi regime studied the works of Bernays carefully, though he maintains he resisted offers to work with them. But the temptation was too great for another pioneer in the field. Soon after Hitler came to power, he arranged a meeting with Ivy Lee. Lee became a paid adviser to the regime, receiving a lump-sum payment and an annual retainer from the German Dye Trust, which worked closely with Hitler. Lee also had dealings with propaganda minister Joseph Goebbels, drafting Nazi policy statements in his U.S. PR office and sending them back to Germany. Goebbels organized a series of press conferences in 1934, likely on Lee's advice.[39] Lee spoke openly about this to a U.S. Congressional committee in 1934. During one of the sessions, a congressman asked him, "Your business is what?" Lee replied, "It is very difficult to describe, Mr. Chairman. Some people call it publicity agent. Some people call it counsel in public relations. But that would give you a general idea of it."[40] As for Goebbels, the impact of U.S. public relations theory was long-lasting. He once confided to a colleague, "After the war, I'll go to America. There at least they will appreciate a propaganda genius, and pay him accordingly!"[41]

In 1985, an unlikely guest made an appearance on the David Letterman show. Here's how Letterman introduced him: "My next guest is a truly fascinating gentleman. He happens to be 93 years old and he is the father of public relations. In the course of his 70-year career, some of his clients have been presidents Wilson, Hoover, Coolidge and Eisenhower, Thomas Edison, Eleanor Roosevelt and Enrico Caruso. It's a pleasure to welcome Dr. Edward Bernays."

Bernays got an enthusiastic reception from the studio audience as he slowly made his way to the interview chair. Letterman began the conversation this way: "I mentioned to the people how old you were. I hope you don't mind me telling them that. And what kind of a doctor are you?"

Public relations coaches tell their students that when they are being interviewed by the media and encounter a question with a double-barrelled thought, it's a golden opportunity to answer just one and ignore the other if they choose to. Bernays gave a lengthy answer, explaining that he might be ninety-three chronologically, but was sixty-one physiologically, forty-five mentally, and even younger socially and emotionally. He ignored Letterman's question about his academic credentials.

After some back and forth banter, Letterman was still intent on discovering the specifics of Bernays's doctorate, so he asked again. Confronted with just a single question, and for the second time, Bernays was forced to confess that his only degrees were honorary ones. But he offered the following explanation: "What we're dealing with really is the concept that people will believe me more if you call me doctor."[42] Bernays died ten years later, at 103, continuing to spin stories to the very end.

Chapter 2

Corporate Propaganda

WE ALL HAVE A PRETTY GOOD IDEA OF WHAT PROPAGANDA is. Wilfrid Laurier University professor Stanley Cunningham developed a helpful checklist. Among other things, he included:

- self-serving reports;
- lies, distortions, fabrications, and exaggerations;
- disinformation;
- selective disclosures and censorship;
- spin — slanted or loaded words;
- mass persuasion, manipulation, and brainwashing; and
- public relations, advertising, rumours, and gossip.[1]

In the boardrooms of corporations around the world, it is safe to say that all these techniques, and more, have been used at one time or another. No, not every company in the world engages in mendacious propaganda — some uphold ethical standards. But the number of times large companies all over the world have been caught in outrageous whoppers is staggering. Capitalism, after all, dictates that the central aim of any for-profit company is to make money. In the end, all other aims, objectives, and missions are secondary. If a profit is not being turned, if shareholder value is not being enhanced, the very basis for the company's existence will be called into question. And companies have historically relied on the media to help them in their central mission. Here are some of the reasons a company might use propaganda techniques to mislead the media, and, in turn, the public:

1. *To sell a product.* This is the most basic imperative for any company, and it's in aid of this that lies, distortions, fabrications, and exaggerations run rampant. Of course, there are companies that carefully stick to truth and facts in describing their products, but the temptation to spin is great. Through reflexive coverage of press releases and press conferences, and uncritical reporting of corporate announcements, media have often been facilitators of deception and disinformation. We'll look at some examples in this chapter.

2. *To cover up reasons for consumers not to buy the product.* Even when science shows that particular products are ineffective, harmful, or even deadly, there will be companies that continue to try to make money by selling them. The Big Tobacco propaganda playbook is particularly instructive to examine, as it was one of the first all-out efforts to deny and cover up a mountain of evidence pointing to the deadly nature of their products. For decades, the campaign was successful in convincing the media to cast doubt on the dangers, which helped industry pressure governments to delay regulations. Some of the same techniques were adopted by companies producing fossil fuels, asbestos, toxic chemicals and minerals, dangerous drugs, and other products.

3. *To discredit or co-opt detractors.* The aim of any company is to recruit the media to amplify their messages, spreading them far and wide in as unfiltered a fashion as possible. This often succeeds spectacularly well, but there are occasions when critics and detractors begin to chip away at the corporate messaging. Attacking the credibility and integrity of detractors has become a key component of modern public relations. Feeding negative information to the media is an important part of this strategy.

4. *To enhance a brand or image.* Brands can communicate a company's vision and mission. But the way companies try to position their brands and images can vary significantly from the reality of their practices and products. More than twenty years ago, oil giant British Petroleum became an early promoter of the term *carbon footprint* when it tried to reposition itself as BP, a company that thought beyond fossil fuels.[2] The idea was to suggest individuals were just as responsible for climate change as industry, perhaps more so. Media quickly adopted the term, and it has become ubiquitous in the discourse around climate change. A focus on individuals helps to deflect attention from the world's oil and gas producers, whose operations and products produce more than 40 percent of global emissions.[3]

Throughout this discussion and in the chapters that follow, I will be referring to *misinformation* and *disinformation*, words that some people use interchangeably. While both involve falsehoods, it's the intention of the purveyors that distinguishes the terms. Your best friend might innocently or ignorantly share false information with you because they have been misinformed. But pushing a message by lying or deliberately omitting crucial context constitutes disinformation.

SELL THE PRODUCT

More than a century ago, renowned U.S. muckraking journalist Samuel Hopkins Adams wrote a series of exposés about patent medicines. These were the medical products of the day that were widely advertised in newspapers and the subject of many media stories. They were tonics and elixirs that promised to cure you of just about everything. Some were infused with heroin and cocaine, while others claimed to have mysterious life-altering wonder oils. Adams was warned when he began his research not to lump all proprietary medicines into one indiscriminate denunciation. But in trying to separate the sheep from the goats, there was a "lamentable lack of qualified candidates for the sheepfold." Here is how his no-holds-barred critique of the well-established industry begins:

Gullible America will spend this year some seventy-five millions of dollars in the purchase of patent medicines. In consideration of this sum it will swallow huge quantities of alcohol, an appalling amount of opiates and narcotics, a wide assortment of varied drugs ranging from powerful and dangerous heart depressants to insidious liver stimulants; and, far in excess of all other ingredients, undiluted fraud. For fraud, exploited by the skilfulest of advertising bunco men, is the basis of the trade.[4]

Adams was just as colourful in his denunciation of the newspapers of the day, calling them accomplices for being either witting or unwitting dupes in the promotion of the miracle cures.

Before you write off the snake-oil medicine excesses as a relic of the early twentieth century, consider some more recent scandals that have all revolved around the insatiable desire of companies to sell their products. A cereal company claimed one of its products could boost the immunity of kids who ate it. A sneakers manufacturer said its shoes were designed to tone muscles and burn off calories. A skin-care company claimed its cream could actually slim your body down. A mouthwash company said its product was just as effective as floss in fighting tooth and gum problems. All of those enthusiastic claims were subsequently withdrawn, sometimes under threat of lawsuits or regulatory actions. Here are some specific examples that affected Canadian consumers:

- Volkswagen actively promoted its clean and green diesel engines, and car columnists faithfully relayed those claims, before the company finally admitted that it had installed "defeat devices" in millions of cars to fake how much pollution was actually being emitted. More than 100,000 Volkswagen and Audi vehicles equipped with the defeat devices had been imported into Canada.[5] The deception lasted years before it was exposed.
- Keurig Canada made misleading claims about the recyclability of its single-use coffee pods. The company agreed

to pay a $3 million penalty after Canada's Competition Bureau found the pods were generally not accepted by municipal recyclers outside of British Columbia and Quebec.

- Facebook paid a $9 million penalty after the Competition Bureau ruled it had made false or misleading claims about the privacy of Canadians' personal information on Facebook and Messenger. The bureau said Facebook gave the impression users could control who could see and access their personal information, but then it didn't limit the sharing of those details with some third-party developers. This came after technology reporters and columnists had provided advice for years about how users could protect their privacy, based in part on representations by Facebook, which the bureau found to be misleading or false.

- Travel website FlightHub of Montreal paid a $5 million penalty after the Competition Bureau found it was charging hidden fees and posting fake customer reviews about its services. Among other things, the bureau said FlightHub gave the impression consumers could reserve seats by selecting specific ones on a seat map, but the company then didn't secure those seats for many customers.[6]

It goes without saying that most examples of corporate lying or propaganda are the ones in which the company actually gets caught. Consider the thousands of occasions when the deception goes undetected.

When Netflix announced the Canadian launch of its streaming service in 2010, the company closed a street in downtown Toronto and invited the media to come and hear its CEO explain how Canadians could now subscribe. What Netflix didn't announce at its press conference was that among the crowd of excited onlookers who just happened to be passing by were paid actors, hired by the company to look enthusiastic and chat up reporters if the opportunity arose.

An information sheet handed out to the operatives instructed them to "play types, for example, mothers, film buffs, tech geeks, couch potatoes, etc. Extras are to behave as members of the public, out and about enjoying their day-to-day life, who happen upon a street event for Netflix and stop by to check it out." The situation was exposed on Twitter, and company representatives apologized, but tried to explain it all away by saying the extras were for a "corporate documentary" and weren't supposed to talk to reporters. That didn't square with the information sheet, though, which explicitly said: "Extras are to look really excited, particularly if asked by media to do any interviews about the prospect of Netflix in Canada."[7]

If the journalists covering the Netflix announcement almost became unwitting dupes, another example showcases a PR strategy of attempting to gain favourable publicity in a more overt way. On the eve of launching its store in Winnipeg in 2012, IKEA held an exclusive event for the media. There was live music, beer and champagne, and gift bags filled with IKEA merchandise for everyone. It was almost certainly the largest media event in the city's history, with about 250 people in attendance. That led one media ethicist to wonder just how many active journalists there were in Winnipeg. In fact, IKEA also invited bloggers and social media practitioners, as well as some people in the world of marketing. When the company announced that everyone would be invited to shop at the store with a 15 percent discount, cheers went through the room.

As managing editor for CBC Manitoba at the time, I sent a reporter to cover the event with instructions not to accept any freebies, and to pose the question of how IKEA could ethically justify offering journalists benefits. IKEA wouldn't answer any questions about the 15 percent discount or how many purchases were made at the media event. "It's really to help, just kind of giving an opening look — showcase our products in a really good way and let people come and enjoy it," said an IKEA spokesperson about the event.[8] Many of the attendees went home with their goodie bags and more merchandise bought with their exclusive discount.

Selling products is serious business for the automotive industry, and one example of a sophisticated technique is worth revisiting in detail for the way in which it played out both with the public and the media. In March of 2000, Toyota invited the media to attend a press conference in Winnipeg. It had decided to use Manitoba and northwestern Ontario as test markets for a new way to price and sell its cars. Knowing that many customers were growing weary of the need to haggle for the best price, the company promised "a nicer way to sell cars." Dealers would get together to establish a "drive-away" price for each car that was below the manufacturer's suggested retail price. All dealerships would agree to sell at that price and could not add any additional fees. In other words, there was no need to haggle. The program was dubbed Access Toyota. The *Winnipeg Free Press* produced a straight-up news story reporting on the new system and quoted several Toyota officials. No independent or critical voices were included in the coverage. It quoted Yoshio Nakatani, president and CEO of Toyota Canada, as saying that if the system worked in Manitoba, it would revolutionize the way cars were sold in North America.[9]

Accompanying the media coverage was an advertising blitz by Toyota. Several pages away from the *Winnipeg Free Press* report of the media event was a full-page ad touting the program. Thirteen more ads, most of them full-page spreads, ran in the newspaper over the next few days. Similar ads appeared in Brandon, Steinbach, and other Manitoba communities. "Over three years, we've taken the whole sales procedure apart and put it back together again," Toyota said. "Access Toyota isn't a marketing scheme, it's a unique overhaul of the way we serve you."[10]

The campaign was clearly a success, and soon Toyota expanded it to Saskatchewan and Alberta. British Columbia and Montreal were next to use the sales system, and plans were in place to roll it out across the country. While all this was going on, it appeared no one in the media was asking, How is this any different from price fixing? The whole idea of healthy competition is for customers to be able to visit different dealerships and bargain for the best price. If all dealers were agreeing on a price in advance, and refusing to budge from that price, did that not frustrate the process? In 2002 the Automobile Protection Association began raising questions about how the system worked. It did some comparisons and concluded that Access Toyota's pricing was higher than in comparable markets that didn't yet use the system.

In 2002 I was the executive producer of an investigative program at the CBC called *Disclosure*, and we decided to look into the sales technique. We sent a team to do some comparison shopping for Toyotas. In order to capture what was actually happening on the showroom floor, we used hidden cameras for the team's visit. In Montreal, a salesperson offered our reporter $386 off the sticker price for a new Camry. He said that was the Access Toyota price and no amount of haggling would result in anything lower. He further announced that the reporter could go to any other dealership in Montreal and would be quoted the same price, which we verified to be true. Toyota's "nicer way to buy a car" amounted to a take-it-or-leave-it price from every dealership in town.

Our reporter then drove to Toronto, where Access Toyota was not yet in operation. At one dealership he was offered the same car, on the same terms, for more than $1,000 below the Montreal price. "You'd better hurry," the sales manager told him, saying that Access Toyota would soon be arriving in Ontario. "There's no discounting whatsoever in Access. Whatever price they tell you, that's it." We visited six other dealers in Toronto, and on average, the price offered for the same vehicle was $500 less than in Montreal. Even when the Montreal dealers were insisting they couldn't negotiate better prices, our reporter showed them the fine print on Toyota's website that claimed "A Toyota dealer is free to set its own retail prices and will not suffer in any way should the dealer choose to sell at a price other than those posted on this website." One of the sales representatives we visited replied, "That's probably there for Toyota Canada to cover itself, you know, legally," while another said, "Listen, this is for Toyota. It's against the law to fix the prices."[11]

Toyota vigorously defended its program and insisted dealers were entitled to sell for less than the Access price, but the Competition Bureau was conducting its own investigation of Toyota, interviewing clients and sending hidden shoppers to locations in several provinces. In a court document, the bureau said a variety of salespeople told it that dealerships would be subjected to fines and possible loss of dealerships if they offered to sell cars for below the Access price or even if they added some incentives.[12] In March of 2003, a month after the *Disclosure* item was broadcast, Toyota and the Competition Bureau agreed to a settlement. There was no formal finding of price-fixing, but the bureau ordered Toyota to revamp its program and make it clear that dealers are entitled to sell for less. A bureau spokesman said the company was intending "to implement a scheme through Access Toyota, including enforcement, that would have included agreements and threats to maintain the price that dealers charge for Toyotas."[13] As part of the settlement, the company agreed to donate $2.3 million to various charities. While the company said it would continue to roll out the revised program across the country, it decided to abandon its revolutionary no-haggle policy about a year later.

The Toyota story illustrates an important theme in the way media cover events. Unless news releases and press conferences are carefully scrutinized, journalists are in danger of becoming unwitting megaphones for misleading messages.

Here's another example from my own experience that reinforces the need for journalists and the public to approach all corporate announcements with caution and healthy skepticism. It concerns a land development deal and an associated investment component, two areas that can be rife with overinflated promises that often leave the media and the public duped.

When it was first announced in 2013, the SkyCity condominium project seemed like a lifesaver for Winnipeg's declining downtown core. The mixed-use retail/office/condo complex would be the tallest freestanding structure between Calgary and Toronto, the developers said. Their proclamations were spread far and wide by all of Winnipeg's media outlets. The plan was to inject $200 million into the city and build a gleaming forty-five-storey tower on a dusty parking lot. Surely this was a good news story that would make every Winnipegger proud. As with the Toyota story, the coverage was largely uncritical. The only people quoted when the announcement was made were developers and representatives of the city. "This city is taking off, and it's because of these kind of projects that we will keep the momentum going," said Winnipeg mayor Sam Katz.[14] CBC did one story looking into the checkered background of the developers, but most media reports celebrated the city's newest skyscraper. Enthusiasm for the project built rapidly. Before too long, developers announced they had sold 50 percent of the 388 planned condo units.

Over the next few years, cracks began to emerge. One of the partners went into creditor protection and dropped out. But the remaining developer wasn't deterred. "Sky's still the limit," boasted a newspaper headline. "The funds are there, the project is healthy, and we still believe in the city."[15] Construction was being financed by syndicated mortgages, investments from ordinary people who were being offered 8 percent returns for buying a small stake in the proposed building. Investors were being told that the government had committed money to the project before those funds were actually in place. Then, in 2017, a CBC investigation showed some investors who had bought bonds were in danger of losing their money when their bonds defaulted. In the meantime, no construction work had even begun on the project.

Three days after the CBC story was released, an item appeared in the Homes section of Winnipeg's leading daily newspaper entitled "Luxury Living Among the Clouds."[16] Accompanied by supplied promotional pictures from the developers, it was a cheery story that promoted the building and invited potential condo buyers to be in touch with the sales office. It even supplied a phone number. There was no mention of any of the reported problems and concerns that had been identified. If the story was a paid advertisement, it wasn't labelled as such. But SkyCity was in trouble. The project eventually collapsed amid regulatory fines and RCMP raids alleging syndicated mortgage fraud. In 2022, after a six-year investigation, the RCMP charged two Ontario men who were behind the SkyCity plan with fraud and secret commissions. All that remains on the site is an empty parking lot. Construction never broke ground. Similar stories unfolded in other cities across the country.

COVER-UP

When an industry is confronted with mounting evidence that its product causes harm, it often tries to cover up the facts and create as much doubt as possible about the truth. Big Tobacco is generally credited with writing the playbook for this strategy. Though smoking was known to be harmful a century ago, the first influential scientific studies began emerging in the early 1950s. When popular media began running with these stories, tobacco sales declined, and the industry turned to public relations giant Hill+Knowlton for help. The Tobacco Industry Research Committee was created, ostensibly to look into evidence about the effects of smoking, but really to suggest to the public there was another side to the "debate." Its first act in 1954 was to run full-page ads in 448 newspapers across 258 cities entitled "A Frank Statement to Cigarette Smokers," promising to fund research to discover the effects of cigarettes on health.

With each peer-reviewed study showing links between smoking and cancer, the industry countered with other studies it had sponsored casting doubt on the evidence. Their mantra for decades was that no conclusive proof existed linking tobacco to cancer. Thirty years later, the Tobacco Institute, a U.S. industry trade organization, was still insisting that "eminent scientists believe that questions relating to smoking and health are unresolved."[17] Industry tactics also included creating front groups of smokers' rights advocates, concealing the addictive qualities of nicotine, and pressuring governments to limit or delay bans on smoking. Many experts believe the lobbying was successful in staving off effective smoking regulations for decades.

Tobacco lobbyists also knew they could make use of the media to further their strategy of covering-up evidence and creating maximum doubt. Industry-sponsored entities such as the Tobacco Institute, the Center for Indoor Air Research, and the Council for Tobacco Research were established, and they quickly became regarded as quotable sources by the media. Their statements often appeared in press reports, until the industry agreed to dissolve them following a comprehensive settlement in 1998 between the four largest U.S. cigarette manufacturers and forty-six states, which also triggered billions of dollars of ongoing payments from the industry to governments.

A *New York Times* article by its public editor in 2008 admits that newspaper conventions often trumped common sense during the years of tobacco lobbying. "When does fairness demand that a newspaper walk down the middle in a scientific dispute, and when does responsibility demand that it take sides?" asked Clark Hoyt. "It is hardly a new question, and the *Times*, historically, has been slow to declare victors. In 1979, fully 15 years after a landmark federal report said that smoking was dangerous, articles in the *Times* still quoted Tobacco Institute spokesmen arguing that it had not been proved."[18]

Hoyt was referring to the 1964 report by the U.S. Surgeon General, which reviewed more than seven thousand medical journal articles and came to the conclusion that smoking was harmful to health. Specifically, it concluded smoking was a cause of lung and laryngeal cancer in men, a probable cause of lung cancer in women, and the most important cause of chronic bronchitis. But the tobacco industry continued to sow doubt, and the *Times* continued to feature that doubt on its news pages. Finally, in 1980, Hoyt said a further government report called smoking the leading cause of preventable death, and the newspaper made no further efforts to present the so-called other side. "The issue was settled." Even so, the industry has never stopped using PR techniques to promote its products and influence public opinion.

The tobacco playbook was studied carefully by the oil and gas industry and continues to be employed to this day. In the same year that the tobacco industry finally agreed to pay reparations for its decades-long campaign of cover-up, the American Petroleum Institute stole a page from the original Hill+Knowlton strategy. Here's how their plans were described in a *New York Times* story in 1998:

> Industry opponents of a treaty to fight global warming have drafted an ambitious proposal to spend millions of dollars to convince the public that the environmental accord is based on shaky science.
>
> Among their ideas is a campaign to recruit a cadre of scientists who share the industry's views of climate science and to train them in public relations so they can help convince journalists, politicians and the public that the risk of global warming is too uncertain to justify controls on greenhouse gases like carbon dioxide that trap the sun's heat near Earth.[19]

Versions of this same campaign have continued and only intensified since then. In its 2022 report, the Intergovernmental Panel on Climate Change blamed "vested economic and political interests" for organizing and financing misinformation and so-called contrarian climate change messages. Even though there is expert scientific consensus on climate change, the panel points to rhetoric that disregards the risk and urgency of the problem, leading to delayed action and indecision on the part of governments.[20]

Over the years, the industry has sought out and funded the tiny minority of researchers with university credentials who believe climate change either doesn't exist or is caused by factors other than carbon emissions. But as with the tobacco experience, that minority got an oversized presence in media reports as journalists looked to find "balance" in their stories on global warming. A study in 2004 found that over a fifteen-year period, a majority of articles in major U.S. publications gave "roughly equal attention" to the views that humans were contributing to global warming and those that argued there were only natural fluctuations at work. "In other words, through 'balance,' US newspaper coverage perpetrated an informational bias … This informational bias has helped to create space for the US government to defray responsibility and delay action regarding climate change," the report's authors concluded.[21]

As climate change becomes increasingly difficult to deny, a new tactic has emerged. This involves acknowledgement of climate change coupled with a calling for delayed implementation of regulation, or for shifting the onus of responsibility onto individuals rather than the large-scale carbon emitters. These arguments also receive a consistent airing in media reports about climate change.

DISCREDIT DETRACTORS

In 2020 I was working with a team at CBC's *Fifth Estate* investigating fashion tycoon Peter Nygard. The Winnipeg-based multi-millionaire had built a clothing empire over the previous fifty years while leading the flamboyant lifestyle of an international playboy. There were persistent stories about his mistreatment of women, but he had successfully avoided any consequences until a lawsuit filed in New York accused him of multiple acts of sexual assault. We had interviewed two women who accused Nygard of rape. They agreed to go public, the first time any Canadian had gone on the record with such an allegation. Our investigation included corroboration from witnesses, family members, and, in one case, an RCMP officer. One of the victims had been a model, and the other a model and an actor. Before we published, we asked Nygard for a response. Nygard wasn't just fighting for his personal reputation, he was trying to ensure the survival of his corporate empire, which depended so heavily on his personal image. We weren't surprised he disputed the allegations, but the nature of the denial went much further.

The official response came from Jay Prober, Nygard's lawyer. He charged that one of the women had "jumped on the perceived money train and has nothing to lose, especially if her legal fees are being paid as we suspect they are. She is a purported actress who is now playing another role."[22] Prober also sent us sworn statements from two people claiming parts of our victim's stories were false. Throughout the year, as more allegations against Nygard piled up, Prober repeated his accusations against the women who were coming forward with stories. "A lot of people see dollar signs [and they're] jumping on the bandwagon," he told the *Winnipeg Free Press*. "They are more of the same by women jumping on the perceived money train who are likely to have been paid to make these fabricated accusations."[23]

Throughout his career, Nygard had used similar tactics to conceal his activities from public view. Whenever someone accused him of sexual impropriety, he would either pay for their silence, threaten them with lawsuits, attack their credibility if they tried to go public, or pressure media outlets to suppress the story.

The essence of Nygard's strategy was to prevent media coverage in the first place or ensure it stopped soon after it began. This is exactly what happened in 1996, when the *Winnipeg Free Press* began an investigation into his treatment of women. After an initial story detailing sexual harassment, reporters were preparing a follow-up piece with first-hand allegations that Nygard had raped one of his employees. Nygard recruited high-profile Winnipeg business leaders to pressure the newspaper to kill the story. The credibility of complainants was called into question, and the newspaper was accused of going on a witch hunt. Years later, in our CBC report, newspaper publisher Rudy Redekop admitted that he bowed to the pressure and ordered an end to any further coverage.[24] It didn't take long for media coverage to resume praising Nygard's business acumen and international stature. He was awarded a key to the city of Winnipeg in 2008 and was often shown in media reports hobnobbing with politicians.

Nygard's luck ran out in December 2020, when he was arrested and ordered extradited to face sex-related charges in New York. He has also since been charged with sexual offences in Toronto, Montreal, and Winnipeg. The story of his rape of a Winnipeg employee finally went public twenty-five years after it had been suppressed.

Discrediting detractors is one of the oldest and most pernicious tactics used by those attempting to manipulate media and the public. When consumer activist Ralph Nader was exposing safety problems in the auto industry in the 1960s, General Motors hired private detectives to dig up dirt on him. They even sent a woman to try to seduce him at a Safeway supermarket, hoping a sex scandal would make people discount the facts he was highlighting about unsafe GM products.[25] In 1971, when strategic analyst Daniel Ellsberg was leaking the sensitive Pentagon Papers, exposing U.S. activities in the war in Vietnam, President Richard Nixon sent his infamous team of covert plumbers into action. They broke into the office of Ellsberg's psychiatrist, hoping to find damaging information they could use to embarrass him. More recently, Facebook was accused in 2018 of hiring a public relations firm to discredit people who had become active in a group called Freedom from Facebook. The PR firm distributed information to the media claiming that key group members were being funded by billionaire George Soros.[26] Facebook acknowledged hiring the company, but severed ties with them soon after media reports exposed the scheme.

The media are frequently manipulated into relaying information that is deliberately disseminated to defame whistle-blowers. Glenn Greenwald, the reporter who broke the story of Edward Snowden's revelations about U.S. covert mass surveillance, said he wasn't surprised when embarrassing details about his past began appearing soon after. A concerted effort was made in 2013 to discredit him personally, and somehow blunt the force of the revelations he had reported on. Many media outlets gladly snapped up the details and reported them, without considering how they were being manipulated in the process.

Some of the stories mentioned that Greenwald had been involved years earlier in a pornography business, while another said he was embroiled in a lawsuit with his condo board over the size of his dog. Someone clearly had done extensive background research into Greenwald and leaked the results to a number of media outlets simultaneously. In a pre-emptive piece he wrote for the *Guardian*, Greenwald said, "When I made the choice to report aggressively on top-secret NSA [National Security Agency] programs, I knew that I would inevitably be the target of all sorts of personal attacks and smears. You don't challenge the most powerful state on earth and expect to do so without being attacked." The *Guardian* itself followed up with an editorial that said, "Those who leak official information will often be denounced, prosecuted or smeared. The more serious the leak, the fiercer the pursuit and the greater the punishment."[27]

ENHANCE THE BRAND

Corporations devote considerable time and expense to managing their images and brands. The field of polishing corporate images has grown so extensively that many universities now include it in their offerings. At the University of Toronto, for instance, students can earn a certificate in Brand Management. Students are taught "how to understand the discipline of brand management and how it drives company value." They also study brand launches, rebranding and "competitive defence."[28] There are numerous techniques involved in burnishing a brand. Companies might attach their names to celebrities, sports stars, and events through sponsorships. They might engage in philanthropy and other acts that could help to boost their corporate social responsibility credentials.

All too often, companies make statements about their products and practices that are inconsistent with reality. This is especially true when it comes to claims that amount to "greenwashing" — the practice of falsely representing products or practices as environmentally friendly when they are not. The use of terms like *green, sustainable,* or *eco-friendly* has become commonplace for many companies, no matter how toxic or harmful their products are. The International Consumer Protection and Enforcement Network conducts an annual review of websites for questionable claims, and in 2022 it looked at companies promoting clothes, cosmetics, and food. It found four in ten sites used misleading and potentially illegal tactics, including the use of vague claims and unclear language designed to suggest that the products are natural or sustainable without adequate explanation or evidence supporting the claims; using eco-labels not associated with an accredited organization; and hiding or omitting information, such as a product's pollution levels, to appear more eco-friendly.[29]

Another way companies try to enhance their brands is by encouraging or paying media outlets to format their messages as disguised news content. In this case the media outlet is complicit in the manipulation of the messaging. Advertorials, or paid advertisements in the form of news stories, have been a staple in many newspapers over the years. But there are more subtle ways advertiser content can be featured in media. A Tim Hortons cup on the anchor desk of a morning television show might appear innocent enough, but it's a form of product placement that aims to exercise influence on viewers. Corporate branding has been attached to weather and business segments, sports shows, and other parts of television newscasts, even on CBC Television, which has guidelines on the separation of editorial and advertising content.

Most weekend newspapers are chock full of sections that purport to cover autos, travel, real estate, and other topics but are often vehicles for advertising content. More ethical outlets will carefully and clearly label advertising content as such, but this is not always done. Even when an item hasn't been completely bought and paid for, there are hidden factors that influence the content. For instance, try to think of a time you have read a newspaper review of a new car or a holiday destination that was not largely positive. Most readers might be unaware that car companies supply free vehicles for one or two weeks for writers to test out, and invite them to all-expense-paid events and shows. Even the Automobile Journalists Association of Canada leaves it to individual members to decide whether to keep products or gifts that are supplied by manufacturers, including such items as tires or helmets, after they have reviewed them.[30] Travel writers are similarly offered trips in which some or all expenses are paid, and this information is not always disclosed in their reports.

The most sophisticated form of media-driven brand enhancement is so-called sponsored or branded content. These are pseudo-stories or segments that are made to blend with the regular content of a media outlet but are actually advertisements. You might watch a television segment in a newscast that discusses the best holiday gift ideas without ever knowing that the seemingly independent interview was a paid placement. For advertisers, the benefit is clear. A segment with the look and feel of a news item will carry more credibility than an outright ad. But the public is often hoodwinked in the process, and the media outlet is complicit.

In September 2020, CBC touched off a controversy with its own staff when it announced a new service called Tandem, dedicated to creating branded content, including promotional podcasts. Allowing advertisers to insert themselves into the core offerings of CBC shows wasn't new. Product placement had been used in dramas, with TD Canada Trust and other companies popping up regularly in shows such as *Little Mosque on the Prairie*, *Heartland*, and *Being Erica*. The CBC Life website also offered sponsored items made to look like news. But the Tandem announcement signalled an expansion of the practice, and it came with an explicit statement of intent from a CBC executive that rubbed CBC journalists the wrong way. Advertising spokesperson Donald Lizotte said, "Clients wanted an integrated, turnkey solution to create quality content and leverage the credibility of our network. I am so pleased that we now offer this."[31] Tandem's first paid placement was a six-part podcast extolling the virtues of Athabasca University. It was hosted by a CBC personality, and visitors to CBC's podcast website could have been forgiven for confusing it with all the authentic journalistic offerings.

Hundreds of CBC staff members objected to the new service, taking the unusual step of releasing an open letter that said it made a mockery of the corporation's journalistic reputation. "In an era of 'fake news,' where misinformation is already rife, it undermines trust," they said. Though CBC journalists are barred from expressing opinions on matters of public controversy, they made an exception, in this case, to ensure the public wouldn't be duped by any of the advertiser content. "Our job is to cover the news, not be the news. But today we are crossing that line to appeal for your help," the open letter stated. "CBC is using its resources to help advertisers trick Canadians."[32]

In response, CBC issued nine guidelines that it said would protect the integrity of the news service while still offering paid content. They included restricting the service to digital platforms, clearly labelling the content as paid, and using a graphic design to differentiate the items. The guidelines, as well as a subsequent CRTC ruling allowing CBC to continue with its program, still left many CBC staff dissatisfied. In its defence, CBC said many other news organizations did the same thing. While that's true, it hasn't been without controversy. The *Globe and Mail* came under scrutiny for printing a double-page spread in its business section from the *China Daily* newspaper. While it was labelled as having been produced by a third party, the newspaper's publisher later said the pages should have been more clearly marked to reflect that it was a paid ad.[33]

In 2021 comedian John Oliver used an unorthodox but effective technique to illustrate a segment about sponsored content on local news shows. He created a fake company called Venus Inventions, which had its own website and a signature product called the Venus Veil, "the world's first sexual wellness blanket." Oliver was mocking a practice that he said had become routine. "It is far too easy to make a ridiculous product that makes outlandish claims and get it on to local TV," Oliver said. "And the reason I know that is, we did."[34]

Oliver hired an actor and then, posing as the blanket's manufacturer, paid three local TV stations in Utah, Texas, and Colorado, to run interviews with his fake company about the blanket. The breathless anchors are shown expressing enthusiastic interest in the blanket, which the actor maintains was "inspired by the biological technique of magnetogenetics, and technology pioneered in Germany 80 years ago." Viewers were told the blanket had proprietary magnetic fibres that improve sexual performance. One of the interviewers was the station's chief medical correspondent, but in none of the cases were any questions raised about the logic of the claims being made. The result was a very funny but revealing episode of Oliver's show.

. . .

Big corporations wield enormous economic power, and their influence extends to their dealings with the media. Millions are spent trying to convince the media and the public that products are useful, safe, and environmentally friendly, whether they are or not. Through various means, these messages make their way into news reports, talk shows, and specialty columns. Most news organizations don't have the capacity to test every claim that is made. Some are willing to repeat assertions even without consulting independent experts for alternative viewpoints. While investigative reporting can catch some of the more outrageous falsehoods, other dupery goes undetected for years. In many cases, media outlets are seriously misled. But there are times when they are willing purveyors of the messages, as the practice of sponsored content demonstrates.

It's troubling enough when the media are misled by the corporate world in the ordinary course of doing business. When they become complicit in the misinformation, the deception is raised to an entirely new level.

Chapter 3

Think Tanks or Spin Factories?

IT'S LIKE CATNIP FOR AN ASSIGNMENT EDITOR DESPERATE to fill a news page or a broadcast lineup. Every May or June, a news release comes across the wire services proclaiming, "Tax Freedom Day." It's supposedly the day of the year when an average taxpayer is free of the burden of paying taxes and can start enjoying all of their income themselves.

A U.S. businessman developed the concept more than seventy years ago, but the Fraser Institute has turned it into a franchise. A proponent of low taxes, less government, and other libertarian ideals, the Fraser Institute knows how irresistible the concept is to newsrooms. It's a simple item to insert into a news lineup, as it comes complete with statistics, graphics, and a built-in outrage factor. Editors picture their readers sitting at home and shouting, "What, I have been working nearly half the year, and I don't have anything to show for it yet?" On their websites, clicks, likes, and shares are sure to follow.

The problem with the concept of Tax Freedom Day is that it is hardly ever subjected to scrutiny for its methodology or underlying assumptions. Academics over the years have pointed to problems with how the Fraser Institute conducts the analysis. As early as 2005, Osgoode Hall Law School professor Neil Brooks wrote a paper calling it a "flawed, incoherent and pernicious concept."[1] He argued that it understated average family income and overestimated the total tax bite. He also questioned why royalty payments made by oil, gas, and mining companies should be included as part of the typical Canadian's tax burden. By misusing the concept of averages, the institute's calculations are "preposterously exaggerated," he said.

In 2012 UBC professor and tax policy expert David Duff also took issue with the logic behind the Fraser Institute's calculations. "I think it's a deliberately slanted way to inform Canadians about the taxes they pay, because it's abstracted from the benefits one gets from government and from the reasons we pay taxes, and it looks at taxes as though it's just money you take and throw into the sea. It gets people to focus only on that side of it," he told the CBC.[2] Every few years since then, other economists and academics have pointed to the problematic assumptions in the Fraser Institute's analysis. While the institute defends its methodology and acknowledges that taxes do pay for government services, it fundamentally associates freedom with the time Canadians no longer need to "work for the government" by paying tax. It continues to send out its press releases, as it has done each year for decades, and many media outlets turn them into news stories without challenging their underlying premise.

The Fraser Institute is one of the dozens of think tanks, institutes, and foundations deemed credible sources by many Canadian media. Once a source achieves such status, their statements are often taken at face value; it's assumed that there's no need to corroborate or verify its claims. The mere fact that a think tank issued a report becomes news worthy of publication. The very names of these bodies exude authority: Atlantic Institute for Market Studies, Frontier Centre for Public Policy, Justice Centre for Constitutional Freedoms, Macdonald-Laurier Institute, the Parkland Institute, the Rideau Institute, and the Montreal Economic Institute. Their success in convincing the media to pay attention to their reports and studies is undeniable.

The Fraser Institute boasted that in 2021 its work generated more than 35,000 mentions in news articles in mainstream media and 1,500 opinion columns in newspapers.[3] "No other Canadian think tank generates as much media, web, and social media attention," it said. While it described itself as an independent body dedicated to peer-reviewed research designed to improve the quality of life of Canadians, the Fraser Institute's objectives align closely with certain sectors of corporate Canada. On its thirty-fifth birthday, it presented thirty-five "big ideas" describing how the institute was changing the world. Among them was a commitment to privatization of government entities, opposition to government meddling on drug pricing, support for private health care, and concern about "overly restrictive labour legislation" such as minimum wage laws.[4] The institute's world view is concisely described in the joint opening message from its president and chairman in its annual report: "We have been one of the only think tanks to consistently push back against the federal government's attempt to destroy one of Canada's most important industries, the energy industry. We were the only think tank to highlight the serious and harmful economic effects of the dramatic increase in the federal carbon tax. We were, and continue to be, the most prominent think tank consistently arguing that Canada needs a change in policy direction — that more government spending, increased redistribution, and new and higher taxes are not the answer."[5]

With such an overt expression of the institute's ideological orientation, one might wonder how journalists can be misled by its statements and reports. In my experience, few journalists think deeply enough about the history and ideologies of the various think tanks. Instead, many reporters view them as trusted sources and easily approachable interview subjects who can always be relied on for a quote. After all, they have the status of being an institute, or a centre, even though such designations have been self-assigned and have little meaning.

An essential first step in decoding the messaging of these think tanks is to examine their history and the funding behind them, which is sometimes a challenging and mystery-laden exercise. In the case of the Vancouver-based Fraser Institute, the key impetus to its founding in 1974 was the election of Dave Barrett's NDP government in British Columbia two years earlier. Barrett moved swiftly on various fronts, increasing the minimum wage, creating a public auto-insurance system, introducing a pharmacare plan, and instituting rent controls. On average, he passed a new law every three days while in power.[6] These developments threw business leaders into a state of panic. They started calling British Columbia the "Chile of the North," a reference to the socialist government of Salvador Allende, which was ultimately toppled by a CIA-led coup. Barrett's introduction of a mineral royalties tax particularly enraged the business sector. Alf Powis, chair of Noranda, concluded that "what was needed was a think tank that would re-establish the dominance of free enterprise ideas, the values of the market, and property rights."[7]

Economist Michael Walker and forestry executive Patrick Boyle got to work establishing such a think tank, and they turned to Britain for expert assistance. Antony Fisher, who founded the London-based Institute of Economic Affairs in 1955, had developed many of the pro-market ideas that helped Margaret Thatcher eventually take power. Inspired by the ideas of Austrian economist Friedrich Hayek, Fisher developed a system of structuring and funding think tanks that would promote free-market ideology internationally. Fisher came to Vancouver and helped the Fraser Institute in its early years. For the business community, Fisher seemed the ideal candidate to combat the policies sprouting from the government cabinet room. A profile of Fisher by one of the groups he helped to create characterized his early motivations this way: "Seeing Britain embrace a socialist economic agenda at the end of the war, Antony was dismayed by the subversion of individual enterprise in service of a government-led centralized policy. He came across an abridged edition of F.A. Hayek's *The Road to Serfdom*, which proposes that central planning inevitably erodes individual liberty and enables tyranny. Hayek's philosophy not only influenced Fisher's own career trajectory but also inspired him to think of ways to drive grassroots-level change that promoted free-market opportunities."[8]

The Fraser Institute, named after a nearby river to mask its ideological bent, quickly signed up more than two dozen corporate and individual members, including representatives of major oil and forestry companies and all five big banks. Within two years, it had 175 corporate members.[9] Over the years, it has received substantial support from foreign conservative and libertarian sources, including the American billionaire Koch brothers. While the institute doesn't directly disclose its list of contributors, many critics have pieced together information about financial backers from different sources. Today, it has annual operating revenues of more than $10 million, and as a registered charity, it issues tax receipts for donations.

Fisher heeded Hayek's teaching that it was important to influence the "second-hand dealers in ideas," which included journalists and commentators. Despite its claim that it was independent and free of political influences, the institute's early publications appeared to be a direct response to legislative initiatives in British Columbia. The first book it published in 1975 was an attack on rent controls and had contributions from Hayek, Walker, and neo-liberal economist Milton Friedman. A planned second book was an attack on Barrett's proposal to start up a provincial savings and trust company, but the project was set aside after the defeat of the NDP government in 1975.[10] In addition to research publications, the Fraser Institute organized conferences and then published the proceedings in book form. B.C. professor and author Donald Gutstein, who studied Fraser's early history, noted that, like its libertarian counterparts in other parts of the world, it relies on the thesis of the "perverse effect" to discredit programs. It's a technique to profess support for the idea behind specific policies, only to observe that the policy will have unintended consequences and often the exact opposite of the desired effect. Employment insurance or social assistance, for instance, will only worsen unemployment and poverty. Rent controls, they argue, will lead to less new housing and ultimately higher housing costs.[11]

Inexperienced journalists particularly seem unaware of the history and ideological underpinnings of the Fraser Institute when they write their stories quoting from Fraser's reports and studies. It's almost as if, by sheer coincidence, the conclusions of all the reports and commentaries churned out by the institute point to the inefficiencies of government and the superiority of the free-market system. When I was head of the CBC Manitoba newsroom, an excited journalist would periodically burst into my office announcing that they had just been selected to attend an all-expenses-paid seminar in Vancouver designed to teach journalists about economics. What a great opportunity, they exclaimed, and it would come at no cost to the CBC. Here is one of the actual emails a journalist received:

> Many of today's pressing issues such as health care, income
> inequality, and the environment have economic implica-
> tions affecting many aspects of Canadian society. Our

seminars will equip journalists with the tools to decipher today's economic and political landscape and the terminology to accurately and confidently report on economic and policy developments.

This graduate seminar-style program is open to journalists from TV, radio, print, and new media from across Canada. Full bursaries are available to cover all program costs, including travel, accommodation, conference tuition, materials, and included meals.[12]

I didn't approve any of these junkets, but journalists from other newsrooms across the country routinely attended them. The institute also organizes a separate course for journalists on how to use an economic lens to analyze Canadian and global policies, including instruction on its concept of unintended consequences. Together with workshops for students and teachers, these courses are funded partly by a multi-million-dollar donation from former Barrick Gold CEO Peter Munk. Fraser's 2021 annual report notes that even during the pandemic it influenced 7,400 post-secondary students and 550 teachers through webinars. According to the same report: "Unfortunately, Canada's education system continues to be dominated by people who believe that government action rather than competitive markets is the best way to improve the lives of Canadians. Through in-person seminars, online webinars, curated resources, and academic contests, teachers, high school and post-secondary students, and journalists are exposed to a more rounded view and are taught about the powerful and positive impact of economic and human freedom."[13]

In 2018 two doctoral candidates in political science at York University decided to attend one of the seminars to see exactly what was being taught. They later described listening to presentations by two George Mason University professors who worked for the Koch brothers–funded Mercatus Center in Virginia, which bills itself as "the world's premier university source for market-oriented ideas." Fraser employees gave two talks: one was entitled "The Global Impact of Economic Freedom," and another was on the "Minimal Impact of the Minimum Wage" in fighting poverty in Ontario.

The students concluded the presentations were "ideologically-constructed propaganda" designed to undercut democratic oversight and advocate for a state that only had a limited and restricted role.[14]

Antony Fisher wasn't content with building a handful of think tanks in Britain and North America. In 1981 he created an organization now known as the Atlas Network. Established with a mission to spread free-market think tanks everywhere, the institute achieved phenomenal success. Today, it partners with more than five hundred think tanks worldwide, promoting its stated vision of "a free, prosperous and peaceful world where the principles of individual liberty, property rights, limited government, and free markets are secured by the rule of law."[15] The president of the Fraser Institute serves as a senior adviser to Atlas's Center for United States and Canada. As with many think tanks and networks, it doesn't trumpet where it raises its money. "To influence public opinion, it is necessary to avoid any suggestion of vested interest or intent to indoctrinate," Fisher said in the founding proposal sent to potential Atlas donors.[16]

Today, it sends more than $6 million in grants worldwide and has a proven track record in influencing public opinion. Convincing the media to amplify its messaging is an integral part of this work. Alejandro Chafuen, a former president of the network and a long-time Fraser board member, articulated the process this way: "Journalists are very much attracted by whatever is new and easy to report," and when a think tank produces a survey, it's an easy sell to the media. "And donors also see this."[17] In 2021 the Atlas Network laid claim to 175 "freedom expanding policy victories" internationally.[18]

Some Atlas Network devotees have created their own institutes. The Canadian Health Policy Institute was founded in 2012 by Brett Skinner, former CEO of the Fraser Institute and Fraser's director of health policy research for eight years. In 2003 Skinner was a co-winner of what was then known as the Atlas Economic Research Foundation's Sir Antony Fisher International Memorial Award, and his work has appeared in free-market publications worldwide. When Skinner is quoted in the media, or writes an op-ed in a newspaper, the public doesn't learn much about his history.

Readers may not realize, for instance, that while running the neutral-sounding health policy institute, Skinner was simultaneously executive director of health and economic policy for Canada's leading pharmaceutical lobby group for four years. It's not surprising, therefore, that most of his advocacy takes issue with attempts to legislate lower drug prices or introduce any form of national pharmacare. Such measures would hurt patients, produce fewer new drugs in Canada, and be costly for taxpayers, he argues, relying on the thesis of unintended consequences. A piece he co-wrote in 2020, critical of a government plan to reduce drug prices, didn't pull any punches: "It is not too much of a stretch to say that the new regime reflects Soviet-style thinking on price controls."[19]

Skinner doesn't hide his past jobs and activities. In some cases, reporters quoting him might not be aware of his long association with free-market ideals. In the case of editors who publish media commentaries, there's less of an excuse as to why his full history isn't mentioned.

DONNER CANADIAN FOUNDATION

Canada saw a rapid expansion of free-market think tanks in the 1990s. Much of this was due to the generosity of the Donner Canadian Foundation, which Donald Gutstein called "the lifeblood of conservative and corporate propaganda in Canada." It was created in 1950 by William H. Donner, a multimillionaire who made his fortune in the U.S. steel industry. In 1938, after an income tax dispute with the federal government, he left the United States for Switzerland. He eventually settled in Canada, set up his charitable foundation, and died three years later in Montreal. The foundation supported uncontroversial causes like health care research and prison reform for many years. But in the 1990s, the more right-wing branch of the family in the United States took control of the foundation and radically shifted its direction. "We changed emphasis in 1993," said Patrick Luciani, the acting executive director of the foundation. "It had been a classic Canadian foundation, quite liberal. But the Donner family saw the country going through a fiscal crisis and they wanted to fund projects that looked at more competition and less government."[20]

Gutstein documented a remarkable list of grants and start-up funds from the Donner Canadian Foundation that changed the Canadian think tank landscape. It provided some core funding to launch or support a series of organizations across the country:

- $450,000 over three years as start-up funds and another $620,000 in programming money for the Atlantic Institute for Market Studies, a Halifax think tank pushing free-market ideas. A search of Canadian Newsstream, a database of newspapers, magazines, wire feeds, and other sources, shows more than five thousand references to the institute since it was founded in 1994. It merged with the Fraser Institute in 2019.

- $435,000 for start-up funding for the Frontier Centre for Public Policy in Winnipeg, which has been instrumental in trying to downplay the devastating role played by Indigenous residential schools. Many rural Manitoba newspapers, from the *Neepawa Banner* to the *Roblin Review*, have regularly run handout opinion pieces supplied to them by the institute. In 2018 the centre hired veteran broadcaster Roger Currie to voice an ad that said it's a myth residential schools robbed Indigenous children of their childhood.

- $500,000 for the Montreal Economic Institute, which produced rankings of schools in Quebec for several years. The ranking list triggered widespread media coverage in Quebec, along with criticism that its focus on marks diminished public schools, which don't pick and choose their students. The *Montreal Gazette* routinely reported on the findings, saying the list was "widely disputed but keenly read."[21]

- $1.4 million was given to start *Next City* magazine, which promoted the privatization of medicare and ending government arts subsidies, among other pet conservative causes, and $400,000 to launch right-wing magazine *Gravitas*.[22]

Donner does not restrict its support to think tanks and libertarian institutes. It says it invests in "creative solutions to critical problems faced by Canada and the world." In 2022 it donated to a wide variety of organizations, including CARE Canada, Doctors Without Borders, and the Canadian Parks and Wilderness Society. But its fidelity to free-enterprise think tanks is unwavering, and in 2022 it contributed nearly half a million dollars in total to the Fraser Institute, the Macdonald-Laurier Institute, and the Montreal Economic Institute.[23]

. . .

Neo-liberal ideology does not entirely dominate the think tank landscape in Canada. There are several left-leaning institutes and organizations that challenge the free market system. The more influential and better-known examples are the Canadian Centre for Policy Alternatives (CCPA) and the Broadbent Institute. Some have also developed a status as trusted sources in news media. With total revenues of more than $6 million, the CCPA is an influential voice in Canadian media. Founded in 1980, it calls itself one of Canada's leading progressive voices in public policy debates, dealing with "issues of social, economic and environmental justice." The centre gets financial support from a variety of trade unions and labour federations, among other sources. It too boasts of its influence on the media, claiming 17,500 mentions in news stories during 2020.[24] The Broadbent Institute, named after former NDP leader Ed Broadbent, is more openly associated with the NDP. Its board includes current and former NDP activists, strategists, and politicians. As part of its media strategy, it funds a newsgathering service called PressProgress. The service focuses on such areas as right-wing politics and extremism, big business, and labour.

A decade ago, the Canada Revenue Agency began auditing the CCPA along with other think tanks and groups to see whether they were violating rules that limited political activities by charities. Part of the reason was that the agency felt the think tank's research and education materials appeared to be biased and one-sided. More than four hundred university professors sent a letter to the federal government questioning why right-wing think tanks didn't appear to be included in the same inquiries. They said the CCPA audit was "politically motivated to intimidate and silence its criticism of your government's policies." While the audits found no violations in most cases, some institutes said the process sent a chill through the community about advocacy work.

Reflecting on the controversy, then CCPA executive director Bruce Campbell said all think tanks had a point of view. "I think all policy research institutes have a bias in that we're informed by a set of values. Those values guide our research, so we have a perspective or an orientation. But that doesn't diminish the quality of our research or the rigour of our standards," he said. The Fraser Institute president at the time, Niels Veldhuis, disagreed. He said the Fraser is not value-based, but driven by data, and it shouldn't even be described as conservative.[25]

Nonetheless, the volume of activity of think tanks broadly espousing libertarian and free market ideas often crowds out alternative voices. Gutstein did a study in 2013 on how many times media stories mention the different think tanks and institutes. He found that the right-wing organizations beat out their left-wing rivals by a ratio of 7 to 1.[26] This research revealed a significant increase in the dominance of right-wing institutions since a more extensive study conducted in 1997 looked at references over six months in fourteen major daily newspapers and the CBC and CTV networks. That study found right-wing think tanks or research institutes received more than three times as much coverage as their left-wing counterparts.[27]

MACDONALD-LAURIER INSTITUTE

One of the most successful and influential think tank figures in Canada is Brian Lee Crowley, who launched the Atlantic Institute for Market Studies in 1994. He has moved seamlessly through the worlds of academia, government, think tanks, and journalism. He focused his doctoral thesis on the social and political philosophy of Friedrich Hayek and has been professing libertarian and neo-liberal ideas ever since. Some of his early work criticized unemployment insurance and other government transfers to individuals and provinces.[28] All the while, Crowley paid attention to the dissemination of his messages through the media. In 1998, he took a two-year leave to serve on the editorial board of the *Globe and Mail* and has written opinion pieces for the newspaper since then.

Former prime minister Stephen Harper once called the Atlantic Institute "dollar for dollar the best think tank in the country." When he took office, Harper invited Crowley to assist the new government. For nearly two years, he was a visiting economist with the federal finance department, working on policy files and redesigning the pre-budget consultation process. Crowley characterized the position, which came with the rank of assistant deputy minister, as the most senior independent advisory role on economic policy within the government.[29]

It might not be surprising, therefore, that Harper's Conservatives were helpful when it came to supporting a new venture Crowley proposed to create in 2009, the independent Macdonald-Laurier Institute. Finance Minister Jim Flaherty held a private dinner at Toronto's Albany Club to drum up support for the plan. The *Globe and Mail* reported that he sent a letter to well-heeled Bay Street figures announcing that he was giving the think tank his personal backing, and he hoped that they would consider doing the same. Flaherty talked about the important ideals his government was trying to push forward, including smaller government, lower taxes, and greater personal responsibility. He then provided an insightful analysis of how the government could use outside actors to help forge a media and public consensus for its policies: "I can speak with some authority when I say that driving change within Ottawa is not easy. There are powerful actors in Ottawa, within the civil service, Parliament, the media and in many non-governmental organizations, that actively resist progress. — Although I have always felt well supported by friends and colleagues, I have clearly felt the need for independent research, support and promotion of these ideals," he wrote. "This important national initiative deserves to succeed. Please join me in ensuring that it does. My office will follow up with you."[30]

Harper himself was well aware of the power of think tanks and lobby groups to shape public opinion. He served as president of the National Citizens Coalition for four years, campaigning for the same causes and ideals that Crowley was pushing. Having a supportive think tank based in Ottawa could only prove useful. In short order, the Macdonald-Laurier Institute was suggesting policies that were in line with government thinking, and it produced research studies that effectively backed up proposed government legislation.

For example, Harper faced criticism for introducing a variety of tough-on-crime bills even as the incidence of crime was declining. Crowley's institute promptly published a report trashing the methodology used by Statistics Canada and arguing that crime wasn't going down after all. You didn't need to read much further than the title of the study to know where it was headed: "Why Canadian Crime Statistics Don't Add Up." Instead of advocating for disinterested, scientific inquiry into the numbers, the study had this conclusion: "The current report demonstrates that the entire process of collection, analysis, and reporting of crime statistics is in urgent need of law-enforcement-led modernization."[31] Some newspapers, particularly in the Sun chain, gave the report major play, while the institute itself offered opinion pieces to other papers to buttress the report's claims.

The relationship between the government and the institute that Flaherty had envisioned could not have been more symbiotic. In 2012 Harper proclaimed, "I commend Brian Crowley and the team at MLI for your laudable work as one of the leading policy think tanks in our nation's capital. The Institute has distinguished itself as a thoughtful, empirically based and non-partisan contributor to our national public discourse."[32]

Governments come and go, but think tanks continue their work no matter who is in power. They also have to develop sophisticated strategies to influence public policy, even when the tide of public opinion appears to be going in the opposite direction. One of the Macdonald-Laurier Institute's programs over the last decade has centred on recruiting Indigenous support for resource development projects. In the face of growing calls to cut carbon emissions, halt pipeline construction, and preserve Indigenous rights over their traditional lands, the institute has developed the type of strategy that one energy industry insider has called the "magic sauce" for shaping debate around resource development.[33] It involves stressing the benefits to Indigenous people of oil and gas projects, and recruiting Indigenous academics and business people to argue in favour of continued development. One of the institute's Indigenous employees, Melissa Mbarki, writes opinion pieces for newspapers outlining the benefits of the oil and gas industry. She has also argued for more transparency from First Nation governments and supported Pierre Poilievre's bid to lead the Conservative party. When quoted in media stories, she is sometimes billed as being an institute employee while other times she is just referred to as an "Indigenous policy analyst."[34]

In 2018 the Atlas Network hailed MLI's efforts to "engage non-traditional allies to create free market change." It especially lauded the institute's creation of a twelve-person Indigenous advisory committee as an adjunct to its work. The committee has provided credibility to MLI's work and "has provided a shield against opponents that is hard to undermine," said the Atlas report. It all involves a "vision of self-sufficiency for the Aboriginal population based on resource development."[35] At the same time, the institute fought against Canada endorsing the United Nations Declaration on the Rights of Indigenous Peoples, which requires free, prior, and informed consent from Indigenous people before resource development projects can proceed. It argued that the declaration would allow even fringe groups to veto projects. "The consequences would have been detrimental to the market-based progress that Canada's Aboriginal population are making."[36]

As for climate change, the institute has cast doubt on the urgency of declaring it an emergency. According to Jeff Kucharski, a senior institute fellow, the green lobby risks a public backlash by promoting radical action: "Politicians and others who warn of an impending climate 'catastrophe,' 'cataclysm' or 'emergency' are being unnecessarily alarmist, thereby raising unrealistic expectations that justify extreme measures."[37]

When quoting the Macdonald-Laurier Institute or reprinting editorial commentaries from them, the media rarely make reference to the institute's financial backers and ideological orientation. Some reporters might simply not be aware of them, or they may think that a prestigious-sounding institute is equivalent to a university faculty. Others might feel that including such context in their pieces would unnecessarily clutter them. Still others believe it's sufficient to flag each institute as either left wing, right wing, or centrist.

A significant chunk of the Macdonald-Laurier Institute's finances over the years has come from the Aurea Foundation, founded in 2006 by gold-mining magnate Peter Munk, which said it gave special attention to the investigation of issues related to the strengthening of the free market system.

In addition to other substantial foundation support, the MLI has received donations or sponsorships from major oil producers, banks, and pharma companies, among others.[38]

CANADIAN TAXPAYERS FEDERATION

Calling itself a citizens advocacy group as opposed to a think tank, the Canadian Taxpayers Federation (CTF) is also a ubiquitous presence in Canadian media, popping up in hundreds of stories each month to comment on various levels of government and how they spend money. Since its founding in 1990, the overlap between CTF staff members and conservative politicians and commentators has been noteworthy. Former Harper cabinet minister and Alberta premier Jason Kenney was its president in the early years. In 2009 Harper tapped several CTF staffers to work in senior positions in the Prime Minister's Office. John Williamson became Harper's director of communications, Sara MacIntyre was his press secretary, and Adam Taylor became an issues-management adviser.[39] Neil Desai, a former CTF Ontario director, worked as a manager of strategic planning for Harper for three years.[40] Close ties between the CTF and some media outlets resulted in staff movements between the two. Candice Malcolm, a former Ontario director, wrote a column for the *Toronto Sun*. Adrienne Batra, a former CTF director in Manitoba, became the same newspaper's editor.

The organization says it is dedicated to lower taxes, less waste, and accountable government. It devotes considerable time and effort to garnering media attention, and it has been undeniably successful in this regard. Each week it sends out its "Let's Talk Taxes" commentaries to more than eight hundred media outlets and journalists across Canada. Journalists know that a Canadian Taxpayers Federation quote is easy and quick to get. When a reporter is on deadline and writing about any topic that touches on government spending, it's a simple matter to harvest a quote from a CTF spokesperson. In 2020 the federation issued 182 press releases and supplied 152 op-eds to the media. It calculated that it was mentioned more than 7,500 times on radio, TV, and in newspapers.[41] It's difficult to go more than a day or two in any given year without seeing some reference in the media to the Canadian Taxpayers Federation.

Some of the group's pet causes revolve around government waste and debt. It runs an annual "Teddy Waste Awards" with a mascot, Porky the Waste Hater, to mock what it considers unnecessary government spending. It has been a consistent and vocal opponent of carbon taxes. It promotes a national debt clock to keep track of the federal debt. Though it maintains it is free of political influence, many of its positions align with federal or provincial Conservative party platforms. It opposes the federal gun registry. It has called for cutting funding to the CBC. It has advocated for ending the public auto insurance monopoly in British Columbia. It regularly calls for cutting government bureaucracy and slashing public service wages. It took credit for convincing the city of Montreal to institute a property tax cut, which included "a few stunts to focus media attention on the issue."[42]

But exactly how does the federation earn the right to represent Canadian taxpayers? Over the years, critics of the group have often questioned who the federation represents. It has consistently refused to disclose its donors, though the Atlas Network has listed it in the past as a partner.[43] Most organizations sign up members who then provide input and have some level of say in what the group stands for. In the case of the CTF, the situation isn't as straightforward. In 2013 Alberta researcher Tony Clark signed up with the CTF to see if it would provide him with more access to its financial statements. A CTF vice-president told him that audited financial statements are only available to members, and that technically the only members of the federation were the board directors themselves.[44]

The federation's website says it has 235,000 supporters. The only people who can determine the federation's policies and direction, though, are its six board directors. Board chair Michelle Eaton's resumé includes positions such as vice-president of public affairs with the Ontario Chamber of Commerce, senior manager with the Philip Morris International tobacco company, director of public policy and regulatory affairs with Manulife, and ministerial press secretary and communications director in Harper-era federal departments.

Stung by criticism about its governance structure, the CTF published a blog entry explaining why it doesn't allow supporters any decision-making power in how it runs the organization: "First, it was the structure handed down by the founders who believed as the organization became more effective that it could be subject to takeover by groups hostile to the CTF. The founders were most concerned about takeover by political parties, but obviously, unions and various other agitators for big government fall into the same category."

But the federation then explained there was a more practical reason as well: "What structure most effectively advances the organization's mission: One bogged down in meetings, procedures and elections or one that is lean, performance-based and nimble? Rather than spending our staff's time and our donors' funding renting halls for AGMs (ours would require the Skydome), we choose to put our resources where our supporters want them most."[45] As for why the federation refuses to name its donors, it says it is not legally obligated to and wants to protect their privacy. "Why would we serve up a list of our donors so that government officials, petty politicians, agitated union activists and various other stalwarts of the entitlement state could target them? Not happening."[46]

Despite its lack of transparency regarding its own financing, the CTF is quick to insist on full disclosure from other groups. Demanding access to budgets and salaries for First Nations has been a continuous theme for the federation, as it was for the Harper government when it introduced its First Nations Financial Transparency Act in 2011. In 2021 a professor and a research assistant at Simon Fraser University published the results of an exhaustive study into how the CTF frames Indigenous issues. They read and analyzed more than four hundred documents the CTF published between 1998 and 2019 on Indigenous topics. They concluded that "the CTF traffics in resentment that fosters white settler backlash against Indigenous sovereignty, Indigenous forms of governance, and the legal concept of 'Indian' itself." The paper says the CTF goes far beyond an analysis of tax policy issues in its portrayal of Indigenous issues, and consistently employs anti-Indigenous political rhetoric and policies. "What we show here is the durability of the CTF's neoliberal settler colonial paternalism, and its opposition to Indigenous sovereignty in the name of 'taxpayers.' From this we can begin to sketch how political advocacy organizations contribute to Indigenous-settler relations, and anti-Indigenous policy formation."[47]

• • •

While think tanks bristle at the notion that their funders could influence the direction of their research and policies, investigations in the United States demonstrate exactly how this can happen. A *New York Times* story in 2016 showed how even the most prestigious think tanks collaborate with donors to tailor their work. Working with the New England Center for Investigative Reporting, the *Times* obtained thousands of pages of confidential correspondence between the Brookings Institution, one of the world's most influential think tanks, and major corporations. What the documents showed was that in return for financial support from the corporations, Brookings would assure them of "donation benefits" that included setting up events featuring corporate executives with government officials, as well as engaging with national media to ensure strong press coverage.

In one specific case, Brookings was wooing the Lennar Corporation for US$400,000 in donations. Lennar was embarking on a US$8 billion project to revitalize part of San Francisco. Brookings promised to provide "public validation" of Lennar's efforts through local and national media coverage. In response to these allegations, an executive vice-president at Brookings insisted the organization was independent. But he acknowledged that the appointment of a Lennar executive as a senior fellow at the institution had created the appearance of a conflict and said Brookings would no longer allow corporations or corporate-backed foundations to make anonymous contributions.[48]

The *Times* reported that similar arrangements exist at many think tanks. "On issues as varied as military sales to foreign countries, international trade, highway management systems and real estate development, think tanks have frequently become vehicles for corporate influence and branding campaigns."

It examined seventy-five think tanks and found that staffers had simultaneously worked as lobbyists or consultants for the companies being profiled by the organizations. In one case, a visiting fellow at the American Enterprise Institute contributed to research pushing for higher spending on new military equipment while also working as a lobbyist for arms suppliers like Northrop Grumman and BAE Systems. The report he helped to write at the institute didn't mention that he was a paid lobbyist. In the end, his client won the contract to supply the very vehicles he was advocating.[49]

Journalists themselves are not immune to the cacophony of messaging that comes at them from every direction. The steady drumbeat of press releases, media stunts, and narratives has an effect on both journalism and the public. According to Donald Gutstein, "Constant repetition over many decades has achieved the desired result, as some ideas have become familiar and even common-sense: economic and school choice are unqualified good things; the tax burden is burdensome and requires relief; government is inefficient because it harbours bloated bureaucracies and overpaid public employees; the private sector is hobbled by red tape; and so on."[50]

But as I will discuss in later chapters, there are ways for media outlets to combat this. Journalists need to use critical thinking to unpack the messages and the motivations behind them. They need expertise in different fields to be able to understand economic, social, and political concepts. And they have to resist the pressure of the punishing deadline and avoid the pitfalls of repeating statements without subjecting them to proper scrutiny. Following the money trail is essential in understanding whose interests are being served by various organizations. Cats have a difficult time passing up the opportunity to roll around in catnip. Journalists need to hold themselves to a higher standard.

Chapter 4

Political Lies

"READ MY LIPS, NO NEW TAXES," FORMER U.S. PRESIDENT
George H.W. Bush once famously said. It was a bold and decisive campaign
promise. But once elected, Bush betrayed his lips. He did what he promised
he wouldn't do, and soon a joke began to spread: How do you tell if a politician is lying? Simple. His lips are moving.

Politicians in Canada have their own versions of the lip-reading mantra.
The lives of Indigenous people will be improved, they say. Young people
will have untold new educational opportunities. Government will create
thousands of new jobs. Climate change targets will be met and exceeded.
Corruption will be eliminated. Transparency and accountability will be the
new standards for government.

When the promises do not materialize, politicians have excuses at the
ready. They say that circumstances have changed, and a new reality demands
different policies. Sometimes this can be true, but more often than not the
explanation is more straightforward. The politicians have just lied. They
have made promises with no intention of ever following through. And once
in government, it often becomes easier to lie than to level with the public.

More insidious than unfulfilled promises is the routine deception that
accompanies many government announcements and actions. With its legion
of communications specialists, social media experts, access-to-information

stonewallers, and image consultants, the government's ability to spread a misleading message has never been as robust as it is today.[1] In an age when the world is awash in disinformation and misinformation, it's especially disconcerting that politicians themselves add to the cacophony. And all too often, they succeed in misleading the media to help spread the lies.

Does every politician of every persuasion lie all the time? No. It would be overly cynical to think that's the case. But for politicians in power, the urge to preserve the status quo is overwhelming, and truth-telling suffers. Politicians vying to be in power are also prone to shading the facts to their advantage. U.S. investigative journalist I.F. Stone wasn't using hyperbole when he proclaimed that "all governments lie."[2] Though it's a distressing conclusion, the public seems resigned to the notion that politicians lie. An Ipsos poll in 2021 showed that just 10 percent of people worldwide feel their politicians are trustworthy. The number is only marginally better in Canada, at 13 percent.[3] But the general public doesn't sit in the galleries of the House of Commons or provincial legislatures and doesn't attend news conferences. Ordinary people rarely get the chance to grill politicians directly on their statements or pronouncements. That's the job of the media, and professional journalists pride themselves on being able to sort truth from fiction.

Usually, the lies are not easy to discern and disprove. They are reported, perhaps paired with comments from people who question them. They often go unexposed, sometimes for decades, sometimes forever. Questions about U.S. president Donald Trump's extramarital relationships with women have swirled for years, but only with his 2023 indictment did detailed allegations of his secret scheme to alter business records and pay for people's silence emerge. As traditional media outlets get smaller, fewer and fewer journalists are assigned to cover the government regularly. In most provincial capitals, only a handful of reporters cover the legislature full-time. The number of journalists who regularly follow proceedings on Parliament Hill has also declined drastically over the years. There is even less attention paid to provincial and federal Crown corporations and agencies, which employ thousands of people and spend billions in public dollars. In some of Canada's smaller cities, where the local TV station and newspaper may have been shuttered, there is literally no media oversight of municipal or provincial affairs. The net result is a low level of scrutiny and more opportunities for politicians to mislead the public.

Even when journalists are present, a bewildering array of techniques are used to spin the messages emanating from the corridors of power. Statistics and data are often presented in such a way as to enhance a government's achievements and downplay shortcomings. Money is shuffled between different accounts to present rosier spending and deficit numbers. Polls are commissioned with misleading questions to claim community consensus for government policies. At press conferences, questions are not answered directly. Instead, ministers and other government spokespeople are trained to pivot the answer to a pre-arranged talking point. This practice was magnified during the Covid pandemic when most journalists were limited to asking a single question and occasionally, one follow-up.

Unavoidable bad news is often buried deep within a budget document or released on a Friday afternoon or in a pre–long weekend statement. Stretched for time and resources, many journalists take the path of least resistance and repeat the talking points. They may be skeptical, but they are also practical. It's easier to rewrite the government's executive summary of a budget than to read the entire thousand-page document.

Politicians also use journalists to help more overtly with their messaging, offering them nuggets of news that are essentially trial balloons to test public opinion before policy changes are announced. More compliant journalists are sometimes handed exclusives, with the quiet understanding that largely uncritical coverage will mean more of the same. Often these scoops are of the most inconsequential variety, such as reporting a cabinet shuffle or a budget policy hours before the actual announcement. But for journalists who feel their careers are boosted by breaking this kind of news first, it can be a powerful reward that is just as easily revoked for bad behaviour.

The system of handing out scoops while obscuring the source of the information has its more sinister side. Journalists are often misled into promoting false and dangerous narratives. This was the case with Maher Arar, the engineer detained by U.S. authorities in New York in 2002 while travelling home to Canada after visiting family in Tunisia. He was secretly transported to Syria, where he was imprisoned and tortured for almost a year. Despite an absence of evidence connecting him with terrorism in any way, several Canadian media outlets repeatedly ran stories quoting unnamed sources suggesting he was guilty. CanWest News, the *Ottawa Citizen*, the Canadian Press, and others ran reports claiming he had trained in Afghanistan and participated in terrorist activities. One described him as a "very bad guy" while another said he was "not a virgin" when it came to terrorism. One anonymous source was quoted as saying they were "100 percent sure" Arar had trained in an al Qaeda camp.

A commission of inquiry eventually exonerated Arar and found that he was the target of a deliberate smear campaign by anonymous and unaccountable Canadian government officials. The journalists who had run with the stories served as pawns in a disinformation campaign. Few reporters ever apologized for their role in the affair, but the *Globe and Mail*'s Jeff Sallot offered this perspective: "Somebody should be trying to find out who deliberately leaked misinformation to smear Mr. Arar. I had sources try to tell me that Mr. Arar was in fact a bad guy who confessed to training in Afghanistan. I never reported these allegations because ... scoops are no substitute for the truth."[4]

Sometimes journalists who realize they were duped feel compelled to expose the people who misled them. In 1994 Canadian defence officials were in crisis over allegations of misconduct by peacekeepers in Somalia. In one incident, Canadian soldiers shot a Somali citizen near their base. Major Barry Armstrong blew the whistle on what really happened, reporting that the man had been shot in the back and wounded, then killed "execution-style" with a gunshot to the back of his head. Desperate to cover up what took place, Canadian officials launched a campaign to discredit Armstrong. An aide to the defence minister called *Toronto Star* reporter Allan Thompson and prompted him to request an autopsy report, which purported to show Armstrong's analysis of the body was flawed. Thompson ran with the story, which called Armstrong's credibility into question. But the revelations from Somalia kept coming. At a subsequent inquiry, it was clear the autopsy report was just one cherry-picked part of a body of evidence that pointed to guilt on the part of the soldiers. Defence officials falsely told the inquiry they had only released the autopsy to the *Star* because Thompson had requested it.

This was too much for Thompson, who would later become head of Carleton University's School of Journalism. "I was duped into helping government officials smear a whistle-blower," he said.[5] Then he did something few journalists do. He wrote a follow-up story, outing his original source and acknowledging that the value of getting a "scoop" may have obscured the nature of the leak. He said the defence department had carefully laid down a paper trail to cover its tracks, deliberately failing to tell the commission that it had coached him to request the autopsy document.

DONALD TRUMP

There is not much question that the Donald Trump era has significantly impacted how journalists view political lying and what they are willing to do about it. As soon as he became president, his torrent of lies began. U.S. presidents before him had also engaged in lying, but many of Trump's lies seemed to carry no strategic importance. He just couldn't help himself. He told a gathering that it hadn't rained during his inauguration, even though it had, and he grossly inflated the size of the crowd in attendance. Those early statements gave journalists something they didn't usually see: lies that are extremely easy to disprove. This encouraged many news organizations to catalogue and debunk the lies regularly.

PolitiFact, a fact-checking website run by the Poynter Institute in the United States, scrutinized hundreds of Trump pronouncements over the years. It judged more than three-quarters of them to be false, mostly false, or in their "Pants on Fire" category.[6] The *Washington Post* eventually concluded that over his four years in office, Trump had made 30,573 false or misleading statements.[7] *Toronto Star* reporter Daniel Dale, who later moved to CNN, made it his personal mission to scrutinize every Trump statement. "I fact-checked every word uttered by this President from his inauguration day in January 2017 until September 2020 — when the daily number of lies got so unmanageably high that I had to start taking a pass on some of his remarks to preserve my health," Dale said.[8] The debunking process had only so much impact. Trump continued to repeat many lies after they had been exposed, claiming that his detractors were pushing fake news. And a not insignificant number of Americans continue to believe his lies. This has led many to conclude that we are living in a post-truth world, where alternative facts and lies comfortably coexist with the truth.

The final lie of Trump's administration was that he had won the 2020 election and that his opponents had rigged the outcome. This message was amplified by various conservative media outlets. Fox News questioned the security of electronic voting machines and accused the Democrats of vastly increasing the number of mail-in ballots for their own benefit. "The 2020 presidential election was not fair, and no honest person would claim that it was," said Fox News host Tucker Carlson. "The system was rigged against one candidate and in favour of another, and not in ways that were hidden from view."[9] Though many other news organizations refuted evidence of election interference, the misleading messaging took hold on social media and had a lasting impact on public opinion. At the beginning of 2022, a poll in the United States found that more than 40 percent did not believe Joe Biden had legitimately won the election.[10]

Even so, it wasn't until 2019 that major media outlets used the word *lie* to describe Trump's statements. In a way, it flies in the face of journalism's traditional approach, which is to confine itself to reporting what both sides say about a situation rather than uncovering the truth about it. Conventionally, Trump would be quoted as saying his inauguration was the biggest in history, while people with opposing views would be included in the same story. Perhaps Trump's enduring contribution to journalism is that he emboldened outlets to call out lies when they spotted them. But what if the frequency of his lies also had the effect of encouraging many Americans not to believe *anything* anymore? It just might be that Americans' lack of trust was a factor in fanning the confusion and disinformation that was rampant during the Covid-19 pandemic. As well, by mocking the triviality of many of Trump's lies, both the media and the public may have been lulled into not scrutinizing some of the more systemic duping that is taking place.

Take the issue of election rigging. Trump's allegations may be far-fetched, but the reality is that U.S. politics are rife with such things as gerrymandering and voter suppression, all designed to deliberately influence the outcome of elections.

...

It may seem hard to believe, but election tampering has also been part of Canada's history. In my own experience, I have witnessed efforts by a provincial government to conduct a secret vote-rigging process to subvert an election. A handful of close races typically decides which party forms the government in Manitoba. To increase their chances in three of those races during the 1995 election, senior Progressive Conservative strategists devised a plan to create and fund a phony Independent Native Voice Party. The idea was to divert Indigenous voters from their traditional NDP allegiances, allowing the Conservative candidates to squeak through. It didn't work, and it was eventually exposed by CBC Manitoba. A provincial inquiry judge who looked into the matter concluded he had never encountered so many liars in a single proceeding. But it took a full three years before the real story emerged in the media, because of adamant government denials at the time.[11]

There were similar denials during the so-called robocall scandal of 2011, when voters received calls directing them to the wrong polling stations on the night of a federal election. An investigation by the *Ottawa Citizen* showed how Elections Canada was looking into the Conservative campaign in Guelph as a source of the dirty-tricks campaign. A court eventually convicted one Conservative staffer in the affair, but the trial judge noted the employee likely didn't act alone.

With so much skullduggery taking place, many of the covert and corrupt activities governments of all stripes engage in never come to the surface. But in one notable Canadian example, they did so in spectacular fashion.

THE SNC-LAVALIN AFFAIR

Robert Fife is no stranger to the world of influence, lobbying, and deception in Ottawa. He began covering national politics in 1978, spending many years developing sources on all sides of the political spectrum. Sometimes those sources were willing to provide information on the condition their names not be used. That was the case in February 2019 when Fife, Ottawa bureau chief for the *Globe and Mail*, broke a story that rocked the Canadian political establishment. He reported that Prime Minister Justin Trudeau's office tried to pressure the justice minister to make a deal with a giant corporation that would prevent a criminal trial for fraud and corruption. The day the story broke, reporters asked Trudeau about it during a press conference. "The allegations in the *Globe* story this morning are false," he said emphatically.

Fife was confident in his sources, but he knew that the truth was not always guaranteed to emerge in the end. He had been told that the justice minister and attorney general, Jody Wilson-Raybould, resisted the pressure and refused to make the deal the PMO requested. It all revolved around Montreal-based engineering giant SNC-Lavalin, which was facing corruption charges based on its dealings years earlier in Libya. The prime minister wanted Wilson-Raybould to negotiate a remediation agreement to allow the company to pay a fine but avoid a criminal conviction. For Fife, Trudeau's firm denial was worrisome. "I was really concerned for the first couple of weeks," he said in an interview with the CBC. "I had a lot of sleepless nights. My biggest fear was: I had no idea whether they were going to get to her and say 'Go out there and deny the story.' Because if she came out and denied the story, I'm dead in the water."[12] Fife, in fact, had been one of the reporters using unnamed sources who made allegations against Maher Arar that were eventually shown to be unfounded. Was he being fed correct information this time?

Sometimes it takes years or decades for the truth to emerge about contentious issues in the corridors of political power. Fife himself acknowledges that the shrinking ranks of journalists means that only 20 percent of federal government affairs get regularly scrutinized in the media. But he didn't have to wait long to see what Wilson-Raybould would say about the matter. She testified under oath that she indeed was pressured by the PMO. In a subsequent book, she details a meeting she had with Trudeau days after the *Globe* piece came out. The prime minister was insisting that neither he nor his staff had lied when they said they weren't directing her to take a position on the SNC prosecution. But she wasn't buying it. Wilson-Raybould reveals what she was thinking at that moment:

> I knew what he was really asking. What he was saying. In
> that moment, I knew he wanted me to lie — to attest that

what had occurred had not occurred ... I told him I had
serious concerns and that my belief in him was very shak-
en. At some point, he asked me what he should say to the
media. He had a media availability ostensibly on housing
later that morning. He mentioned a line they were thinking of using: "Her presence in Cabinet speaks for itself ..."
Can you believe it? I told him I was not going to give him
communications advice. How ridiculous. In my opinion,
there is no spin on dishonesty.[13]

The entire SNC-Lavalin affair is an instructive case study in lobbying, influence, and spin, and how powerful forces try to keep journalists and the public in the dark. It began in February 2015, when RCMP filed charges against the company, alleging it used bribery to get government business in Libya. The company said the allegations pertained to people who were no longer with the firm. It immediately began a sustained and sophisticated lobbying and PR effort to convince the government to use a "deferred prosecution agreement" system, which would permit the company to bypass a trial just by paying a fine. It would also avoid a formal conviction, which could have barred the company from bidding on government work for ten years.

Within months, the company was buying image-building ads on all the major networks and in Canadian dailies under the slogan "Proud to Build What Matters."[14] Soon afterwards op-eds began appearing in newspapers touting the benefits of deferred prosecution agreements. One was written by John Manley, a former Liberal cabinet minister and head of a leading Canadian business group.[15] Later in the year, the Institute for Research on Public Policy brought together a number of business leaders and academics to discuss deferred prosecutions. It issued a press release in March 2016 urging the government to adopt the system. Its press release nowhere mentioned that the study was partly funded by SNC-Lavalin itself, along with other business groups. That information was buried in the footnotes of the report.[16]

Simultaneously, the company initiated the first of dozens of lobbying meetings with government officials. By February 2018, the company was approaching staff in the minister of finance's office suggesting the deferred prosecution system could be introduced in the next federal budget, even though it involved a change to the Criminal Code. Twenty-five days after that meeting, the government did just as it had been asked, announcing the change and then tucking the provision into its 582-page budget bill. Few if any journalists knew what was going on, and some of the government's own members didn't even notice. Two months later, some MPs realized what was happening when they were given fifteen minutes to discuss the provision at a committee meeting. Liberal MP Greg Fergus told the committee he had read through most of the budget bill before the hearings but had no idea about the deferred prosecution provision. The proposal received Royal Assent at lightning speed, without ever being scrutinized by the House of Commons Justice Committee, which usually reviews Criminal Code changes.

SNC-Lavalin had successfully prompted a change to Canadian law, with the full co-operation of senior government officials. There was just one problem. On the eve of the law coming into effect, the director of public prosecutions decided the company wouldn't be offered a deferred prosecution, and Wilson-Raybould backed up that decision. Months of pressure from the PMO and top officials wouldn't get the minister to back off. Eventually, she was shuffled out of her portfolio and then resigned from the cabinet. It was one of the biggest and ugliest scandals in Trudeau's administration, but it's likely none of it would have become public if Wilson-Raybould had not stood her ground. Mario Dion, the federal conflict of interest and ethics commissioner, eventually ruled that Trudeau breached the Conflict of Interest Act:

> I find that Mr. Trudeau used his position of authority over Ms. Wilson-Raybould to seek to influence her decision on whether she should overrule the Director of Public Prosecution's decision not to invite SNC-Lavalin to enter into negotiations towards a remediation agreement. Because SNC-Lavalin overwhelmingly stood to benefit from Ms. Wilson-Raybould's intervention, I have no doubt that the result of Mr. Trudeau's influence would have furthered SNC-Lavalin's interests. The actions that sought to

further these interests were improper since the actions were contrary to the constitutional principles of prosecutorial independence and the rule of law.[17]

There was one final note of irony in the story. In December 2019, SNC-Lavalin agreed to plead guilty to a single charge of fraud relating to the Libyan affair. In return, federal prosecutors dropped the bribery charges. The company paid $280 million in fines and was placed on probation for three years. But most importantly, it retained the right to bid on federal contracts, the key thing it was worried about all along. Company shares jumped 20 percent when the news was announced.

Summing up the whole firestorm he helped to trigger in Ottawa, Fife mused, "Now that they pulled back the curtain, now you see how things really operate in this town."[18]

In trying to mislead journalists and the public, Trudeau had walked a fine line between lying and just sidestepping an issue. When pressed about whether he pressured the minister, Trudeau kept repeating that he never directed her to do anything. He ignored the reality that the *Globe* story never accused him of doing so, only of pressuring her.

It was reminiscent of former Toronto mayor Rob Ford, who once scolded a gaggle of reporters for failing to ask him the right questions in their pursuit of allegations that he used crack cocaine. In 2013 a video circulated purportedly showing him smoking crack. When asked if he was a cocaine addict or whether he smoked crack, he repeatedly said no. Then, while accosted by reporters one day outside his office, he asked them to rephrase the question again. "Do you smoke crack cocaine?" someone finally asked. His tortured reply: No, he doesn't now, and he isn't an addict, but yes, he had done so in the past. "I wasn't lying," he insisted about his answers over the previous few weeks. "You didn't ask the correct questions … You ask the question properly, I'll answer it."[19] President Bill Clinton used similar linguistic chicanery when he looked into the cameras sternly and stated, "I did not have sexual relations with that woman." Only later did he acknowledge an "improper physical relationship" with Monica Lewinsky, a White House intern.

When it comes to misleading the media, politicians are forever trying to portray themselves as tireless workers who are always on the job in the service of the public. Most people wouldn't criticize a hard-working politician for taking a regular vacation. Still, it seems it's far easier for them to be sly about their whereabouts than to share holiday details publicly. It can also be useful to obscure ethically suspect behaviour.

Prime Minister Justin Trudeau got into trouble when he decided to take a trip to the Aga Khan's private island in the Bahamas over the Christmas holidays in 2016. His daily itinerary, which is made available to the media, merely said, "Personal," leaving the impression he was spending holiday time at home with family.[20] Media inquiries about his whereabouts went unanswered for several days until the Prime Minister's Office released a statement saying he had gone to Nassau. There was no mention that he had been staying with the Aga Khan.[21] A few days after the release of the first statement, Trudeau finally revealed where he had been, though his office still didn't disclose the presence of another Liberal MP and party officials on the same trip.

The ethics commissioner eventually ruled Trudeau violated multiple sections of the Conflict of Interest Act by making the trip and travelling on the Aga Khan's private helicopter. The holiday cost Canadian taxpayers more than $200,000, including meals, accommodations, and Jet Ski rentals for the prime minister's personal protection detail.[22]

Then there was Trudeau's ill-considered decision to take a family vacation to Tofino on September 30, 2021, Canada's first National Day for Truth and Reconciliation. In a clear effort to mislead, his official itinerary said he would be in Ottawa for "private meetings." But when a Global News reporter spotted him walking on the beach in British Columbia, the jig was clearly up.[23]

BRIAN PALLISTER

A far more elaborate and long-term scheme to keep the public in the dark about vacation time occurred in Manitoba when it was revealed that the soon-to-be premier was spending nearly one-fifth of his life outside the country at his plush holiday retreat. In the spring of 2016, while a provincial election campaign was underway, the CBC's investigative unit was hard at work poring through the Panama Papers — a leak of more than 11.5 million financial and legal records from a Panamanian firm showing who had offshore bank accounts and holdings. The documents had been provided to the International Consortium of Investigative Journalists in the United States, which shared them with the CBC. A check of prominent Manitoba political names didn't turn up any offshore assets, but we did spot the presence of Donny Lalonde, a former national boxing champion. Since leaving Winnipeg, he had become involved in questionable real estate transactions in Costa Rica. Working in collaboration with Costa Rican journalists on the Lalonde story, we discovered something interesting: the country tracks everyone's entry and exit trips and is happy to make that information public.

To my knowledge, Costa Rica is the only country that considers such information a public record. It was a valuable tool in our investigation of Lalonde, but suddenly another idea occurred to me. Brian Pallister, the Conservative leader vying to become Manitoba's next premier, was known to have a property in Costa Rica. He hardly ever talked about it, and even personal aides and staff were unaware of the details. I asked our team to see if we could get Pallister's travel records. Sure enough, the Costa Rican General Immigration and Foreign Citizens Bureau provided us with a detailed list of every occasion when he had entered and exited the country, going back years.

The result was a bombshell revelation on the eve of the provincial election. The headline said it all: "Brian Pallister spends nearly 1 in 5 days of his time in Costa Rica, travel logs show." We thought it would be fair to track his trips back to when he became a member of the legislature in 2012 and found he had spent about 240 days either en route to or in the Central American country.[24] That was over about three and a half years. It's not hard to understand why. Photos posted by the construction company that built "Residencia Pallister" show a lavishly appointed 7,700-square-foot home complete with a basketball court, forest views leading to the ocean, and a large infinity pool. For someone who was campaigning that he would work hard for the people of the province every day, it was a challenging story to explain away, especially since he had misled the media about his holiday trips.

In 2014 Manitoba had experienced extensive summer rainfall, which caused it to declare a state of emergency and ask for military assistance in battling the flood waters. It was a tense time, and estimated damage eventually totalled more than $1 billion. During the height of the crisis, reporters noticed that Pallister, leader of the Opposition at the time, appeared to be missing in action. In a year-end interview several months later, the *Winnipeg Free Press* asked him explicitly to account for his time during the flood. He responded: "I was at a family wedding in Alberta in July. The first week of July was when the unprecedented rainfall occurred one day in parts of western Manitoba. But prior to that time, I had visited every potential flood area — some of which had been flooding — in the province. But I didn't take a film crew with me. I guess I'm learning as I go. I suppose I have to tweet you guys every time I go to something."[25]

Now that we had official confirmation of Pallister's trips, it was clear his statement was false, designed to cover up his absence at a critical moment in the province's history. Travel logs showed that he was on a fourteen-day stay in Costa Rica between June 29 and July 12, 2014, right at the height of the state of emergency. Faced with this revelation, he acknowledged that the family wedding had occurred on June 28. "Mr. Pallister has repeatedly stated that he does not believe times of crises should be politicized," said his spokesperson.

More evidence that Pallister was hiding his Costa Rica trips came from an examination of an answer he had given in early April of 2016 when the *Winnipeg Free Press* asked each party leader where they travelled the last time they had left Canada. Pallister responded that he had visited a favourite bar and restaurant in a North Dakota border town the previous fall. But, again, the travel logs showed this to be untrue. He had been in Costa Rica for twenty-five days over Christmas and New Year's and spent another eleven days at the end of January and into February 2016. "This was an oversight, an unfortunate lapse in memory," said his spokesperson.

Despite Pallister's dissembling on his Costa Rica vacations, he went on to win the provincial election handily and became premier. Voters were too angry at NDP premier Greg Selinger for his own difficulty with sticking to a story when he raised the provincial sales tax after telling voters he wouldn't.

Yet Pallister had a troubled time in office, often beset by problems of his own making. Like Donald Trump, he made bold statements that often didn't stand up to factual scrutiny. He claimed he wouldn't and didn't cut health care in Manitoba, even though the signs of deep cuts were everywhere. During the pandemic, he blamed everyone from Justin Trudeau and Joe Biden to the pharmaceutical companies for foiling Manitoba's efforts to vaccinate the public, even when the evidence showed none of his assertions were accurate. He repeatedly boasted that Manitoba had enacted the strictest preventive measures, and sooner than any other province, when that was demonstrably false. As *Winnipeg Free Press* columnist Dan Lett said, "In times of adversity, great political leaders are usually able to find the words and solutions that fit best with the challenges they are facing. In Manitoba, faced with a raging wildfire of new infections, Pallister has given us histrionics and lies. And the worst part is that no one seems able to stop him."[26] In the end, he stopped himself by stepping down as premier in mid-pandemic.

. . .

Deception in the political arena is so commonplace that when journalists stand toe to toe with politicians, they often experience an overwhelming feeling they are being fed a lie. Much rarer is the time when the journalist has immediate access to proof.

That happened several times in my career, perhaps most spectacularly in November 1984 when I interviewed federal finance minister Michael Wilson. Just two months after the Progressive Conservative government led by Brian Mulroney was elected, Wilson visited Manitoba as part of a tour of the West to meet with his provincial counterparts. Ottawa had just unveiled plans to slash government spending in every direction, consistent with the deficit-fighting ethos sweeping many Western countries at the time. *Austerity* was the new buzzword, and no part of government spending would go unexamined. That included fundamental aspects of Canada's social safety net, including child benefits, Old Age Security payments, and unemployment insurance. According to this plan, the provinces would have to do their part in the belt-tightening process, and Manitoba's share of anticipated cuts to its federal transfer payments was $72 million.

Wilson scheduled a meeting with Manitoba's finance minister, Vic Schroeder, at the downtown Westin Hotel in Winnipeg. The two politicians emerged from their ninety-minute chat and sat in the hotel lobby for an impromptu news conference. Wilson placed a bundle of file folders on the coffee table in front of him and told the throng of reporters that he was there to listen and consider Manitoba's position. No decisions had yet been made, no judgments rendered, and Manitoba would not be treated differently or more severely than any other province, he said. After a few minutes, Wilson dashed off to attend a luncheon at the hotel where he was to deliver the keynote address. The assembled reporters scattered to file their reports. I lingered behind, and after reporters from all the other media outlets had left, I noticed the file folders were still exactly where Wilson had put them.

Five minutes passed. Then ten. After fifteen minutes, when no one had come to retrieve anything, I sat down at the coffee table and gingerly opened a file. Inside was a black book stamped *Secret* with instructions on how Wilson should handle his meeting in Manitoba. I had no intention of taking the folders with me, or even so much as moving them, but I reasoned that if a politician was so imprudent as to leave them abandoned in a public place, I was justified in reading them. It was a decision my bosses at the *Winnipeg Free Press* backed up, despite furious blowback from Wilson and the prime minister himself. What I found inside revealed that Wilson had not been forthright at the news conference. Memos from his deputy minister confirmed Manitoba was the hardest hit province regarding the transfer payment cuts and said no compelling evidence had been presented to indicate Ottawa should back away from the plan. At the same time, Wilson was being secretly urged not to deliver too hard a message to Manitoba during these meetings, given the controversy the cuts had stirred. It all appeared to be a stage-managed exercise in public relations.

The entire time I read through the file, dictating portions into my tape recorder, I expected someone to burst into the lobby and grab the material back. It never happened. After more than an hour, I approached one of Wilson's aides and told them about the wayward files, and they retrieved them. But after the luncheon ended, I decided to test Wilson again on how truthful he would be. One of the memos addressed to Wilson said that if Manitoba succeeded in avoiding the funding cut, other provinces would make similar claims and the cost to Ottawa would be $1.3 billion. It was an exact calculation, and it was clearly spelled out in the brief to Wilson. Well before Wilson knew I had read through the memos, I asked him explicitly what this cost would be. I used the identical language as that in the memo. He looked me straight in the eye. "We don't know," he replied. "It's hard to say."

The affair became known as the hotel papers caper, triggering intense Opposition questions in Parliament. For the federal Liberals and New Democrats, it was the perfect opportunity to bash the new government for its lack of transparency. "Did he mislead the people of Manitoba?" asked Liberal leader John Turner in Question Period on the same day my story was published. "Will the Prime Minister instruct the Minister of Finance to consult from now on in a more honest and open way?" chimed in Manitoba MP Lloyd Axworthy. Mulroney defended his minister, calling him a man of "unimpeachable integrity." Always quick to try to take the offensive, Mulroney went further and accused me of "pilfering" the documents. That led NDP leader Ed Broadbent to proclaim, "It is a curious world when a cabinet minister is so sloppy and careless to leave behind a document that the Prime Minister accuses someone else of pilfering. It is a strange government we have."

The next day, Axworthy jumped to my defence over the pilfering accusation in the House of Commons: "Now that he has had the opportunity to check the record, and recognizing that the press person in question was only living up to the standards for open communication by the government, which the Prime Minister has called for, is he prepared to apologize for that remark and begin to repair the breach of trust he has with members of the media?" To which Mulroney replied: "Mr. Speaker, if I have offended anyone, including the Hon. Member, I apologize."[27]

It's the closest I ever got to an apology from the prime minister of Canada.

The episode came early in Mulroney's eight-year tenure as prime minister, but it foreshadowed a culture of dishonesty and deceit that plagued his government. Allegations of dirty land deals, fraud, conflicts of interest, and various other misdeeds were rampant during Mulroney's government. Most scandalous of all were the revelations that Mulroney himself took secret cash payments from a German lobbyist. All the while, he fought back with his trademark smile and bombast. He was soon given the nickname "Lyin' Brian."

I have often thought back to the Michael Wilson story and wondered whether Mulroney might have seen it as a warning about what can happen when you engage in lies and then get caught. Many years after the incident, I delivered a training session to journalists on the federal Access to Information Act. I pointed out to students that cabinet documents are secret but can be requested under the Access to Information Act after twenty years. When I got home that evening, it suddenly dawned on me that I could now see how the episode had played out in Brian Mulroney's cabinet at the time. Were ministers encouraged to be more upfront in their dealings with provincial counterparts? Did the cabinet have a robust discussion on increased political transparency?

I filed an official request for the cabinet minutes of December 1984, one month after the hotel caper. My hunch was correct. The agenda for one cabinet meeting contained an item called "General Discussion: Security of Classified Material." Instead of a lecture about truth in politics, Mulroney had other things in mind. The minutes detail a comprehensive list of new procedures for ensuring government material remains secure, including keeping documents in locked security briefcases when travelling and prohibiting the removal of cabinet papers from Ottawa without the express approval of the Privy Council Office. "The prime minister reminded cabinet of the importance that must be attached to maintaining proper security of classified and other sensitive documents by ministers," the minutes said. "He underlined that this was a matter of personal responsibility with particular care and prudence being needed when ministers travel outside the National Capital Region where facilities for safekeeping of documents may not be readily available."[28]

One of the oldest adages in journalism is: "If your mother tells you she loves you, check it out." It's a reminder that verification is the essence of good reporting. Governments, and politicians generally, are constantly telling people they love them. As the stories in this chapter show, they are not always being truthful. Media are often the conveyor belts for misleading information, even outright lies. Sometimes it's difficult to find out the truth about a political attempt to mislead. The need to file a story quickly to meet the next deadline can often be the worst enemy of verification. But journalists who display a consistent level of skill, skepticism, critical thinking, and persistence are able to expose some of the lies. Carl Bernstein, part of the famous *Washington Post* duo who exposed the Watergate scandal in the 1970s, reflected on this in a speech several years ago. "Almost inevitably, unreasonable government secrecy is the enemy," he said. "And when lying is combined with secrecy, it's usually a road map to what the real story might be."[29]

Chapter 5

Thin Blue Lies

AS A YOUNG REPORTER WORKING THE NIGHT BEAT, ONE OF my duties was to call the police department every hour. "Anything new to report?" I'd ask the sergeant. There would be a shuffling of papers, and the officer might inform me about an assault, a break-in, an arrest, or a charge. It was a quick and easy way to provide fodder for the newspaper, and in those days, it didn't even occur to reporters to question the validity of any of the information offered. Nor did our editors ever suggest we try to get the perspective of the person charged before running their name in the paper. Police were considered an authoritative source, worthy of trust and able to supply unchallenged facts about everything from minor incidents to shootings and murders. To a large extent, this remains true today. Crime news has been a staple of the media for centuries. It's seen as urgent and entertaining, something everyone will want to read. Even the smallest newsrooms are guaranteed a reliable stream of stories from their police calls, and many local news outlets traditionally assign a reporter exclusively to the police beat. A U.S. study once found that nearly 14 percent of all full-time reporters said they covered crime or police.[1]

Imagine, then, what a police reporter would have concluded after reading the following press release from the Minneapolis Police Department.

MAN DIES AFTER MEDICAL INCIDENT
DURING POLICE INTERACTION

May 25, 2020 (MINNEAPOLIS) On Monday evening, shortly after 8:00 pm, officers from the Minneapolis Police Department responded to the 3700 block of Chicago Avenue South on a report of a forgery in progress. Officers were advised that the suspect was sitting on top of a blue car and appeared to be under the influence.

Two officers arrived and located the suspect, a male believed to be in his 40s, in his car. He was ordered to step from his car. After he got out, he physically resisted officers. Officers were able to get the suspect into handcuffs and noted he appeared to be suffering medical distress. Officers called for an ambulance. He was transported to Hennepin County Medical Center by ambulance where he died a short time later.

At no time were weapons of any type used by anyone involved in this incident.

The Minnesota Bureau of Criminal Apprehension has been called in to investigate this incident at the request of the Minneapolis Police Department.

No officers were injured in the incident.[2]

The headline of this police communication might just as well have read: "Nothing to see here, folks. Move along." Police officers were merely detaining someone in a forgery case. They noticed he was in medical distress and helpfully called an ambulance. Unfortunately, he died, though thankfully no officers were injured in the process. No weapons "of any type" were used in this incident. Based on this press release, it's unlikely this would have even made the local news. Instead, the murder of George Floyd triggered worldwide protests and a racial reckoning in society that continues to reverberate far beyond Minneapolis.

Fortunately for the truth, seventeen-year-old Darnella Frazier captured the scene on her phone and posted it online for the world to see. It shows all the things the Minneapolis Police Department's press release carefully omits: that a police officer, Derek Chauvin, pressed his knee against Floyd's neck for nine minutes and twenty-nine seconds; that Floyd repeatedly protested he couldn't breathe; that other officers stood by and didn't do anything. The press statement didn't just lie by omitting crucial evidence. It also misrepresented the sequence of events, pretending that Floyd was in medical distress as he was being handcuffed when the police themselves were the cause of his distress. It was an attempt to dupe the media, and it might have worked if not for the video evidence of what actually happened.

Such blatant misrepresentation of facts is common in police reports, especially where police misconduct is a factor. When Los Angeles police infamously brutalized Rodney King in 1991, they wrote reports claiming he had suffered only minor cuts and scrapes. In 2020, when police shot and killed an innocent Breonna Taylor in Kentucky, officers were charged with fabricating evidence to justify a "no knock" warrant and conspiring to cover up the truth.

. . .

In Canada, police departments have been known to jump to the defence of officers who shoot suspects before independent investigations have even begun. Perhaps the most famous example was the shooting of Indigenous leader J.J. Harper in Winnipeg in 1988. Harper was misidentified as a suspect in a crime, confronted by police officer Robert Cross, and then shot to death. Within two days, Winnipeg's police chief exonerated Cross, blamed Harper for the events, and declared racism was not a factor in what happened. But Winnipeg's Indigenous community was outraged, and the case was soon investigated intensively by Manitoba's Aboriginal Justice Inquiry. It concluded that Harper's detention was inappropriate, that Cross had altered his story, and that an "official version" was concocted by police to mask what had really happened. The inquiry concluded it was Cross, through his unnecessary approach and inappropriate attempt to detain Harper, who set in motion the events that resulted in Harper's death. It also said racism played a part in what happened. More broadly, the inquiry concluded that the Harper killing was just one example of a wider problem. "The justice system has failed Manitoba's Aboriginal people on a massive scale."[3]

Thomas Nolan, a former Boston police lieutenant who became an academic, says he used to coach officers on how to frame their reports to paint victims as aggressors and themselves as valiant defenders of the law. Police routinely use contrived forms of expression when communicating with the media. They might describe "a male suspect exiting his vehicle" or a car that is "blue in colour." But when describing serious matters, they have invented legalistic-sounding euphemisms like "officer-involved shooting" and "police interaction," designed to obscure the truth. According to police press releases, officers never shoot people. At the most, they might "discharge their weapons," which then strike individuals. Nolan says this is a deliberate strategy:

> This stilted, imprecise "legalese" is the commonly used verbiage found in the police lexicon and forms the base of the narrative that police use throughout the United States. The purpose of the narrative is ultimately to exculpate the police from any blame or allegation that the use of force being described was unnecessary, inappropriate, excessive, or unlawful. It also serves to shield the use of force incident from any meaningful examination, review, or criticism from interlopers, those meddlesome and irksome outsiders such as members of the media, the defense bar, and residents of communities of color who might express skepticism, question, challenge, and even interrogate the police version of incidents when officers use force.[4]

I cringe whenever I hear or read these manufactured phrases pop up in media reports, as they frequently do. It's a signal the reporter is being manipulated. If police have shot and killed someone, it's pure doublespeak to refer to the incident as an "interaction."

Deception and lying aren't just restricted to communication with the media. They often continue into the courts. In 2012 an investigation by the *Toronto Star* found more than one hundred cases across Canada where police used illegal techniques, excessive force, and racial profiling and then covered it up with false testimony in court. The newspaper found that a common technique would be for police to assault a suspect and then begin their cover-up by charging their victim with assault and obstructing justice. "Some of the victims were guilty of nothing more than a bad attitude." In reviewing court transcripts of cases where police lied, the *Star* made note of words judges used to describe their evidence: "lie," "fabricate," "evasive," "absurd," "ridiculous," "subversive," "disturbing," and "pure fiction."[5]

The *Star* also noted that many officers who were accused of lying by judges never faced any consequences. Some were identified as repeat offenders. In many cases, the lying wasn't reported to the internal discipline divisions of police departments, while other police forces seemed unconcerned by the findings. A spokesperson for the Toronto police told the newspaper its investigation couldn't be taken seriously since many of the judicial statements were "throwaway comments" of little value. "A judge can comment on anything he or she wishes. Such comment, however, does not amount to a finding of guilt," the spokesperson said. "The criminal justice system works on evidence, on examination, cross-examination, and decision. It does not work on throwaway comments unsupported by evidence."[6]

Systematic lying in court is so common in the United States that officers have coined a term for it: *testilying*. A New York mayoral commission investigating police in the mid-1990s found that officers often perjured themselves on the witness stand. "Perjury is perhaps the most widespread form of police wrongdoing facing today's criminal justice system," the report said.[7] A quarter of a century later, the *New York Times* revisited the issue to see if anything had changed. It found lying in court was a recurring problem. Similarly, a *USA Today* investigation in 2019 collated police misconduct records over ten years. It found 2,227 instances of perjury, tampering with evidence or witnesses, or falsifying reports.[8]

For people who work in the criminal justice system, the findings of these media investigations do not come as a great surprise. Toronto criminal lawyer Reid Rusonik took to the pages of the *Toronto Star* in 2012 to give his perspective:

As a young criminal defence lawyer, I was taught that I must approach every case with the assumption that all police officers lie all of the time. I was taught that to analyze their anticipated evidence from any other starting point would be gross negligence. As a white, middle-class man from small-town Ontario, I was shocked and incredulous about the idea of using this assumption even merely as an intellectual exercise. Over the years, however, employing this analytical discipline in more than one thousand cases has invariably produced evidence of its soundness in instances where there was room for a police officer to fabricate.

Many times, the lies were merely exaggerations. Often it was a question of omitting truths as opposed to distorting them. Far too often, however, analysis of this type has exposed instances of blatant fabrication on critical points of evidence.

In these last instances, I am not referring to fabrications borne out of the existence of contradictory evidence from another human being whose credibility was also in issue. I am referring to lies in the face of completely independent evidence: audio and videotapes, computer records, the laws of physics, and notes made by the officers themselves. As a result of my own experience, twenty-five years later, I teach new defence lawyers the same thing I was taught.[9]

Academics have found that lying is woven into the fabric of police culture. Arresting officers realize they can lie to secure confessions. Senior officers know they can exaggerate to lobby for bigger budgets. For some, a form of "noble cause corruption" is at play — a sense that any means will justify the ends of securing social order and making sure the bad guys go to jail. Ottawa Police, for example, tricked a suspect into providing a DNA sample by pretending they were doing a door-to-door survey and giving away prizes to anyone participating. In the same case, they issued a fake news release in 2014 for the sole purpose of seeing how a suspect who was being monitored by a hidden camera would react.[10] The police were unconcerned that reporters would be duped because the bigger prize was catching the "bad guy."

The problem is that "bad guys" often end up being the marginalized and dispossessed in any given community. Most of the suspects Derek Chauvin restrained with his knee over the years were people of colour. While Black people make up about 20 percent of the population of Minneapolis, they are involved in 60 percent of incidents where police use force.

We found the same systemic racial bias in policing when, at CBC Manitoba, we conducted a comprehensive review of deadly encounters involving police over seventeen years in Canada. While individual cases of shootings and deaths are generally reported when they occur, police departments deliberately obscure the total statistics so that it's difficult to draw conclusions about trends. The vast majority of police departments also refuse to report statistics about the race of suspects, people arrested, and people killed. Our team spent six months going through police and coroner reports, media stories, court transcripts, and other sources, including interviews with family members, to build a database of all deaths that had occurred between 2000 and 2017. We found more than 460 incidents in all. About 70 percent were fatal police shootings, while the rest involved people dying in restraint or after physical struggles. Some happened after the use of baton strikes or stun gun shootings.

To understand who the victims were, we tried to identify the gender, age, race, or ethnicity of the victim, how they died, how they were armed, and whether they had mental health or substance abuse problems.[11] The findings confirmed what many people had suspected for years. Black, Indigenous, and people of colour were vastly overrepresented. For instance, Black people in Toronto represented nearly 37 percent of the victims, but at the time were about 8 percent of the population. In Winnipeg, two-thirds of the victims were Indigenous, even though they were about 10 percent of the population. Another telling finding was that in 70 percent of the cases, mental health or drug use was a factor. In all the cases involving fatal encounters, we could only identify eighteen where criminal charges were laid against an officer. Of these, there had been two convictions. After all, most deadly encounters have no independent witnesses other than the police themselves. As

Thomas Nolan pointed out, "A bedrock tenet of the police subculture, and one taught to me very early in my career in law enforcement, is that another officer's judgment, particularly as it pertains to his or her use of force, is never to be questioned or second-guessed."[12]

The entire CBC investigation painted a picture of police targeting people of colour who were in mental and drug-induced distress. It was a time-consuming and expensive project for a media outlet to pursue, and many people wondered afterward why the information was so difficult to obtain in the first place. In effect, by refusing to gather and release the available data, police departments were deliberately covering-up how they did their work and who ended up being victimized in fatal encounters. Analyzing the results of the investigation, retired Ottawa police officer Syd Gravel said, "My initial reaction was that there is a failing here in our society."[13]

INNER CIRCLES AND OUTER CIRCLES

In their efforts to manipulate reality, police rely primarily on the media to convey their messages to the public. Sociologist Richard Ericson identified two types of reporters who typically cover the police beat: the inner circle and the outer circle. Inner-circle reporters usually come from outlets that rely heavily on crime news to fill their pages and news lineups. These would include radio reporters who have little time for anything other than the briefest reports, and rarely venture beyond spot news. But it would also include beat reporters for major newsrooms who depend on good relations with police to be kept in the know. Many police departments in big cities provide office space for journalists right inside the station. The inner circle reporters often spend the bulk of their working day there and tell their assignment editors what the breaking news stories are. In effect, the police are able to define the news agenda for these reporters. "The repertoire of inner-circle reporters rarely included explanations or secondary understanding," Ericson writes.[14]

When not covering breaking crime news, inner-circle reporters produce features that typically show police in a positive light. They focus on the life of officers and how they do their jobs, along with the tools and techniques they use. Such reporters are frequently rewarded with scoops. They are the first to be notified about a drug bust or a significant investigation. They might be invited on a ride along when police intend to make an arrest. Police departments in many places arrange "perp walks," which involve tipping off friendly reporters or photographers to a location where officers will parade a suspect in handcuffs down the street. This serves two purposes: to reward reporters with an exclusive, behind-the-scenes view of an arrest in action, and to embarrass a suspect they don't like for one reason or another.

This practice was taken to its extreme in New York in 1995, when police took a suspect from the station for a ride around the block and brought him back to the precinct to parade him in front of a TV crew that had arrived late. The man sued the police and won, with the judge concluding that there was "no legitimate law enforcement objective or justification" other than to shame him.[15]

Inner-circle reporters also tend to print the names of most people charged with crimes, no matter how minor the offence. In their defence, they argue that they are merely passing along what the police have told them, and it's in the public interest to know who is charged with offences. The problem with this practice is that charges are often downgraded or thrown out altogether before there is any trial, and even cases that proceed to court sometimes result in an acquittal. But the follow-up is rarely reported in the media, because the sheer volume of crime reports is hard to track. The net effect is that the media are only reporting half the story.

This practice began to have serious consequences in the internet era, where a search for a person's name would reveal an original charge that might or might not have been dropped. News organizations have begun to recognize the problem and are starting to adjust how they handle routine police briefings about minor crimes. In 2021 the Associated Press announced it would no longer include the names of accused people in such stories. The news service's vice-president of standards made a frank admission: "Usually, we don't follow up with coverage about the outcome of the cases. We may not know if the charges were later dropped or reduced, as they often are, or if the suspect was later acquitted."[16] The ethics advisory committee of the Canadian Association of Journalists has also criticized the practice of always naming suspects. "Significant research shows the extent of over-policing in racialized communities and also illustrates how that coverage can reflect so-cietal priorities and/or can stigmatize communities. Further, a focus on spot-news coverage of minor crimes contributes to stereotyping by displacing opportunities for better-rounded news coverage in affected communities."[17]

Outer-circle reporters, on the other hand, detach themselves from po-lice sources and have more of a mission to "police the police" rather than to co-operate with them, according to Ericson. This often leads to conflict between police and reporters. I spent much of my career operating in this outer circle, as a reporter and manager. While other reporters might get ex-clusives about police busts, I put greater value on having my newsroom look critically at the policies and actions of officers. It often led to tense moments, with police departments refusing to provide information on critical issues.

Throughout my time as news manager at CBC Manitoba, there would be disputes, recriminations, and periodic meetings at the police station to sort out thorny issues. No matter which circle a journalist or newsroom inhabit-ed, however, senior police officials ultimately controlled what information to release and what facts to withhold. Police could decide whom to name and whom to shame. For example, when a police department decides to crack down on drunk driving, it will sometimes release the names of offenders to the media and hope they'll be published as a deterrent. When someone is released after serving their term in jail, police will occasionally put out a statement warning the community that the person remains a danger to the public. Many media outlets reflexively publish such information without in-dependently verifying the facts or weighing the consequences to the person who has served their time.

. . .

Police also attempt to eliminate entirely media reporting of certain crimes. Decades ago in Winnipeg, if the police didn't want media scrutiny of a particular case, they would ensure the accused appeared before a judge in a suburban courtroom where reporters rarely ventured.

An interesting example of a clumsy cover-up by both police and a Crown prosecutor occurred early in my career. One day, I was walking through the ornate halls of Winnipeg's law courts building when a waving hand appeared from behind a door. A provincial court judge beckoned me into a room. "You will want to be in Courtroom 103 this afternoon at 2:00 p.m.," he said.

I didn't need any further encouragement. A quick check of the court docket indicated nothing of interest, just a succession of guilty pleas to minor offences. There would be no reason for the media to be in attendance that day. But I knew something was brewing, so I came to the courtroom and patiently waited as a series of accused appeared before a judge for sentencing. Finally, a forty-eight-year-old man pleaded guilty to a hit-and-run incident. He was driving carelessly and hit another vehicle, injuring two people. Then he left the scene of the accident. The Crown attorney recited the facts of the case briefly, and both he and the man's defence counsel jointly recommended a light sentence be imposed. Provincial court judge John Enns paused for a moment and then admonished both lawyers for "studiously avoiding" mentioning that the accused was a Winnipeg police officer. "You should know better," he scolded them.[18] It was a telling example of how police use their influence to mislead and cover things up, with complicity from the Crown. In this case, though, a judge refused to play ball. The following year, an internal city report not meant for public distribution showed how police routinely hid the occupation of police officers who had been charged with criminal offences.

By exercising control over what they release and what they hide, police departments can significantly mislead the media and the public about the extent of crime in the community. Over the years, the Local News Research Project has studied the issue in Toronto. Even though the *Toronto Star* does strong investigative work when it comes to policing practices, it also relies on routine police communications to fill the pages of its newspaper and website. One study found that police and crime-related news dominated its coverage of disadvantaged city neighbourhoods, even though police statistics showed violent crime was more prevalent in other areas.[19]

When the research project looked at the Toronto edition of the Chinese-language newspaper *Ming Pao*, it found that police and crime-related news was the number one local news topic. Principal investigator and university professor April Lindgren thinks she knows why. "The local news pages must be filled every day and crime stories are more readily available than other news because police forces run sophisticated media relations units that issue regular press releases and make officers available to brief journalists," Lindgren says. "One phone call to a police media relations officer can net a reporter numerous items; writing stories about other issues is more time consuming and less certain in terms of results."[20] Because police are considered an authoritative source, it's deemed acceptable to repurpose a press release with no further reporting.

The problem is that ethnocultural newspapers introduce newcomers to the culture and conditions in their adopted countries. Anyone reading a steady diet of crime news might believe their city is infested with crooks and violent offenders, even when statistics show crime declining. Lindgren sums up the situation in this way:

> This research is a wake-up call about how everyday news-gathering practices, when combined with sophisticated public-information units run by police organizations, can result in distortions to reality. A pessimist would argue that little can be done to address this problem in an era when newspapers are under increasing pressure to do more with less. Much of the time, reporters are so busy putting out the news they don't have time to see the bigger picture. An optimist, however, would argue that committed journalists are not in the business of deliberately misleading their audiences and that greater awareness of how police media units can and do influence the mix of news can lead to changes in practice.[21]

RACISM

One of the most long-standing and pervasive ways police departments have misled the media and the public over the years is how they describe Indigenous people. Historically, whenever police called a press conference to discuss a missing or murdered Indigenous woman or girl, they would invariably paint negative images of the victims themselves. Often there would be references to drug use, prior criminal involvement, or the ubiquitous euphemism that the victim was "known to police." Police would also bandy about the term *high-risk lifestyle*, a reference to drugs and the sex trade. The implication was that the victim voluntarily chose to engage in the sex trade, knowing that such a practice carried high risks.

The use of these tropes amounted to victim-blaming and diminished the magnitude of the crime and the urgency of locating a missing person. The message was that victims were somehow at fault for their own victimization. The police statements suggested the victims' "lifestyles" were a matter of individual choice and that they ought to have known what the consequences might be. They ignored the entire history of colonization in Canada and the social and economic forces that led to the devastation of Indigenous people. In many cases, police would release mug shots of the murdered victims or the missing women, showing them in an unflattering light and further victimizing their families. By picking up and repeating these victim-blaming narratives, the media became complicit in diminishing the impact of the crimes.

During the National Inquiry into Missing and Murdered Indigenous Women and Girls, many people decried these police tactics and the subsequent reports in the media. Jamie Lee Hamilton shared the following with the inquiry: "When we've had trans people — Two-Spirited, trans people that have been murdered, the police routinely would disclose to the media that they're trans. And they have no right to do that because it sets in motion this defence that's used, the panic. We call it the homosexual panic defence of, 'Oh, the perpetrator was triggered because of this.' When in actual fact, they're hate crimes."[22]

Other testimony at the inquiry highlighted the value media place on official sources, especially the police, over sources deemed less credible. For example, even when a story revolves around a specific victim, the media will often defer to police accounts instead of collecting first-hand information from families.

As Kim M. told the inquiry, in relation to the media portrayal of her sister:

Media needs to be educated on how they report on missing and murdered Indigenous women and girls. They need to be respectful and honourable … When media was trying to post pictures of my sister, they were not very representative pictures, and I actually phoned a number of places that were posting pictures and I said, "We're sending you pictures. Use these." Even the way how they described my sister when they first announced that she was murdered, they described her as a sex-trade worker. So, I phoned them and I said, "How can you — why are you calling her that?" So, media, get your facts straight and treat us with honour and respect.[23]

Alongside the systemic racism that led police to downplay crimes against missing and murdered Indigenous women was the deliberate refusal to keep statistics on the extent of the phenomenon. Just as they had with data about deadly force incidents, the police ignored the issue as it grew and become more pronounced. Community groups, political organizations, and academics tried to fill this gap over the years with their own research.

At CBC Manitoba, we began a project in 2014 to count and document as many unsolved cases of missing and murdered Indigenous women and girls as we could. As a starting point, we used lists generated by organizations like the Native Women's Association of Canada, and university researchers. In the end, we found more than 250 unsolved cases stretching all the way back to 1951. We also found that many had been subjected to little or no investigation by police forces. The project involved interviewing more than one hundred family members of the victims. Many said the call they had received from CBC News was the first time anyone had contacted them about their relative. When asked to rate the quality of the police investigation in each case, on a scale of 1 to 10, the families assigned an average rating of 2.8. "I feel like the police are not taking interest in anything that has anything to do with the aboriginal people," said Mary Pia Benuen, whose best friend, Henrietta Millek, disappeared from St. John's in 1982 and was never found.[24]

Countless people told the national inquiry that police would routinely minimize or devalue their concerns that a family member had gone missing. Sometimes they would be left waiting in police stations for hours before anyone would take them seriously. In some cases, they were told to wait for twenty-four hours or longer before police would even be prepared to take a report. Police would insist the missing person might be drunk and on a bender. At other times, police would ignore or not be interested in suspicious circumstances that accompanied someone's disappearance.

As a follow-up to our initial reporting, we looked intensively at thirty-four cases involving an Indigenous woman's death or disappearance in which authorities insisted there was no foul play. In all of those cases, families said they didn't accept the findings of police and suggested murder might be involved. We found evidence in many of those incidents pointing to suspicious circumstances, unexplained bruises, and other factors indicating further investigation was warranted.

Perhaps the most troubling example was that of Nadine Machiskinic, a twenty-nine-year-old mother of four who fell ten storeys down a laundry chute in a Regina hotel in 2015. Police decided there was no foul play, despite the clear evidence of suspicious circumstances. Surveillance video, for instance, showed that two men had accompanied her in the elevator to the top floor, but police never located those men. In fact, police took more than a year to issue a public appeal for information about the men in the video. The implication left by the police investigation was that she was either drunk, high on drugs, or suicidal, a common theme in the nearly three dozen cases we examined. An RCMP review of the Regina police investigation concluded that it didn't meet professional standards. Still, no one has ever been charged with Machiskinic's death.

Canadian police attitudes toward Indigenous murder victims and those who go missing have not gone unnoticed in other parts of the world. Several international organizations have pointed to systemic racism in Canadian policing. Human Rights Watch, which reports on abuses worldwide, conducted two fact-finding missions to Canada and came away with a troubling picture of police practices in Indigenous communities. It documented violent abuse against Indigenous women at the hands of police, including young girls being pepper-sprayed and tasered, a twelve-year-old girl being attacked by a police dog, strip searches by male officers, and injuries due to excessive force used during arrests. In some cases, these occurred during "wellness checks," when police were called to help someone in distress. It recommended Canada stop enforcing laws in ways that effectively criminalize people for their poverty or lack of housing, substance use, mental health, or status as a victim of gender-based violence. It also recommended Canada collect and make public comprehensive race and gender data on victims of crime, police stops and searches, police use of force, and complaints of police misconduct.[25]

Police departments across Canada have historically said they don't collect race-based data, or if they do, they don't think it's valid to release the statistics. Media organizations have occasionally pried loose such data through Access to Information requests, despite police efforts to delay their release and redact documents extensively.

The most impactful example was the *Toronto Star*'s attempt to get data from the city's police department. In 2000 it asked for the police database of arrests, which recorded the skin colour of people charged. The request was denied, but after two years of appeals and a ruling by the provincial privacy commissioner, it received a massive database of incidents and charges. Analyzing the data allowed the newspaper to conclude that Black people arrested by Toronto police are treated more harshly than white people. When focusing on drug charges, they showed Black people were taken to police stations more often and held overnight at twice the rate of white people. After fighting vigorously to prevent the release of the data in the first place, Police Chief Julian Fantino then rejected any implication of racism and told the newspaper it was "barking up the wrong tree."[26] The Toronto Police Association launched a multi-million-dollar lawsuit alleging every Toronto officer had been defamed. The suit was dismissed.

When the Toronto police finally decided for the first time to release race-based statistics voluntarily in June 2022, it revealed that Black, Indigenous, and Middle Eastern people were all overrepresented in strip searches and use of force by officers.[27] This is consistent with every formal and informal study conducted on the issue. The results confirmed what many media reports, advocacy groups, and individuals had been saying for decades.

Though mainstream media have been historically complicit in the repetition of racist and sexist messaging promulgated by police departments, the efforts by some journalists to hold police accountable for their actions are often actively thwarted. Nowhere is this more glaring than in the protests organized by Wet'suwet'en hereditary chiefs and their supporters to defend their land from incursions by the construction of the Coastal GasLink pipeline in British Columbia. The RCMP actively prevented the media from gaining access to cover the story, particularly when officers were carrying out enforcement actions. They set up large "exclusion zones," which banned reporters from critical geographical areas and impeded their work. Police employed similar tactics during protests against old-growth logging at Fairy Creek, B.C., and in the dispersal of homeless camps in Toronto city parks. Even though a judge warned police in the Fairy Creek situation not to interfere with journalistic rights in this regard, the problem resurfaced in Wet'suwet'en.

Matters came to a head in late 2021 when police arrested two journalists, Amber Bracken and Michael Toledano, and accused them of violating Coastal GasLink's injunction, which stops opponents from impeding work on construction. After spending several days in jail, they were released and charges were eventually dropped, but press freedom groups from around the world decried the assault on their ability to report from the front lines. Bracken, who along with The Narwhal is now suing the RCMP for wrongful arrest and violating her Charter rights, explained the need to be present on the ground to report on complex issues:

> Coastal GasLink ... runs a sophisticated press strategy. Its
> narrative — of economic benefit for all, including nearby
> First Nations — gets coverage in the regular news grind,
> often generated by industry-supplied press releases. It's much
> more difficult to tell the untold sides of the pipeline story.
> I've talked to journalists from multiple outlets who have also
> been frustrated by half answers or no answer at all to questions about the pipeline from company spokespeople.

In the face of this situation, she decried police actions to stop journalists from seeing the reality for themselves:

> Police use exclusion zones, arrest and the threat of arrest to control media access to newsworthy places: places where Indigenous people and land defenders are resisting industry, government and corporate mandates on their territories, and where the RCMP or the OPP are spending millions in militarized response. No one in Canada should tolerate police efforts to intimidate journalists or limit news coverage. There is no doubt in my mind that my arrest was intended to frighten, humiliate and deter me from continuing to cover this story.[28]

DEFENDING AGAINST DEFUNDING

A palpable shift in the public's attitude toward police took place after George Floyd's murder. The incident sparked massive demonstrations in the United States and many other parts of the world. In Canada, a series of deaths following police "wellness checks" on people in racialized communities contributed to the mounting anger against law enforcement. "Defund the Police" became a rallying cry for the Black Lives Matter movement and other activists, and the media began intensively scrutinizing police budgets and practices. A *Globe and Mail* analysis found that police budgets had escalated rapidly in recent years. Between 2009 and 2018, for instance, budgets grew by 66 percent in Alberta. In Ontario, the growth was 34 percent, compared to a 24 percent increase in social and family services and an 8 percent decline in spending on social housing. Some cities spent a significant portion of their total municipal budgets on policing. In Longueuil, Quebec, spending on police amounted to 29.8 percent of the entire city budget, while in Winnipeg it was 26.8 percent.[29]

The movement to defund police in the United States scored some initial successes. In budget votes throughout 2020, advocacy groups lobbied for and won cuts of $840 million in more than twenty police departments, with some of that money redirected to community services. Some cities, like Denver and Oakland, decided to eliminate police officers from schools.[30]

Police departments everywhere faced an existential crisis. They were encountering criticism and increased pressure at every turn. One of their key strategies in response to this problem was to figure out how to get the media and the public back onside. Some insight into this strategy emerged in an online webinar organized at the end of 2020 by ShotSpotter, a U.S. company that sells technology to police departments. The target audience for the webinar was police chiefs and public information officers (PIOs) for departments. The title of the webinar was: "Best Practices for Media Relations in a Time of Defund the Police," and among the topics covered were "strategies to avoid landmines and change the narrative, and how to leverage social media and data to get the public on your side."

Ron Teachman of ShotSpotter set the table for the conversation: "It's likely that no police agency will be spared from having insufficient resources, unrealistic demands and expectations of service placed on them, and subsequent scrutiny of their performance, particularly from the media." All this, he said, when "there is civil unrest in our streets and rapidly escalating violent crime."

The two speakers, representing police departments in New Jersey and Virginia, echoed his concern, and one even mused about the ultimate survival of their profession. But they also offered potential solutions. Reach out to victims of crime, one suggested, and get them to speak publicly about the excellent job police are doing. "Share positive stories from your community validators, let them sell it. In today's landscape every positive story needs to be amplified." One speaker talked about a police force in New Jersey that was hit with massive layoffs in 2011 and had to rebuild itself. "The main driver for re-establishing credibility was the media," he said.

The webinar featured some wistful nostalgia about the old days of inner-circle reporting. "We lived in a day and age a decade ago where we kind of had a standard group of reporters that we worked with, beat reporters, who worked for the 6 o'clock and 11 o'clock news. The paper got published the next morning. Today that all has changed. Everybody has a platform. Everybody has a presence."

In the end, it was good old-fashioned public relations and brand management that were presented as the key to surviving the crisis. As one of the experts noted, "If you're not using your PIO as your brand ambassador, your corporate reputation risk manager, then you're running in some pretty dangerous territory. The way you look, your interactions with the community, everything has to be thought about in a marketing and a trust-building fashion."[31] For Toronto police, one solution was spending more than $300,000 to produce its own podcast to give people a "behind the scenes" look at policing.[32]

Managing risks while maintaining the brand has been a complex balancing act for police departments. Many have tried diversifying their ranks and putting more effort into building community support, while still maintaining the need for strong budgets to fight what they typically claim to be ever-increasing violent crime. By the end of 2021, many U.S. politicians who had initially embraced the "defund" movement reversed course. A measure to restructure and reform the Minneapolis department was defeated. "I think allowing this moniker, 'Defund the police,' to ever get out there, was not a good thing," Minnesota's Democratic attorney general Keith Ellison said.[33]

In Canada, meanwhile, strategic police attempts to appease racialized communities have been met with mixed success. In June of 2022, Toronto police chief James Ramer tried to rationalize why statistics showed police were targeting Black, Indigenous, and other diverse groups. "As an organization, we have not done enough to ensure that every person in our city receives fair and unbiased policing," he said. "As chief of police and on behalf of the police, I am sorry and I apologize unreservedly. The release of this data will cause pain for many. We must improve and we will do better."

The announcement didn't impress Beverly Bain, of the No Pride in Policing Coalition, a coalition of queer and trans people. She called it a public relations stunt and an insult. "Chief Ramer, we do not accept your apology. This is not about saving our lives. What we have asked for you to do is stop. To stop brutalizing us. To stop killing us."[34]

. . .

Police departments are unique institutions, among the most powerful in society. Members carry weapons and are afforded the discretion to arrest people and charge them with crimes. They are also, under certain circumstances, given licence to exercise deadly force. Given the enormous powers the police have at their disposal, society expects them to act in an unbiased, ethical, and responsible fashion. Yet, as we have seen in this chapter, there are fundamental problems with police attitudes and practices. Media have a critical role to play in holding police accountable for their actions, but too often they are misled or co-opted by the very people they need to be scrutinizing. Over the years, there have been important reports by investigative journalists delving into policing, which can serve as inspiration to all reporters. Despite the pressures facing journalists and news organizations, these reports show that holding powerful institutions accountable is an achievable objective.

Chapter 6

Military Lies

IN THE SPRING OF 2019, THE CANADIAN MILITARY WAS REEL-ing from a torrent of criticism over the presence of racists and neo-Nazis in its ranks. The issue was hardly new. A quarter century earlier, Canadian soldiers had beaten a Somali teenager to death while on a peacekeeping mission, sparking an inquiry that would expose the ugly side of racism in the military's ranks. While politicians initially tried to blame it all on "youthful folly," the Somalia Inquiry led to scathing condemnation of the armed forces. The Department of National Defence (DND) eventually promised to enforce a zero-tolerance policy on racism and harassment.

Every few years, there was yet another reminder that this wasn't just an isolated problem. In 2017, for instance, five Canadian Armed Forces members who disrupted a Mi'kmaw ceremony in Halifax proclaimed they were members of the Proud Boys, a violent, fascist movement. The following year, officer cadets at the Royal Military College in Quebec desecrated a Qur'an. The military repeatedly failed to address the problem. It allowed one soldier who had made racist remarks on a white nationalist podcast to return to duty. As for the soldiers who had declared themselves to be members of the Proud Boys, which the government later designated as a terrorist organization, the military decided it would not lay charges. The officers were put on probation but resumed their regular work. The Proud Boys tweeted their joy at the military response: "We win, our brothers the Halifax 5 are returning to active military duty with no charges, let the SJW [social justice warriors] tears pour. Proud of our boys."[1]

The tempo of criticism increased when reporters got hold of a document from the Military Police Criminal Intelligence Section called "White Supremacy, Hate Groups, and Racism in the Canadian Armed Forces." It found that fifty-three different members had been linked to six hate groups since 2013, and thirty of them remained in the military. In addition to the Proud Boys, it identified the Atomwaffen Division, La Meute, Hammerskins Nation, Three Percenters, and Soldiers of Odin. The report argued that this didn't represent a significant problem compared to the total numbers in the armed forces. But that didn't impress anti-racism activists, who called on the armed forces to take immediate and decisive action to root out the cancer from within its ranks.

For the public affairs experts at the DND and the Canadian Armed Forces (CAF), this was an image problem rather than an existential crisis. Between May and July of 2019, a series of emails inside the department between PR gurus and senior officials discussed how best to blunt the force of the criticism. One of the techniques involved identifying so-called champions in the ranks of academics and retired generals, people who could act as cheerleaders to deny that the problem was extensive and to say that it was being well managed. The key objective was to avoid having military leadership offer a reactive response that would give validity to the critics. Instead of tackling racism in their ranks, the officials were intent on counteracting the sting of the critics who were becoming more vocal. "Whether or not they are accurate in their assessment matters comparatively little as there is a reputational risk to the CAF with any such allegations and a counter-narrative may be required," one email said.[2] Translation: The truth doesn't matter. All that matters is our reputation.

The emails were made public by David Pugliese of the *Ottawa Citizen*, who has covered defence issues for decades. He reported that officials created dossiers on journalists who they thought would likely cover the topic of racism in the military. One of them was CBC reporter Murray Brewster, who has written frequently about the subject. The intelligence file noted,

"He's familiar with the defence system, and his reporting, while factual, often emphasizes the mistakes and shortcomings of DND and the CAF."

As police departments do with inner- and outer-circle reporters, defence officials were trying to calculate how best to spin individual journalists. As it turned out, though, the entire plan to create a counter-narrative was abandoned when more high-profile incidents of racism continued to surface. Even as the departmental emails were circulating, the *Winnipeg Free Press* reported that army reservist Patrik Mathews was a recruiter for the white nationalist hate group The Base. The following year, army reservist Corey Hurren stormed Rideau Hall with loaded firearms in a deranged attempt to arrest the prime minister. Under such circumstances, getting any "champions" to step forward would be tough. In April 2022, a ministerial advisory council said the defence department and armed forces hadn't correctly addressed twenty years' worth of recommendations to combat systemic racism. The suggestions "were poorly implemented, shelved or discarded," according to the report.[3] "Racism is not a glitch in the system; it is the system."[4]

The aggressive tactics to create a counter-narrative and influence specific reporters indicated a PR initiative at national defence headquarters that Pugliese covered extensively. He first reported in 2015 that Chief of the Defence Staff General Jonathan Vance wanted to "weaponize public affairs." The general didn't deny using the term but tried to put a benign spin on it. "It's no surprise to me that there are those who would see weaponization as an aggressive, attack mode," he said. "What I am talking about is operationalizing the public affairs branch. I want to make the public affairs branch better."[5]

Pugliese learned from public relations officers that some tactics would be the age-old techniques used in many branches of government: leak positive stories to friendly reporters and target critical journalists by calling them out in different ways. This strategy might include authoring letters to the editor for publication in newspapers, calls to the reporters' bosses, and the use of other means to discredit them.

It eventually became clear that Vance also had more sophisticated ideas in mind. Throughout 2020, defence department insiders leaked information to Pugliese that exposed questionable PR practices. Here are a few:

- Concerned about potential civil disobedience during the pandemic, the military proposed a propaganda campaign styled after its efforts in Afghanistan. To some observers, the government appeared to be proposing something like the psychological warfare techniques that had included, bizarrely, using loudspeakers on trucks to transmit government information. Officials scrapped the plan before it became fully operational.

- In another aborted plan, social media messages supportive of government policies would be sent from the personal accounts of military staff. The idea was that all the posts would be covertly crafted and pre-approved by the defence department.

- The military conducted a training exercise in Nova Scotia in 2020 designed to test how local populations would react to disinformation. They blared wolf noises in the woods through loudspeakers and drew up a fake letter warning that wolves were on the loose in specific areas. It has never been made clear whether the intent was to conduct internal training or to observe how unsuspecting people would react. The army, which never told the Nova Scotia government what it was doing, eventually apologized.[6]

Matters came to a head in November 2020 when Pugliese reported that the military intended to create a new organization called the Defence Strategic Communication group to target the Canadian public with propaganda operations. He quoted from a leaked document that said the group would advance "national interests by using defence activities to influence the attitudes, beliefs and behaviours of audiences" internationally and domestically. A U.S. researcher had already revealed that the Canadian forces spent more than $1 million on "behaviour modification" training from the parent company of Cambridge Analytica, a firm that was embroiled in a scandal over its data-harvesting techniques. These revelations and leaks over such a short span were too much for the federal government. The defence minister said he didn't support the controversial plans, and that no new organization would be created. Even though the military had already held town halls to brief staff about the changes, General Vance ordered a halt to the weaponization initiative. Officials sent a memo to staff: "Our efforts to enhance the formal range of duties of Public Affairs Officers in the Information Operations/Influence Activity domain have come to an end."[7]

Brett Boudreau served with the armed forces for close to thirty years, including spending twenty-two years as a public affairs officer. Now a private consultant, he says words like *enemy*, *target*, and *threat* are appropriate for the battlefield but not for the home front. "That is not just a reasonable expectation but a necessary condition for public trust and confidence in a national institution with real power and profound responsibilities as its raison d'être." Boudreau chronicled the entire effort to weaponize public affairs and came to the conclusion that the military risked losing what it needs most of all: public credibility and trust.

> [Organizational] reputation and institutional credibility are existential conditions for Defence and have valuation like bankable assets. When tasks such as support to long-term care facilities or help to First Nations communities fighting a pandemic go well, the goodwill account balance increases. When the DND/CAF do poorly, such as their long-standing challenges of managing major procurements, or dealing with military sexual misconduct and inappropriate behaviour, the account is drawn down. Too many withdrawals from the available reserve have real consequences that impact recruiting, retention and the willingness of decision-makers to buy the military's preferred choices of multi-billion dollar equipment. This trust balance also directly impacts public willingness to support military operations outside Canada, especially those that could or do result in deaths and casualties.[8]

DND PR

Despite the apparent shutdown of the most recent version of weaponized public relations, the reality is that similar tactics have been used for many years. The Canadian military has the largest and most sophisticated public relations operations of any government department or agency. Hundreds of people work directly on shaping, enhancing, and communicating military messages to the armed forces, politicians, the public, and potential recruits. An assistant deputy minister is devoted exclusively to public affairs, and the DND website lists sixty-one military media PR offices across Canada. Between 2004 and 2010, military public affairs staff grew by 66 percent, and funding increased by 89 percent.[9] If this seems like overkill, consider that there are likely fewer than half a dozen journalists working full-time on the military beat at any given time in Canada.

But it's not just the staff assigned directly to PR that works full-time to polish the military's image. There is a network of institutes, agencies, think tanks, museums, and other assets dedicated to different aspects of military affairs. Some receive direct funding from the defence department, while others supplement their budgets with individual donations and sponsorships, including from arms manufacturers.

The extensive reach of military influence became clear to me in 2011, when I was invited to participate in an old-fashioned debate at the University of Manitoba. The topic was the Ethics of Wikileaks. Months earlier, the organization had released a trove of documents relating to the U.S. war in Iraq and Afghanistan. Working with some of the world's leading media outlets, Wikileaks founder Julian Assange revealed a range of secret files and memos that threw light on military operations that had previously been covered up. New information showed the extent of torture conducted by Iraqi forces, for instance. Documents calculated sixty-six thousand Iraqi civilian deaths, far higher than had previously been disclosed. One of the most graphic leaks involved a video from a U.S. Apache helicopter showing U.S. forces shooting a group of civilians in Baghdad. The Apache's fire also destroyed a civilian van that stopped to help the wounded people. It was carrying adults and children. A Reuters photographer and his assistant were among the dead. The U.S. Army had previously rejected Reuters' request to disclose the details surrounding the 2007 incident. For Wikileaks, the incident amounted to "collateral murder."

The university debate centred on the ethics of whistle-blowers and people who leak sensitive military secrets. I argued this was an essential aspect of journalism.

Throughout history, whistle-blowers have provided critical insights into how society works on all levels. Particularly when they relate to military matters, where secrecy and disinformation are pervasive, leaks provide a valuable way to learn the truth. I pointed to Daniel Ellsberg's leak of the Pentagon Papers in the 1970s as an example of a disclosure that brought vital information about U.S. involvement in Vietnam to the public's attention. But, as in the case of Wikileaks, some people raised questions about the legality and ethics of what Ellsberg had done. The U.S. administration targeted Ellsberg, first by trying to discredit him and finally by pressing charges under the Espionage Act. He was eventually cleared of all wrongdoing. Now it seemed the current U.S. administration was following a similar playbook with Assange.

My debate opponent was Jim Fergusson, director of the university's Centre for Defence and Security Studies. Instead of dealing with the substance of the Wikileaks revelations, he was concerned about the integrity of military intelligence. All of his talking points aligned with arguments put forward by the Pentagon. He said it was up to the military and government to decide when to declassify documents, and he mocked anyone else's "self-defining" right to do so. Releasing unfiltered information put people's lives at risk, he argued, though even today proponents of this theory are hard-pressed to provide evidence this happened. As for Assange, Fergusson said his actions were akin to terrorism and treason. Pentagon officials argued the same, as they were keen to dissuade future whistle-blowers from releasing unauthorized material. It was also prescient on Fergusson's part, as Assange was finally indicted in 2019 by the United States under its Espionage Act.

At the time, it didn't occur to me that the Centre for Defence and Security Studies was anything other than a regular university department, like sociology or psychology. I subsequently learned DND helped to launch military studies at the university and provided funding over the years for the centre.

The Manitoba centre is one of a dozen similar "centres of expertise" that have been supported in different ways by DND and are housed at universities across Canada, including York University, Université du Québec à Montréal, Wilfrid Laurier University, Université Laval, McGill University, the University of British Columbia, the University of New Brunswick, Carleton University, Dalhousie University, the University of Calgary, and Queen's University.

In 1967 the Canadian defence department created a branch called the Security and Defence Forum (SDF) to fund the academic community. The aims were "to sustain and expand domestic knowledge of, and interest in, security and defence issues of current and future relevance to Canada."[10] In addition to core funding, the forum sponsored conferences, special projects, and specific academic research. In return, the centres were often expected to teach a certain number of courses, produce publications, do outreach, or interact with the media. While the Manitoba centre no longer receives core defence department funding, it continues to apply for government and DND grants and it remains closely allied with the armed forces. "As Winnipeg is the home of the Royal Canadian Airforce and the Canadian NORAD Regional Headquarters, the [Manitoba centre] serves as an important resource for the Canadian Armed Forces here in Manitoba," the centre says. Under "Student Resources" on its website, it offers a link to "find out how you can contribute [to] the defence and security of Canada by becoming a civilian employee with DND."[11]

Some academics are troubled by the funding relationship. Amir Attaran, a professor at the University of Ottawa, believes the military and government have politicized academic grants. "The same bureaucrat who administers SDF grants to scholars also manages DND's liaison with cabinet and Parliament," he wrote in 2008. "When DND needs a kind word in Parliament or the media — presto! — an SDF-sponsored scholar often appears, without disclosing his or her financial link."[12] Indeed, the defence forum kept careful track of the impact its funding was having in the media and broader community. In Brett Boudreau's terms, it was investing money from its bankable assets and was interested in seeing a return.

An evaluation for the 2006–7 year counted 14,457 students enrolled in 316 courses offered by its fleet of centres. In aid of shaping public opinion, professors and students engaged in 1,213 media interviews and wrote 115 editorial pieces in newspapers, while there were 420 outreach events.[13] By 2014–15, the department boasted an average of four media engagements for each of its "targeted engagement grant projects." These are grants to fund conferences, workshops, and symposia. One of the funding conditions is that DND has the right to send a certain number of attendees to each event. "Attendance provides an opportunity to network with national and international subject matter experts and facilitates the transfer of information and knowledge, in addition to what may be provided through post-event media engagement," DND says.[14] While staff at the various university centres say the funding they receive is arm's-length and comes with no strings attached, the head of Dalhousie's foreign policy institute once said that "it would be fair to say that the bulk of people associated with SDF centres would take a traditional view on security and defence."[15] The defence forum has since morphed into various other DND entities, but academic funding remains integral to the department's effort to mould public opinion.

With so many centres, institutes, and think tanks operating in the sphere of military research, it is difficult for the media and the public to sort out connections and allegiances. It's important for the public to understand how different researchers and experts are funded and affiliated. But it isn't always apparent. In December 2021, for instance, Rob Huebert wrote an opinion piece for the *Globe and Mail* entitled "Canada Must Do Its Part to Defend the Arctic. That Requires F-35 Purchases and NORAD Modernization."[16] His byline identified him only as an associate professor of political science at the University of Calgary. That's true, but he was also a research fellow with the Centre for Military Security and Strategic Studies and a fellow with the Canadian Global Affairs Institute (CGAI). In other words, he worked with entities that received support from the Canadian military and companies that supply military hardware. Huebert didn't hide those connections, but a casual reader would have not known his full background.

The CGAI is a think tank that derives sponsorship and support from various sources, including some of the world's biggest arms manufacturers, such as Lockheed Martin, manufacturer of the F-35 aircraft; Boeing; General Dynamics; BAE Systems; and others. Knowing that General

Dynamics, the manufacturer of light armoured vehicles that Canada sells to Saudi Arabia, is a sponsor of the institute is relevant when considering the institute's policy papers. In 2016, for instance, an institute fellow noted that the controversial Canada-Saudi relationship was "a deeply flawed but necessary partnership." Why? "It is the least bad option. It is a difficult arrangement, but the alternatives are worse." It doesn't hurt that the deal is also very good for Canada's defence industry, he added.[17] CGAI maintains that its funders don't determine the content of the institute's activities.

For years, the CGAI ran a nine-day military journalism course in concert with the University of Calgary. Journalism students won scholarships to hear what organizers called "media-military theory" in a classroom setting, coupled with field visits to army and reserve units. "Through this education the media will become a better conduit to communicate defence and foreign affairs issues to the Canadian public," the institute said.[18]

The CGAI has also partnered with the Conference of Defence Associations (CDA) to sponsor the Ross Munro Media Award, an annual prize for journalists who cover defence issues. But there has been controversy over the years about whether journalists should apply for prizes sponsored by government-funded entities, especially ones with a specific advocacy mandate. Amir Attaran noted in 2008 that the CDA had received a substantial grant from the defence department the previous year, and in return pledged to "support activities that give evidence of contributing to Canada's national policies."[19] In fact, the CDA, an umbrella group of about forty associations representing 400,000 active and retired armed forces members, has been supported by the defence department since its founding in 1932. The president of the CDA acknowledged to a *Maclean's* reporter that the obligation also included producing a quarterly magazine, conducting symposia for students, and writing op-ed pieces in the press.[20]

"Someone tried to nominate me once [for the Ross Munro award]," Pugliese said. "I said under no circumstances will you ever do that. That award is a joke."[21]

The award was especially troubled in 2008 because the CDA Institute president, Scott Cowan, used his convocation address that year at the Royal Military College to issue a broadside against reporters and "the remarkable dumbing down of the media over the past 40 years." In the middle of Canada's Afghanistan engagement, he felt journalists were not providing informed reporting. It was a vitriolic display of contempt by a representative of an organization that tried its best to influence the media and public opinion. "Unlike 40 years ago when journalists were amongst the best-educated and best-informed citizens, today many of them are neither literate nor numerate, and do us the huge discourtesy of assuming we aren't either," he said.

After decrying most print and broadcast reporters, he had this to say about a typical television news report produced by the national public broadcaster, a comment that also encapsulates his opinion about the general public: "The CBC version is half filled with the opinions of reporters and pollsters, which is the high point, because during the other half they show scenic postcard views or stick microphones under the noses of whatever slack-jawed-gum-chewing vagrants they can find on the street to ask them what they think about oil prices or border security or equalization payments."[22]

SEXUAL ASSAULT IN THE MILITARY

As with systemic racism within its ranks, the armed forces considered the rampant sexual assault epidemic that permeated all levels of the military a public relations problem. Reports of inappropriate sexual conduct, and a lack of will among leadership to do anything about it, have circulated for decades. A Statistics Canada survey in 2016 found more than a quarter of all women in the military had been victims of sexual assault at least once in their careers. Over the previous year, 80 percent of all armed forces members witnessed some form of inappropriate sexualized behaviour.[23] These revelations didn't surprise anyone who followed the issue closely. A year earlier, retired Supreme Court Justice Marie Deschamps had identified inappropriate sexual conduct in the armed forces as a serious problem and called on the leadership to address it. In response, General Vance created a program called Operation Honour and promised a thoroughgoing effort to end the abuses. In reality, it was all a PR effort meant to dupe the media and the public.

In 2021 our team at CBC's *Fifth Estate* examined Operation Honour and spoke to sexual assault victims, former military officers, and experts in the field. A former military investigator we interviewed said his commanding officers routinely interfered in his sexual assault cases, and he had trouble getting military prosecutors to advance charges within the system. Even though Deschamps had recommended the creation of an independent centre outside the armed forces to receive reports of inappropriate sexual conduct, this had never been implemented. The statistics spoke for themselves. In the four years since Operation Honour began, the military had a 14 percent conviction rate for sexual assault, one-third the ratio in the civilian judicial system. In many cases, prosecutors pleaded the cases down to discipline violations. Officers who had committed rape or other serious sexual offences were getting slaps on the wrist.[24]

But Vance, apparently conflating the disciplinary decisions with criminal convictions, touted the supposed success of Operation Honour at every opportunity. In 2018 he told a Senate committee that everything was under control. "Our overall conviction rate for sexual misconduct has been 87 percent since we began Operation Honour," he said. "This puts our conviction rates higher than in the civilian justice system for both sexual assault and lesser offences, speaking to both the effectiveness and necessity of our military justice system."[25] What Vance didn't mention was his own history. He was subsequently investigated for having a twenty-year relationship with a military subordinate and fathering two of her children. Accused of asking her to lie to investigators about the matter, he was charged criminally and pleaded guilty in 2022 to obstruction of justice.

In 2020 the government asked former Supreme Court Justice Morris Fish to examine aspects of the National Defence Act. In considering how the military should handle sexual assault cases, he had this to say when he released his report in 2021: "Sexual misconduct in the Canadian Armed Forces remains persistent, preoccupying and widespread — despite the CAF's repeated attempts to address the problem and to curb its prevalence."

Even as he was gathering his evidence, the number of cases involving senior armed forces staff who were ensnared in inappropriate conduct investigations grew to staggering proportions. They included two chiefs of defence staff, the vice-chief of defence staff, two commanders of the navy, the commander of a navy fleet school, the commander of special forces, the commander of military personnel, the top Canadian at NORAD, and the head of military human resources. The government's response to all this was to appoint yet another former Supreme Court Justice to prepare yet another report. Louise Arbour went over much of the same ground that her predecessor had covered in 2015. But this time, some current and retired armed forces members who spoke to Arbour also shared their perspectives with Pugliese at the *Ottawa Citizen*.

One senior retired officer told Arbour's team that National Defence and the Canadian Forces typically respond to sexual misconduct allegations by trying to undercut victims and protect the senior leadership. Sexual misconduct is seen as a public relations problem, the officer added. "The institution minimizes the problem, attacks accusers and places a desire to protect senior leaders with positive/neutral [media] coverage ahead of any concern for the well-being of victims and other members of the Defence Team," the officer noted in the presentation to Arbour.

When she delivered her report in May 2022, Arbour predictably concluded that the armed forces had failed to root out sexual misconduct. She had forty-eight recommendations for what should come next. The government promised it would act.

MILITARY DECEPTION IN WARTIME

A little more than a month after Russia's invasion of Ukraine began, NBC News came out with a scoop. Here is how the quadruple-bylined story began:

> It was an attention-grabbing assertion that made headlines around the world: U.S. officials said they had indications suggesting Russia might be preparing to use chemical agents in Ukraine.
>
> President Joe Biden later said it publicly. But three U.S. officials told NBC News this week there is no evidence Russia has brought any chemical weapons near Ukraine. They said the United States released the information to deter Russia from using the banned munitions.[26]

The story said this was part of a new "information war" the United States was waging. But there is a more straightforward way to describe it: it was a lie, strategically used to mislead the media and the public in a time of war. During the Ukraine conflict, there has been no shortage of misleading claims and lies from all sides. But this story was immediately reminiscent of another U.S. claim nearly twenty years earlier. In February 2003, then secretary of state Colin Powell strode into the United Nations Security Council chamber bearing binders, recordings, and a vial filled with a suspicious-looking white substance. It all added up to convincing evidence, he said, that Saddam Hussein's regime possessed weapons of mass destruction. It would be compelling evidence to justify the U.S. invasion of Iraq. "My colleagues, every statement I make today is backed up by sources, solid sources. These are not assertions. What we are giving you are facts and conclusions based on solid intelligence," he said.[27] The U.S. media bought the presentation in its entirety. The *Washington Post* called the evidence "irrefutable," and the *New York Times* said it made the case that Hussein was violating U.N. resolutions. The world now knows that the "evidence" Powell presented was not just exaggerated but, in some cases, fabricated.

U.S. examples of big lies are almost too numerous to mention, but the most egregious ones are tied to aggressive military ambitions. The sinking of the battleship *Maine* in Havana Harbor in 1898 led some American politicians to invent evidence that blamed Spain. Leading U.S. newspapers took up the battle cry "Remember the *Maine*" to whip up war sentiment. With the public onside, the government of the day launched the Spanish-American War, which resulted in the capture of Cuba. Sixty years later, there were echoes of this incident in the Gulf of Tonkin affair. In 1964 President Lyndon Johnson claimed North Vietnamese forces had launched an unprovoked attack on U.S. naval vessels. Once again, facts were exaggerated and evidence was fabricated, but the incident was used to justify launching a military strike and ramping up U.S. intervention. And once again, many media outlets unquestioningly reported the "facts" as presented.

Americans don't have a monopoly on lying during wartime. Winston Churchill once famously proclaimed, "In wartime, truth is so precious that she should always be attended by a bodyguard of lies." He might have been channelling Otto von Bismarck, who remarked, "People never lie so much as after a hunt, during a war, or before an election." Some argue that deception and strategic lying is necessary during war to confuse the enemy and preserve the security of your troops. More common are the lies that are used to justify aggressions, bigger military budgets, or simply to avoid the public relations fiascos of admitting to defeats and casualties.

When the *New York Times* published the leaked Pentagon Papers in 1971, it revealed years of U.S. deception about the military's role in Vietnam. Similarly, the *Washington Post* fought for years to access a federal government evaluation of the Afghanistan conflict that showed U.S. officials made pronouncements throughout the eighteen-year war they knew to be false. The head of the federal agency that conducted the evaluation, which included four hundred interviews with military insiders, acknowledged to the newspaper that the documents show "the American people have been constantly lied to." One of the interviews the agency conducted was with Bob Crowley, an army colonel who was a senior counter-insurgency advisor to U.S. military commanders in Afghanistan. He said lying was commonplace. "Every data point was altered to present the best picture possible."[28]

Canadian media were tightly controlled during both world wars, and many of their reports consisted of information military authorities wanted them to transmit back home. The disastrous Battle of the Somme in the First World War was portrayed in its early days as an Allied victory, even as thousands of troops were being slaughtered. This kind of deliberate misrepresentation was a common tactic employed by all sides during the war. British politician and activist Arthur Ponsonby documented twenty major falsehoods that circulated during the conflict. He summed up the strategy in a way that applies not just to the First World War, but almost every other one since:

> A government which has decided on embarking on the hazardous and terrible enterprise of war must at the outset present a one-sided case in justification of its action, and cannot afford to admit in any particular whatever the smallest degree of right or reason on the part of the

people it has made up its mind to fight. Facts must be distorted, relevant circumstances concealed and a picture presented which by its crude colouring will persuade the ignorant people that their Government is blameless, their cause is righteous, and that the indisputable wickedness of the enemy has been proved beyond question. A moment's reflection would tell any reasonable person that such obvious bias cannot possibly represent the truth. But the moment's reflection is not allowed; lies are circulated with great rapidity. The unthinking mass accept them and by their excitement sway the rest. The amount of rubbish and humbug that pass under the name of patriotism in wartime in all countries is sufficient to make decent people blush when they are subsequently disillusioned.[29]

Charles Lynch worked for Reuters news agency during the Second World War and was one of nine Canadian reporters to land with the troops at Juno Beach on D-Day. He had a lengthy and successful career in journalism, becoming chief of Southam News, and was eventually inducted into the Canadian News Hall of Fame. Of his war reporting, he had this to say: "It's humiliating to look back at what we wrote during the war. It was crap ... We were a propaganda arm of our governments. At the start the censors enforced that, but by the end we were our own censors. We were cheerleaders. I suppose there wasn't an alternative at the time. It was total war. But, for God's sake, let's not glorify our role. It wasn't good journalism. It wasn't journalism at all."[30]

Since the end of the Second World War, Canada has carefully cultivated an image as an international peacekeeper and neutral third party. While the United States has engaged in numerous direct conflicts worldwide, Canadians have often stressed their preference for neutrality. But a closer look at the facts reveals that the image is illusory. A number of exposés over the years have shown that Canada quietly but consistently backed the U.S. involvement in Vietnam. This included large-scale sales of aircraft, munitions, and even the defoliant Agent Orange, which the Uniroyal Chemical

Company in Elmira, Ontario, routinely shipped to Vietnam.[31] Canadian weapon sales to the United States actually doubled from 1964 to 1966, and peaked in 1967.[32] Canada's role in the International Control Commission, set up to monitor accords after the partition of Vietnam, often served as a proxy for U.S. interests in the region. Instead of acting as a neutral broker, it facilitated the U.S. escalation of the conflict in Vietnam.

The same kind of deception was at play during the 2003 U.S.-led invasion of Iraq. While U.S. president George Bush was recruiting a "coalition of the willing" to topple the Saddam Hussein regime, Prime Minister Jean Chrétien rose in the House of Commons to declare that Canada would not join the effort. This was widely hailed as a symbol of Canada's neutrality. Only years later did the Wikileaks trove of documents reveal the whole story. On the same day Chrétien made his statement, a senior Canadian official secretly pledged military support for the U.S. mission. A confidential note written by a U.S. diplomat reported discussions at Ottawa's foreign affairs headquarters between Canadian, British, and U.S. officials. It revealed that Canadian foreign affairs official James Wright made it clear that contrary to public statements by the prime minister, Canada would use its naval and air forces "discreetly" to support the American mission. "This message tracks with others we have heard," the U.S. diplomat reported back to his superiors in Washington. "While for domestic political reasons ... the GOC [Government of Canada] has decided not to join in a U.S. coalition of the willing ... they are also prepared to be as helpful as possible in the military margins."[33]

Canada's longest and most protracted war was in Afghanistan. Between 2001 and 2014, some forty thousand troops were deployed. Canada spent an estimated $18 billion on fighting and reconstruction efforts. Throughout the conflict, another battle was also taking place. As in other wars, the military was trying to present a positive spin on its actions. While this succeeded to some degree, some journalists resisted being contained and managed. A debate emerged over the wisdom of embedding with the military. Reporters were aware of prior conflicts and the pitfalls of becoming too close to the people they were covering. But convenience and perceived safety concerns often trumped those worries. CBC correspondent David Halton, who covered numerous conflicts throughout his career, reflected on his experience in Vietnam and felt that the benefits of embedding outweighed any drawbacks:

> I found it easier (and generally safer) covering a war with regular army units, as opposed to reporting independently. In Vietnam, for example, the U.S. Army provided reporters with fairly accurate information about situations at the fronts you wanted to visit, and transportation to get there. Ditto with the Canadian ICCS [International Commission of Control and Supervision] force I deployed to Vietnam with…. Operating independently with just a cameraman, or sometimes a local fixer, was much more hazardous, especially in areas where the [Viet Cong] might be in control at night but not during the day.[34]

Many would be surprised at Halton's assessment of the accuracy of U.S. Army briefings, and many more were skeptical of the advantages of embedding altogether. Sherry Wasilow wrote her Ph.D. dissertation on the topic at Carleton University in 2017. Her overall assessment was that the embedding program gave the military more control to frame and promote issues of benefit to them. This aligned with several other academic studies of embedding conducted in other countries. She interviewed sixteen journalists who had covered the war in Afghanistan, finding diverse opinions on the topic. She also discovered that the more junior the journalist, the more likely they were to be embedded. While some reporters felt it was helpful and often necessary, others were critical. "The whole game [of embedding] was to get journalists locked into a system so they will just behave and tell the stories the government wanted to be told," said Paul Watson of the *Toronto Star*. "There's only one thing you need to know to be a good war correspondent: all militaries lie. If you're only going to write down what you're told, you're just a stenographer for propaganda. You need to question everything you're being told."[35]

The Canadian embedding program was unique in allowing reporters to go "outside the wire" and re-enter the embedment. The Americans were critical of Canada for allowing the practice. But Wasilow found that few embedded reporters took advantage of this possibility. She attributed it to inexperience, fear, directions from their home desks, lack of interest, and sometimes even "sloth." Even some of the critics of getting too close to the military acknowledged that embedding had its advantages, as long as it was balanced by a desire to go out independently. "If you are stuck inside the wire, you are dependent on what they tell you in briefings, which can be limited and misleading," a *Globe and Mail* reporter told Wasilow.[36] Some journalists acknowledged that being in close quarters with the Canadian troops inevitably put pressure on them to write patriotic and positive stories. From the military's point of view, working relationships were more cordial with embedded journalists than with those who chose independence. One CBC journalist declined to be interviewed for the project, saying it would "risk critical relationships with the military needed for future reporting."[37]

A clear example of how the military tried to use embedded journalists to their advantage came in 2008, when the *Globe and Mail* revealed documents from two years earlier showing the PMO expressing concern that not enough positive stories were emanating from the media. The office told the armed forces to push development and reconstruction stories with embedded reporters. A military public affairs manager wrote back with a list of positive stories planned by Canadian journalists in the coming days. "I think you will see from the movements of the embeds below and the coming plans for interviews that the [public affairs officers] have been quite successful in their efforts to get the embeds to focus their attention elsewhere than the military kinetic [combat] operations," the manager wrote.[38] It was confirmation that, as in previous wars, the military did not want stories about combat operations, which would show that Canada's war effort was flagging. Pugliese noted that there were military officers at the highest level throughout the Afghan war saying that the Taliban were on the verge of defeat. "There were journalists who were more than willing to parrot that line," he said.[39]

Pugliese has paid the price for relentlessly holding DND to account. Department officials, all the way up to the minister, have tried to get him fired on four occasions. They have complained to his bosses about alleged unprofessional conduct but could offer no actual proof. Pugliese has been accused of being a Taliban supporter and a Russian sympathizer and has been the subject of elaborate and costly internal schemes inside the department to discredit him. Once, he got a phone call from military police threatening to come to his home to collect a secret document he used for a story. "I have the document right in front of me. It's stamped unclassified," he told them. It's little wonder he isn't liked inside DND. He has persistently foiled their efforts to dupe the public. But he also recognizes the odds are still in their favour. Over the years, he has seen the *Ottawa Citizen* newsroom dwindle from 180 people to thirty-five. When he eventually retires, he isn't confident he'll be replaced. Officials at DND headquarters will be relieved. "They'll be able to get away with a lot more stuff."

It's unlikely the vast majority of Canadians have any idea about the many ways the military seeks to shape and manipulate public opinion. Significant staff and resources are devoted to this purpose, and the main conduit the military uses to get its message across is the media. In part, this is accomplished directly, through the legion of public affairs officers and publicists employed by DND. But indirect means are also used, through the funding of university centres and think tanks whose research and advocacy align with the objectives of the department. At times of crisis, the military reacts as many corporations and governments are prone to do: instead of being forthright and transparent, they tend to cover up and obscure problems and pretend everything is just fine. But unlike many other organizations, the military wields extraordinary power in society, particularly in times of conflict and war. This is why it's crucial for journalists to hold them to account in an independent, responsible, and consistent way. The public interest is being served when journalists carefully parse military messages and combat any attempts to be misled.

Chapter 7

Spies and Their Lies

IN 2019 U.S. SECRETARY OF STATE MIKE POMPEO DELIVERED a lecture on diplomacy at Texas A&M University. In a follow-up question and answer session, he reflected on his military academy training and how that played out during his one-year term as director of the CIA. "What's the cadet motto at West Point? 'You will not lie, cheat or steal or tolerate those who do,'" Pompeo said. Then he added, "I was the CIA director. We lied, we cheated, we stole."[1]

By their very nature, intelligence agencies engage in deception. Whether it involves combatting foreign adversaries or advancing the interests of their national governments, they operate in a shadowy world of cover stories, duplicity, and pretense. Spies are trained to lie and to do so convincingly. Spy agencies are assigned tasks that their elected governments would just as soon keep secret. These jobs might include influencing the affairs of foreign governments, organizing regime changes, even carrying out extrajudicial killings.

In the spring of 2023, stories began circulating that China had attempted to influence the course of Canadian elections. Global News and the *Globe and Mail* quoted unnamed security officials as saying there was an organized Chinese foreign interference network at work. The idea that big foreign powers used their intelligence agencies to meddle in each other's elections didn't strike security watchers as surprising in itself, but the specifics of the allegations and the alleged lack of government response was noteworthy. Global News, for instance, said security officials gave an urgent briefing to the prime minister's senior aides three weeks before the 2019 election, warning about the Chinese interference network.

How credible are the unnamed security sources who provide anonymous information to the media? It's impossible to say for sure, but the deputy commissioner of the RCMP told a parliamentary committee that he hadn't received any "actionable intelligence" to justify initiating a criminal investigation into interference during the 2019 or 2021 elections. David Morrison, Canada's deputy minister of foreign affairs, told the same committee that intelligence gathered by security agencies "rarely paints a full or concrete or actionable picture" of what's happening. "It is often inaccurate or partial or incomplete, or in fact designed to throw us off our track."[2]

Throwing the media off track is a favourite tactic of security agencies. During the U.S. "War on Terror," the CIA developed a system of what it called "enhanced interrogation techniques" that included waterboarding and sleep deprivation. Critics classified it as torture. The U.S. Senate Select Committee on Intelligence released a report in 2014 that documented the lengths to which the CIA went to manipulate public opinion about its program. "The CIA's Office of Public Affairs and senior CIA officials coordinated to share classified information on the CIA's Detention and Interrogation Program to select members of the media to counter public criticism, shape public opinion, and avoid potential congressional action to restrict the CIA's detention and interrogation authorities budget," the committee report said, adding that much of the information it provided was inaccurate. Quoting from an email sent by the CIA's deputy director of its counterterrorism centre to a colleague, the report says the officer explained, "When the [*Washington Post/New York Times*] quotes 'senior intelligence official,' it's us ... authorized and directed by OPA [CIA's Office of Public Affairs]."[3]

MIND GAMES

To understand the full extent of intelligence operations and how they attempt to influence public opinion, it's necessary to look at some historical context. The Cold War spawned many of the current agencies and operatives.

In place of open warfare, East and West resorted to covert manoeuvres and propaganda to expand their spheres of influence. Lying was rampant on all sides, and it became increasingly difficult to discern what was true and what was false. People from different walks of life were recruited to aid in the Cold War battles. Some were aware of what they were doing, while others were lost in the maze of illusions. Journalists played a role in this process too, often cajoled and duped into repeating seemingly innocuous narratives that had geopolitical objectives far beyond their understanding.

"At the dawn of the Cold War, the human mind became a covert battleground contested with new weapons of mass persuasion and individual interrogation," writes historian Alfred McCoy.[4] Fears of alleged Soviet and Chinese "brainwashing" techniques, eventually popularized in movies like *The Manchurian Candidate*, led the CIA to embark on a massive project to discover ways of controlling the human mind. It created various programs and operations with colourful code names until it eventually landed on MKUltra as the umbrella designation of its secret activities. For more than a dozen years, it funded research and carried out experiments in mind-control techniques, including LSD, hypnosis, sensory deprivation, electroshock therapy, and mind depatterning. CIA officials wanted to perfect interrogation methods and were fascinated with the idea that drugs or psychological torture could convince people to renounce their long-held beliefs.

Early in the process, Montreal became the epicentre for Canada's contribution to this research effort. McGill had an international reputation for excellence in mind research. Psychology department head Donald Hebb had published an influential book in 1949. He began assembling a team of academics and researchers that could do cutting-edge work. When the governments of Canada, the United States, and Britain decided to convene a meeting of defence and research experts in Montreal to discuss the issue of brainwashing, they invited Hebb to participate. Hebb told the gathering that sensory deprivation research might provide clues about psychological coercion and interrogation methods. By cutting off all sensory information, Hebb said, "the individual could be led into a situation whereby ideas, etc. might be implanted."[5] All the representatives at the 1951 meeting, including Caryl Haskins and Commander R.J. Williams of the CIA, endorsed the idea.

Ottawa's Defence Research Board quickly provided Hebb with a secret grant called X-38. For the next three years, he conducted the research, paying students to lie in a specially designed isolation box while wearing light-diffusing goggles and cardboard tubes over their forearms so that they couldn't use their hands for tactile perception of the environment. All the while, they were subjected to white noise through earphones. Some students likened the process to torture. Many reported hallucinations and delusions. Hebb also noted they had an increased susceptibility to persuasion. "The contract is opening up a field of study that is of both theoretical and practical significance," Hebb concluded. His results were shared with the intelligence agencies of all the countries that had attended the meeting.

Although all aspects of the program were cloaked in secrecy, it was just a matter of time before news of the unusual experiments leaked. Early in 1954, media reports began to emerge about the program. But participants had been fed a cover story that the research was intended to study how monotony could cause problems for workers in fields like long-haul truck driving. Once the experiments were exposed, McGill staff amplified the dupery by providing interviews to the media about the supposed practical applications of the research. These explanations were reproduced in newspaper reports with no questions asked. "It [the research] began with a practical problem of the lapses that may occur when a man must give close and prolonged attention to a job in which nothing much happens to stimulate the senses," reported the *Montreal Gazette*. "Watching a radar screen hour after hour is a good example. When, after a long, monotonous wait, something at last does happen, the watcher may fail to respond."[6] Canadian media didn't pursue the story any further until June of 1956 when researchers testifying at a U.S. congressional committee revealed that Hebb was conducting brainwashing experiments at the behest of the Canadian military. Even then, it would take another thirty years before the CIA's involvement became public.

Before Hebb's work was complete, one of his associates, John Zubek, accepted a position as head of the University of Manitoba's psychology department. His ambition was to turn Manitoba into the new centre for sensory deprivation research in Canada. He convinced the Defence Research Board that he could do longer, more elaborate experiments than even Hebb had envisioned. The board responded with annual funding over fifteen years, starting in 1959. Following Hebb's lead, Zubek recruited students and armed forces personnel to act as guinea pigs. Some of his early experiments confined volunteers for up to fourteen days, a period of time that other researchers considered dangerous. He also constructed a coffin-like box for volunteers to lie in for days at a time. Although university administrators were delighted that Zubek was bringing in so many research dollars, they were apprehensive about his methods. "The immobilization can be expected to result in an increased incidence of psychotic ideation and sensory experiences — hallucinations, delusions, disorientation, etc.," said one administrator. "The possibility of individuals predisposed to psychotic illness having some continuing reaction to this experience is thereby increased."[7] Despite the warnings, Zubek put more than five hundred people through his lab over fifteen years, and there has never been a follow-up study to determine whether any suffered lasting effects.

Zubek was determined to avoid the public relations mistake of trying to keep the project secret, so he made himself the first test subject and called a press conference when he emerged from isolation. But the key message was a cover story, and he succeeded for years in duping the press into believing this was all a harmless scientific endeavour. "We are studying the effects of the adverse environment on man. It is purely basic research," he said. The Defence Research Board stressed that the findings would be helpful for people going on long interplanetary flights.[8] This explanation seemed to fire the media's imagination, as reporters were engrossed in the race to space between the United States and the Soviet Union. Nearly every media story about Zubek's experiments mentioned how valuable the research would be for space flight.

By the early 1970s, some of the CIA's secret activities were being revealed in media reports and leaks. The United States created two commissions to investigate intelligence operations, which led to the first public revelations about MKUltra and many other covert operations. No similar public commissions have ever delved into Russian, Chinese, or other foreign intelligence agencies. Books that try to piece together details about the KGB's espionage operations have often relied on accounts by defectors, former spies, and dissidents. But even the U.S. commission's findings were incomplete, as the CIA had already destroyed many of its records.

Zubek's cover story began to evaporate in 1972 when a British army official told a parliamentary committee in London that Zubek's research had informed interrogation techniques in dealing with Irish Republican Army militants. Moreover, the committee found similar interrogation measures had been used by the British in Kenya, Cyprus, Brunei, British Guiana, Aden, Malaysia, the Persian Gulf, and other regions. The revelations led to demonstrations and denunciations on the University of Manitoba campus and calls for all military-funded research to end.

Contacted by the media to comment on the furor, Zubek stressed the applicability of his research to northern living and prison confinement. "There have been statements that we are involved in brainwashing techniques, and that is not the case at all."[9] Despite the denials, Zubek's reputation was tarnished. Faced with a lack of research grants and continuing controversy, he fell into depression. He died of an apparent suicide in 1974 at the age of forty-nine. The university never used the sensory deprivation chamber again.

That's where John Zubek's story might have ended, except for the accidental discovery twenty years later of sixteen boxes of Zubek's private records. One file included an instruction sheet for participants in a prolonged perceptual deprivation experiment. "During the course of isolation you are not to exercise, walk about, sit up (except when eating), sing, whistle or engage in any other activity to relieve your boredom." Zubek never released these instructions to the media because they smacked of coercive internment and contradicted the narrative that the research could inform monotony suffered by truck drivers, pilots, or people watching radar screens. In fact, the instruction sheet warned, "Under no circumstances are you to relate your experiences to other people. Failure to comply with this instruction may result in forfeiture of your payment," which increased the longer someone stayed in isolation.

According to historian Alfred McCoy, sensory deprivation has been a constant and recurring theme in interrogation and torture techniques used by U.S. military and intelligence forces over the last sixty years. It is a "no touch torture" philosophy that leaves no visible wounds but terrorizes inmates and softens them up for questioning.

McCoy considered the abuses of inmates at Abu Ghraib prison in Iraq an outgrowth of the sensory deprivation research, arguing that the United States in particular has used these methods with impunity. "As an elusive phenomenon, mental abuse resists prosecution and lends itself well to the politics of impunity. Psychological torture thus emerged as a persistent, albeit covert adjunct to U.S. foreign policy during Washington's rise to global power."[10]

The CIA eventually acknowledged it had secretly funded human behaviour control research at eighty institutions, including prisons, hospitals, and forty-four colleges and universities. There were 185 non-governmental researchers involved in 149 separate projects. Admiral Stansfield Turner, CIA director in the 1970s, said most of the institutions were unaware of the covert funding.[11] While no single piece of evidence points to direct CIA funding of Zubek and his work, it didn't much matter since the agency could freely access the research findings through its agreement with the Defence Research Board. Board chair C.R. Myers said the financial support of U.S. intelligence and defence agencies was critical in building up psychology departments in postwar Canada. "There appears to be no other scientific discipline in Canada that is so dependent for research support on U.S. sources."[12] That such a massive program could operate covertly for so many years indicates the extent of control exercised by intelligence agencies in the postwar world.

THE CIA

The CIA was responsible for funding and orchestrating a bewildering array of front groups that exercised influence in every social, political, educational, and cultural field. One of the agency's founders, Frank Wisner, likened the system to a mighty Wurlitzer — a reference to an organ on which he could play any tune on demand. CIA inventions ranged from the Congress of Cultural Freedom, which included writers, artists, and intellectuals, to the National Students Association, a group purportedly representing student interests. To combat the newly enlarged Communist bloc, the CIA created a variety of committees and coalitions for émigrés and people seeking to overthrow Communist rule. Even groups with respected names, like the International

Commission of Jurists, were found to have been created with CIA money, though many members did not know it at the time. These groups were all quoted repeatedly in the press without acknowledgement of their secret ties.

The CIA paid particular attention to manipulating media coverage wherever it sought to exercise influence. This might include direct ownership of a media outlet, recruiting journalists with favours or bribes to do its bidding, setting up covert news services to distribute items to legitimate publications, and influencing publishers to turn out books with favourable themes. In the wake of congressional hearings into covert CIA activities in the mid-1970s, the *New York Times* set out to take stock of the worldwide propaganda network the CIA had built to that point. The newspaper estimated that, at its peak, the agency influenced more than eight hundred news and public information organizations and individuals. According to one agency official, they ranged in importance from "Radio Free Europe to a third-string guy in Quito who could get something in the local paper."[13]

The *Times* noted that broadcasting was an early concern for the agency, as radio transmissions provided a valuable tool for propaganda efforts in many countries. If a radio station in those days had the words *free* or *liberty* in its name, there was a good chance it was getting help from the CIA. Sometimes the funding was masked through front organizations, while at other times it was more direct. The pattern was similar when it came to publications. *African Forum* and *African Report* used money that flowed through the American Society of African Culture and the African-American Institute. In Kenya, the CIA set up the *East African Legal Digest*. The Vietnam Council on Foreign Relations published a slickly produced magazine in Saigon that was entirely financed by the agency and distributed to U.S. senators and congressional representatives.

In some cases, the CIA owned publications outright, such as the *Rome Daily American* and newspapers in Greece, the Philippines, Japan, and many other countries. Often stories that originated in CIA-controlled foreign publications migrated back to the United States and Canada, creating a propaganda loop that masked the true origin of news items. The CIA even ran its own news service, Forum World Features, that supplied pieces to unwitting newspaper editors across Canada and the United States. And in the field of book publishing, *New York Times* reporter John Crewdson estimated that between the mid-1940s and mid-1970s, more than one thousand books were produced or subsidized in some way by the agency.[14]

When the media were not being influenced by stories planted by CIA-funded entities, they sometimes collaborated more directly. Information about CIA recruitment of journalists began emerging in the 1970s, with the U.S. Senate Church Committee into intelligence activities making some preliminary findings in 1976. Carl Bernstein, who partnered with Bob Woodward to expose the Watergate scandal, left the *Washington Post* in 1977 to study the issue of CIA influence among journalists. He spent six months investigating, and he finally published a twenty-five-thousand-word cover story for *Rolling Stone* magazine with some surprising results. Bernstein concluded that more than four hundred American journalists had secretly carried out assignments for the CIA over the previous twenty-five years.

> Some of these journalists' relationships with the Agency were tacit; some were explicit. There was cooperation, accommodation and overlap. Journalists provided a full range of clandestine services — from simple intelligence gathering to serving as go-betweens with spies in Communist countries. Reporters shared their notebooks with the CIA. Editors shared their staffs. Some of the journalists were Pulitzer Prize winners, distinguished reporters who considered themselves ambassadors without-portfolio for their country. Most were less exalted: foreign correspondents who found that their association with the Agency helped their work; stringers and freelancers who were as interested in the derring-do of the spy business as in filing articles; and, the smallest category, full-time CIA employees masquerading as journalists abroad.[15]

Bernstein named names, including many of the most prominent U.S. reporters and columnists of the day. He said senior management of many organizations directly co-operated with the agency. The most valuable CIA relationships were with major outlets such as the *New York Times*, CBS, and *Time* magazine, he said. Political analyst and *Time* columnist Stewart Alsop and *New York Times* publisher Arthur Hays Sulzberger had both carried out assignments for the CIA. Bernstein interviewed a CIA official who told him that the *New York Times* provided cover for about ten CIA operatives between 1950 and 1966. As for CBS, the working relationship was extensive. The network provided cover for CIA employees, supplied outtakes of news films to the agency, gave the agency access to its film library, and allowed reports by correspondents in the Washington and New York newsrooms to be routinely monitored by the agency.

• • •

While no one has ever undertaken a similarly exhaustive look into the connections between intelligence agencies and Canadian journalists, reporter John Sawatsky documented some examples from the 1970s. In his groundbreaking book on the RCMP Security Service, *Men in the Shadows*, he devotes a few pages to showing how specific journalists worked with the RCMP. "Some successful informers have been journalists, including members of the Parliamentary Press Gallery in Ottawa. Journalists usually are paid off not in money but in kind. In effect the two sides trade information to mutual but not always equitable advantage. Journalists are valuable to the Security Service because their cover is almost perfect. They can snoop around and ask questions without arousing suspicion."[16]

Sawatsky also provided specific examples, citing reporters from the *Toronto Telegram* and *Toronto Star* as informers. The *Star* reporter "was one of the most prolific suppliers of information and in return received more exclusive information than anybody else," Sawatsky said. He also described recruitment efforts by an RCMP officer who approached members of the Parliamentary Press Gallery in Ottawa, trying to get them to spy on Soviet journalists attached to the gallery. Even if journalists didn't formally collaborate with the intelligence agency, Sawatsky was critical of many media outlets for not pursuing accountability for their actions. When stories began emerging in the 1970s of RCMP illegal activities and dirty tricks, he said the press was slow in picking them up. He urged his fellow journalist colleagues to rely less on officially sanctioned sources and more on independent investigation.[17]

While the CIA was furiously trying to perfect ways of reprogramming the human brain, the U.S. military was hard at work preparing for possible chemical, biological, and nuclear warfare. As with the mind control experiments, they didn't hesitate to use unsuspecting civilians in their tests. And once again, Canadian citizens were also in the crosshairs.

Canadian officials have repeatedly lied to the media and the public about the extent of government production and testing of biological and chemical weapons. John Bryden, a journalist and politician who exposed Canada's role in this realm, quotes a speech in 1970 from Canada's ambassador to the United Nations Conference of the Committee on Disarmament: "Canada never has had and does not now possess any biological weapons," said George Ignatieff. For Bryden, it symbolized the ongoing deception and falsehood surrounding the issue. "This, then, is the real negative consequence of the secrecy that has surrounded Canada's chemical and biological warfare program. It has made Canada a liar in the councils of the nations," Bryden wrote.[18]

Also kept secret was Canada's willingness to test nuclear weapons. Between 1953 and 1959, the government agreed to use land near Churchill, in northern Manitoba, as a testing ground for Britain's first nuclear bomb. It was called the Blue Danube and had a slightly bigger capacity than the ones dropped on Hiroshima and Nagasaki. The idea was to test about a dozen nuclear bombs over several years. But the plan was never carried out, because Britain ultimately chose Australia as its testing ground. The agreement wasn't made public until fifty years later, when a nuclear arms expert acquired the secret document that laid out the plan. Had the experiments gone ahead, he said the fallout would have altered the landscape of northern Manitoba and drifted as far afield as Europe.[19]

Routinely duping the media was essential to human experimentation and weapons testing, especially when large-scale operations could not be entirely concealed from the public. The plan to test nuclear weapons in Churchill, for instance, was accompanied by a public relations strategy. "Every effort must be made to keep secret the nature of the trial before the event ... Once detonation has occurred, there will be little hope of keeping secret the fact that an atomic explosion has taken place. Some cover name must be invented to explain why men and equipment are being taken into the base, but if the base is a research station, such as Churchill, it seems possible that no special attention will be called to the preparations."[20]

No matter how the spin doctors planned to explain away nuclear fallout in Manitoba, Canadian government officials didn't appear terribly concerned about the consequences. The explosions were planned for a site near the mouth of the Broad River, about one hundred kilometres southeast of Churchill. "The area is waste land suitable only for hunting and trapping," the document said. It is "uninhabited except for the occasional hunter or trapper."[21]

If the cover stories and efforts to dupe the public sometimes seem far-fetched, consider how long it has taken for many of them to be exposed. On January 22, 1953, a four-paragraph story appeared in the *Winnipeg Free Press* announcing that civil defence authorities from Ottawa were going to study smoke behaviour in Winnipeg. The brief report said the city's health committee approved the plan, but not before councillor H.B. Scott sardonically observed that "they'll find out smoke goes up." The study was said to be part of a national plan to study air currents in built-up areas. Ten days later, the proposal went to the city council, where it got the green light. Reporters who covered these events were duped, as were the politicians who voted on the proposal. In reality, the U.S. Army Chemical Corps was planning to use unsuspecting Winnipeg citizens in an experiment to simulate how radioactive fallout from a nuclear explosion would be dispersed by air currents. It took another twenty-seven years before the public became aware of the true nature of the tests, but to this day the impact on people's health remains unknown.

The truth about the experiments wasn't revealed until 1980, when U.S. authorities released documents under the Freedom of Information Act. Incredibly, nearly three decades after the Canadian government had complied with U.S. requests to spray the city, a defence department spokesman said they were still investigating whether the chemical was harmful to the population at the time.

It might be argued that secrecy is essential in times of conflict, whether it's a hot war or a cold one. Philosopher Sissela Bok acknowledged this reality in her book *Secrets: On the Ethics of Concealment and Revelation*. But she issued a significant warning, especially when it comes to military secrecy touching on public safety, saying that "it carries immense risks of spreading, of creating bondage, of shielding incompetence and corruption, and of delaying advances in knowledge." Scientists have an added responsibility to exercise restraint in this field, because military secrecy "insulates from criticism and feedback, and thus opens the door to abuse."[22]

• • •

How many secret experiments, tests, and projects are under way today? What is the nature of the dupery and cover stories, of the front groups and phoniness that are used to mask what is really going on? By its very nature, we can never know the full answer to this question. Trying to ascertain the truth of many world events is difficult to do in real time, especially when intelligence agencies actively try to obscure the truth. The sabotage of the Nord Stream pipeline in 2022 is an interesting case in point. Current and former intelligence officials from many countries, sometimes speaking anonymously, have fed wildly different stories to the media about who might be responsible. It will be up to investigative journalists to discover the best obtainable version of the truth.

What's clear, though, is that a major front of the intelligence agency battle has moved online. For instance, U.S. special counsel Robert Mueller found systematic and widespread Russian attempts to interfere in the 2016 U.S. election. Through the Russian Internet Research Agency and other entities, agents created fake accounts and groups, amplified phony messages, and fabricated articles. Mueller also determined that Russia's military intelligence service hacked the Democratic National Committee and the party's campaign committee, and then leaked files in an effort to embarrass the Hillary Clinton campaign. The investigation didn't establish that members of the Trump campaign conspired with the Russian government in the interference, but Mueller pressed criminal charges against thirteen Russians and three Russian entities, including the Internet Research Agency.

Though it criticizes attempts by foreign state actors to interfere domestically, the United States maintains a sophisticated mass surveillance capability at home and aggressive online disruption strategies internationally. Edward Snowden's revelations provided concrete proof of surveillance and meddling operations by the National Security Agency. He revealed the existence of the Office of Tailored Access Operations, an Orwellian agency that engages in cyber warfare on behalf of the security apparatus. In 2013 the *Washington Post* reported that U.S. computer operatives routinely break into foreign networks so that they can be placed under secret U.S. control. It quoted budget documents that showed the project had put covert implants and malware on tens of thousands of machines every year, with plans to increase coverage to millions.[23]

One of the most explosive of Snowden's disinformation disclosures related to a series of documents generated by the Government Communications Headquarters, one of Britain's intelligence agencies. Snowden revealed the existence of a unit inside the agency called the Joint Threat Research Intelligence Group (JTRIG). This group's mission was to disrupt, degrade, and destroy its enemies through a series of covert dirty tricks. Journalist Glenn Greenwald, who first wrote about the unit's operations, said the two main tactics were injecting false material onto the internet to destroy the reputation of its enemies and using techniques to manipulate online discourse for its own aims. A slide from a top-secret presentation prepared by the unit for sharing with Anglo-American intelligence agencies discussed ways to discredit a target. One was the age-old "honeytrap," which uses sex to compromise or discredit an enemy. Other, more modern online strategies included changing a target's photos on social networking sites, writing a blog purporting to be one of their victims, or emailing and texting their colleagues, neighbours, and friends.[24]

A JTRIG document from 2011 detailed some of its global aims: discrediting the Iranian leadership, regime change in Zimbabwe, preventing Argentina from taking over the Falkland Islands, and countering Islamic radicalization by, among other things, hosting extremist sites so it could collect intelligence.[25]

Manipulating the media is also cited as a tactic by the intelligence unit. Under the heading of how to discredit a company, JTRIG recommended: leaking confidential information to companies and the press via blogs, posting negative information on appropriate forums, and stopping deals by ruining business relationships. Its secret list of tools and techniques include:

- Sylvester, "a framework for automated interaction/alias management on online social networks";
- Pitbull, "capability, under development, enabling large scale delivery of a tailored message to users on Instant Messaging services";
- Clean Sweep, "masquerade Facebook Wall Posts for individuals or entire countries";
- Gateway, "ability to artificially increase traffic to a website";
- Underpass, designed to "change outcome of online polls";
- Slipstream, "ability to inflate page views on websites";
- Bomb Bay, "the capability to increase website hits/rankings"; and
- Gestator, "amplification of a given message, normally video, on popular multimedia websites (YouTube)."

"Don't treat this like a catalogue," advised the JTRIG document. "If you don't see it here, it doesn't mean we can't build it. If you involve the JTRIG operations teams at the start of your operation, you will have more of a chance that we will build something for you."[26]

In today's world, a technician with a joystick can fire a Hellfire missile from a drone thousands of miles away. Similarly, spies sitting behind their laptops can create havoc and confusion in countries around the world. Media organizations need to be constantly vigilant and develop the expertise to monitor the activities of intelligence agencies, avoid getting caught in their webs of deception, and expose secret attempts at public opinion manipulation whenever they can.

Chapter 8

Science or Junk?

THE PRESS RELEASE SEEMED TOO GOOD TO BE TRUE. IT WAS titled "Slim by Chocolate," and it reported that a new study had just found a surprising way to accelerate weight loss. "Can you indulge your sweet tooth and lose weight at the same time? If it's chocolate you crave, then the answer seems to be: yes. That is the surprising conclusion of a study by German researchers published this week in the *International Archives of Medicine*."

The 2015 release went on to quote Dr. Johannes Bohannon, research director of the non-profit Institute of Diet and Health. It described a clinical trial of people aged nineteen to sixty-seven who were divided into three test groups. One group followed their regular diet, a second ate low-carb food, and the third maintained a low-carb regime but consumed forty-two grams of dark chocolate daily. The low-carbohydrate group lost weight, but the chocolate chompers lost 10 percent more. "To our surprise, the effect of chocolate is real," Bohannon said.[1]

This was a story the media couldn't resist. The German newspaper *Bild*, Europe's largest daily, featured it on its front page. Reports quickly followed in the *Times of India*, the Huffington Post, *Cosmopolitan*'s German website, the *Irish Examiner*, and TV shows in the United States and Australia. News outlets and websites in twenty countries and in five languages ran with the story. Diet magazines were particularly interested in the research, and many articles also featured close-ups of women taking giant bites out of chocolate bars. The item was widely shared on social media.

There was just one problem. The Institute of Diet and Health was nothing more than a website, and its "research director" was actually John Bohannon, a journalist. He was working with a German documentary crew to demonstrate how easy it is to dupe the media into reporting on junk science.

That isn't to say the research was completely phony. Bohannon organized an actual clinical trial, with paid subjects randomly assigned to different diet regimes. What he didn't mention in the press release was that the number of participants was laughably small, only fifteen people, and the differences in weight loss were minuscule. Bohannon explained that they tested for eighteen different measurements, including weight, cholesterol, sodium, blood protein levels, sleep quality, and others. He was banking on science's dirty little secret: if you measure a large number of things about a small number of people, chances are there will be a finding that can be highlighted and hyped.

Bohannon said many outlets ran with the story without requesting an interview. Few who contacted him asked how many subjects were tested, and no one reported the number. No independent researchers were consulted to comment on the quality of the study. Even a Google search would have confirmed that "Johannes Bohannon" and his purported institute were illusory. So how did the official-sounding *International Archives of Medicine* come to publish the study? Bohannon explained that it was posted online two weeks after he sent the publication a cheque for six hundred euros, and not a word was challenged or changed.[2] The journal later claimed it had posted the study by accident.

If Bohannon's test seems like a dirty trick that isn't representative of what journalists frequently encounter, consider what happened at the University of Maryland later that same year. The university issued a press release about a new study showing how drinking chocolate milk affected high school athletes' cognitive and motor skill tests. Only one brand of chocolate milk was surveyed, but a university researcher found that it improved the athletes' test scores and reduced concussion-related symptoms. Media outlets picked up the story, and the ensuing publicity convinced some schools to start providing chocolate milk to their athletes. But after a health news blog picked apart the shaky science in the press release, which was silent about the heavy sugar content in the milk and the nature of the alleged improvements in performance, the university began an investigation. It turned out that the chocolate milk manufacturer had partly funded the study. University officials disavowed the study and said that in the future it wouldn't issue news releases unless the research had been peer-reviewed.[3]

. . .

The stakes are much higher when exaggeration and disinformation invade the realm of serious health topics. In the early months of the Covid-19 pandemic, the CBC asked me to head up a team that would try to spot and debunk misinformation related to the virus. Our small crew of reporters and researchers could barely keep up with the tsunami of outlandish claims and outright lies that flooded social media. We did story after story debunking claims that bleach, mushroom sprays, oil of oregano, or special hats could have any impact on reducing or treating Covid symptoms or preventing infection by the virus. Any time Donald Trump mentioned an unproven remedy or theory, it gave rise to widespread social media speculation. Other theories were pushed by alternative medicine practitioners such as Dr. Thomas Cowan of the United States, who posted a viral video claiming 5G wireless technology had something to do with the pandemic. A reputable radio station in the United Kingdom was one of several to give oxygen to the theory before it was debunked.[4] We pointed out numerous claims by some chiropractors — registered practitioners whose services are covered by insurance plans across Canada — that spinal adjustments could boost immune function. The World Health Organization eventually dubbed the flood of unsupported claims an "infodemic." Our CBC team dealt mainly with claims that could be debunked relatively easily and quickly.

Far more problematic were the studies and abstracts from seemingly reputable sources that didn't stand up to rigorous scrutiny. Take the case of a report by the American Heart Association journal *Circulation*. In November 2021, it published a three-hundred-word abstract of a research paper claiming that mRNA vaccines "dramatically increased" heart inflammation in some people. It's usual for an abstract to be accompanied by the full study, but in this case only the summary was published. When several critics pointed out that the abstract was rife with errors, the Heart Association posted a notice saying, "There are no statistical analyses for significance provided, and the author is not clear that only anecdotal data was used."[5] The journal later changed the article's title to stress that the study didn't prove cause and effect. There was no control group nor any convincing analysis of the results. It turned out that the study's author was a surgeon who sells health products with names like "Mushroom Vitality" and "Total Restore" on his website.[6] Despite the corrections, the abstract had already been picked up by many news outlets and shared widely on social media. It became a weapon in the arsenal of people who advised anyone against getting a vaccine.

A scientific study exudes the aura of absolute truth for the average person. But there are many reasons a study can be exaggerated, flawed, or otherwise rendered unreliable. University researchers and academics are under continuous pressure to publish results, and institutional reputations often depend on the number of papers that appear in journals. Public relations offices of universities are always eager to highlight exceptional and groundbreaking results, and sometimes exaggeration is employed to achieve that end. In their quest for sustainable funding, universities and other institutions look for corporate sponsors to support their laboratories and researchers. This inevitably leads to tensions when a sponsor has a preferred outcome, since it can be implicitly or explicitly made clear that continued funding is dependent on the achieving of positive results.

As Bohannon demonstrated with his chocolate trial, a study can be shaped to get a result that appears to be significant. But would scientists deliberately alter the design of a study to satisfy a funder or secure a desired outcome? That's what Brian Martinson of the HealthPartners Research Foundation in Minnesota wanted to find out when he sent an anonymous survey to thousands of scientists in 2005. He got responses from more than 3,200 people and was astonished to find that one-third of the scientists admitted to at least one of the ten most serious offences on a list of misbehaviours. Just over 15 percent of respondents said they had changed the design, methodology, or results of a study in response to pressure from a funding source, a disturbing admission that points to the dangers of having sponsors involved in bankrolling research. Another 12.5 percent admitted to overlooking the use of flawed data by other scientists, and amazingly 1.5 percent said they had plagiarized or falsified results.[7]

Whether deliberately or inadvertently, the authors of scientific studies and their accompanying press releases sometimes mistake correlation for causation. Just because two data sets appear to correlate with each other does not mean that one phenomenon caused the other. Tyler Vigen of Minnesota provides an instructive and funny example of how the media and the public can be misled on this front. While attending law school at Harvard, he created a website called Spurious Correlations. It shows a series of charts demonstrating convincing correlations between seemingly unrelated things. By looking at the charts and being mesmerized by how closely the lines of the graphs track each other, readers could be forgiven for thinking that certain events cause others to happen. Some of Vigen's actual data show the following:

- The number of people who drowned by falling into pools correlates with the number of films Nicolas Cage appeared in.
- Per capita cheese consumption correlates with the number of people who die by becoming entangled in their bedsheets.
- The divorce rate in Maine correlates with per capita consumption of margarine.
- People who drowned after falling out of a fishing boat correlates with the marriage rate in Kentucky.[8]

Vigen's website always draws a laugh, but actual examples of the confusion about causation appear regularly in serious scientific papers. A study published in the *British Medical Journal* in 2014 looked at 462 press releases on biomedical and health-related science issues from twenty leading U.K. universities, along with their peer-reviewed research papers and news stories that were based on the topics. The findings are disturbing for anyone who places blind faith in how universities promote their published scientific literature. Researchers found that 40 percent of the press releases exaggerated the advice provided in the associated journal article. In 33 percent of the releases, the claims relating to causation were also exaggerated. More than a third of the releases also inflated claims about the applicability of animal research to humans.

Whenever the university press release was exaggerated, it was more than likely that accompanying news articles would be as well. This finding suggests that most journalists don't have the expertise to spot inflated claims, or don't bother checking the underlying studies to see if the hype in the release was backed up with actual data. Still, the study's authors are not quick to single out the media alone for spinning the message: "Although it is common to blame media outlets and their journalists for news perceived as exaggerated, sensationalized, or alarmist, our principal findings were that most of the inflation detected in our study did not occur *de novo* in the media but was already present in the text of the press releases produced by academics and their establishments ... The blame — if it can be meaningfully apportioned — lies mainly with the increasing culture of university competition and self-promotion, interacting with the increasing pressures on journalists to do more with less time."[9]

Because science commands so much authority, it's a prime target for everyone seeking to influence opinion or push a particular point of view. In their groundbreaking book *Bending Science*, Thomas McGarity and Wendy Wagner show how governments, industry, and others can "manipulate, undermine, suppress or downplay unwelcome scientific research." They list some of the techniques:

- shaping science, usually by commissioning research to produce a predetermined outcome;
- hiding science by burying findings that are harmful to their interests;
- attacking science, which involves challenges to methodology or data interpretation; and
- harassing scientists, a time-honoured technique of undermining the integrity of researchers who produce uncomfortable results.[10]

One of the aspects of bent science most difficult to detect is the suppression of reports that ought to be published but aren't. The only way such information can come to light is through a whistle-blower, or in the course of litigation. Clinical trials are a particular area of concern since companies use these tests to convince authorities to approve their products. When a trial demonstrates a product's effectiveness, it is published and forwarded to the government. When it doesn't, it is often buried. A group of western Canadian researchers tried to gain insight into the problem in 2021 by conducting interviews with clinical trial investigators, research administrators and coordinators, and trial participants. They concluded that about 40 percent of randomized controlled trials in Canada were never published, "leading to publication bias and less informed clinical decision-making."[11] Several people told the researchers they believed the sponsor of the studies had influenced the decision not to publish the findings.

The requirement to produce documentation during lawsuits has uncovered numerous instances of suppressed science. McGarity and Wagner point to some famous cases in which companies and industries have concealed research about their products' adverse health impacts. These include lawsuits relating to ultra-absorbent tampons, the Dalkon Shield contraceptive device, silicone breast implants, vinyl chloride, pesticides, and asbestos products. By the time the truth comes out, the authors point out, many innocent people may have already been severely and irreparably injured.[12]

GOVERNMENTS VS. SCIENCE

Governments also have a long history of shaping and hiding science when it serves their political ends. Following the World Trade Center attack on September 11, 2001, the Environmental Protection Agency (EPA) assured New Yorkers that the air was safe to breathe. The EPA issued five press releases in the first ten days after the attack, and eight more in the following months. The consistent message was that the public shouldn't worry about airborne contaminants. This was critical information for all the rescue and relief workers who rushed to the scene on 9/11, and for the thousands of people who lived and worked in the immediate area. Within a week, the agency charged with protecting America's environment had definitive advice.

On September 18, then EPA Administrator Christine Todd Whitman said, "Given the scope of the tragedy from last week, I am glad to reassure the people of New York and Washington, DC that their air is safe to breathe and their water is safe to drink."[13]

But the media were being duped. Two years after the attack, the EPA's own Office of Inspector General issued a report calling into question the reassuring statements that had been made. For instance, when the agency told New Yorkers on September 18 that everything was safe, "the agency did not have sufficient data and analyses to make the statement," the inspector general's report says. In particular, there was no air monitoring data for several pollutants, including PCBs and particulate matter. In retrospect, it's hard to imagine how the EPA could have known the consequences of the high-temperature incineration of millions of tons of building materials and thousands of litres of jet fuel. What's more, the inspector general pointed to political interference. "The White House Council on Environmental Quality influenced, through the collaboration process, the information that EPA communicated to the public through its early press releases when it convinced EPA to add reassuring statements and delete cautionary ones," the report said.[14]

The inspector general quoted the EPA's chief of staff saying that final approval of all the press releases came from the White House. "She also told us that other considerations, such as the desire to reopen Wall Street and national security concerns, were considered when preparing EPA's early press releases."[15] Due to political interference and agency complicity, people were misled about safety in the area. There were an estimated 360,000 building occupants and others who worked and lived in the area, as well as 15,000 children and staff in nearby schools.[16] More than ninety thousand rescue and recovery workers and volunteers came to Ground Zero as well. The reassurances of government officials misled them all. Thousands of cancers and respiratory ailments have been identified in the years since. It is estimated that more people have died from the after-effects of the events than from the initial attack.

The Canadian government and its agencies are not above distorting scientific information when it serves their interests either. I came across a telling example of this tendency in 2014 when our investigative unit at CBC Manitoba looked into the presence of pesticides on organic fruits and vegetables. We filed an Access to Information request and were surprised to learn that testing by the Canadian Food Inspection Agency (CFIA) showed about 20 percent of supposedly organic produce contained pesticide residues. The testing results were public, but the agency analyzed and quantified the findings. When our unit scrutinized the data and the analysis, we concluded that residues were actually present in 46 percent of the tested samples. The CFIA eventually agreed with our numbers.

Sometimes organic products are unintentionally contaminated when pesticides drift over from neighbouring fields. But we also discovered that 8 percent of all the organic samples had so much residue that it was a good indication there was deliberate application of synthetic pesticides. Our audience, which pays significantly more for organic produce in the belief that it is pesticide-free, was surprised when we published the story. For the CFIA, charged with monitoring organic production in Canada, our findings were a potential embarrassment.

But the story didn't end there. To blunt the force of the media coverage, the CFIA said it routinely sent the test results to organic food certification bodies for follow-up. "If there (are) non-permitted substances found in organic products, we would notify the CFIA-accredited certification body who would request the organic operator to take corrective action," a CFIA spokesperson told us. "So we have the system in place, and we have the confidence in our system, and we have the mechanism to address any non-compliances if they arise."[17] That's a comforting statement for any consumer of fruit and produce. Except it wasn't true.

After publishing our story, including the CFIA's reassuring message about its routine corrective action, we received a tip from an insider that no such follow-up with certification bodies had yet taken place, weeks after the CFIA had told us it was. When confronted with this allegation, the agency changed its position. It said it was still trying to figure out a protocol for how to do the very thing it had repeatedly assured us it was doing all along. "We apologize for misleading you, but that wasn't our intent," said the agency's director of its issues, communications, and media relations unit.[18]

Hiding scientific information became a routine government practice when Stephen Harper was prime minister. Soon after taking office in 2006, Harper ordered strict muzzling of scientists in the public service. Centralizing and controlling communications was an overarching strategy of his government, and it was especially zealously enforced when it came to environmental data. Throughout his tenure, Harper strongly preferred making as little evidence as possible public in this area. He cut programs that monitored air and water quality and eliminated the capacity of government scientists to track conditions affecting wildlife. He closed observation stations that measured fossil fuel pollution and its impact on the ozone layer. He laid off nearly two thousand scientists across multiple sectors. At the same time, he criticized international efforts to curb greenhouse gas emissions. Before becoming prime minister, Harper had denounced the Kyoto Protocol to cut emissions as a "socialist scheme to suck money out of wealth-producing nations."[19] Finally, in 2011, he withdrew Canada from the accord.

By limiting what scientists could say publicly, Harper attempted to control the media narrative about his government's statements and policies. Over time, public servants began decrying the practice and offering examples of how the government was silencing them. One Natural Resources scientist wasn't allowed to talk about a thirteen-thousand-year-old flood in northern Canada without ministerial approval, which came too late for it to be included in media reports. A fisheries scientist was prohibited from speaking to the media about her research, which linked viral infections to higher salmon mortality. A water researcher with Environment Canada was blocked from talking about two papers she had written that showed the presence of chemicals and drugs in Saskatchewan's Wascana Creek. Scientists who had discovered that snowfall near Alberta's tar sands was contaminated with petroleum-based pollutants were ordered to decline official comment, and instead to direct reporters to scripted statements that claimed an earlier government study had found no toxins in the area.[20] The government's strategy achieved its desired results. Climate Change Network Canada received internal Environment Canada documents via an Access to Information request showing that the volume of media stories dealing with climate change research had declined. Since the new communications process had been introduced, there were 80 percent fewer media reports.[21]

By 2012 Harper's treatment of the government's scientists was attracting international attention. Academics and scientists from around the world denounced the suppression of evidence and commentary from their Canadian colleagues. For many, Harper's general antipathy to science and evidence was perhaps best epitomized by his elimination of the mandatory long-form census. It was hard for many to understand why a government wouldn't want as much demographic information about its population as possible. Hundreds of scientists and their supporters marched on Parliament Hill that same year. Dressed in white lab coats, people held a mock funeral to mourn the death of evidence and the muzzling of scientists.

Finally, in 2013, the University of Victoria's Environmental Law Centre filed a formal complaint with Canada's Information Commissioner, who is charged with policing the Access to Information Act. The law centre provided detailed evidence of how various government departments had violated the act. None of these measures dissuaded the Harper government from its direction, which continued in full force until it lost power in 2015. After an investigation that lasted more than four years, the information commissioner released a report in 2018 confirming that scientists had been muzzled and that the environmental group's complaint was well-founded.[22] Significantly, though, the residual effects continued. More than half of the three thousand scientists surveyed by their union in 2017 felt they still couldn't speak to the media freely and without constraints about the work they were doing.[23]

CANADA'S LOVE AFFAIR WITH ASBESTOS

Canada's asbestos industry is almost as old as the country itself. At one time the world's top producer, Canada accounted for two-thirds of the global supply. Asbestos was highly valued for being robust, flexible, and resistant to heat and fire. It was used heavily in cement, drywall, shingles, tiles, and other construction materials. It was also deadly. Ontario environmental researcher and advocate Jim Brophy once said that all anyone needed to know about the root causes, the cover-ups, and the human impact of occupational cancer could be learned from the example of asbestos. "It also tells you everything you need to know about the reality of our economic system, what it values and what it fails to protect," he said. "It teaches about the collusion between government and industry. It addresses the issue of so-called 'junk science' and how the powers that be control information and public health policy."[24]

Occupational cancer is Canada's leading cause of work-related deaths, outstripping falls and accidents. Lung cancer and mesothelioma, usually caused by asbestos exposure, represent most of the claims for deaths from occupational cancer.[25] Yet the Canadian government downplayed the risks of asbestos for years, defending an industry that had become deeply rooted in the national landscape. When dozens of countries were banning the manufacture and sale of asbestos, Canada resisted international efforts to place the substance on a list of hazardous substances. Despite overwhelming scientific consensus on the dangers of asbestos stretching back decades, the government didn't finally ban it outright until 2018. Over the years, industry and government tried their best to convince the media and the public that the product could be used safely.

As with tobacco, there was evidence all along of the health dangers associated with asbestos. The industry successfully downplayed concerns for years, but the task became more complex in the 1960s when Dr. Irving Selikoff of New Jersey published a report in the *Journal of the American Medical Association* highlighting its dangers. He looked at 392 asbestos workers with more than twenty years of exposure, finding that 339 had asbestosis. Lung cancer was seven times more prevalent among the workers who had died. The asbestos industry went into damage control. One company executive proclaimed, "This man Selikoff has got to be stopped somehow." Another said, "Our present concern is to find some way of preventing Dr. Selikoff from creating problems and affecting sales."[26]

Over the years, PR companies drew on their tobacco experience to develop strategies for combatting the threat to asbestos sales. A lawsuit in Maryland in the early 1980s provided some insight into their tactics. One document showed that PR firm Hill+Knowlton represented U.S. Gypsum, an asbestos user. A memorandum advised U.S. Gypsum that "the spread of media coverage must be stopped at the local level and as soon as possible."

Part of the strategy was to plant stories in newspapers "by experts sympathetic to the company's point of view," which would defend the safety of asbestos.[27]

Selikoff's research was causing concern in Canada as well. The Quebec Asbestos Mining Association said in 1965 that it sought an "alliance with some university, such as McGill, so that authoritative background for publicity can be had."[28] Minutes of an association meeting in 1965 show a consensus that companies needed to take research matters into their own hands so that they could be in control. "As an example, it was recalled that the tobacco industry launched its own process, and it now knows where it stands. Industry is always well advised to look after its own problems," according to the minutes.[29]

In 1966, the mining association set up and funded the Institute of Occupational and Environmental Health in Montreal. That institute sponsored Professor J.C. McDonald at McGill to research Quebec asbestos miners. His primary focus was chrysotile asbestos, which is different from other varieties and the main form of the mineral mined in Quebec. Over the years, he concluded that chrysotile asbestos was innocuous except at astronomically high levels of exposure and declared that workers could be exposed to safe levels of chrysotile without adversely impacting their health. This was consistent with asbestos industry arguments, and McDonald voiced his opinions in journal articles, at conferences, and in front of regulatory agencies.

A 1971 article in the *Globe and Mail* showed how valuable McDonald's research was for the industry. J.R.M. Hutcheson, president of Johns-Manville Ltd. in Canada, said his company had known since the early 1930s that asbestos fibre affects human lungs. "It's a problem that is controllable and is being controlled in today's industry," he said. Hutcheson said millions of dollars had been spent on reducing the hazards, "and I believe we have achieved the objective." He pointed to research by McDonald that tracked thousands of Quebec miners, showing that the mortality rate was lower than the general population of workers. Only miners exposed to high dust concentrations, about 5 percent of all the workers, had higher mortality rates. But he claimed those miners worked in conditions that had "absolutely no resemblance" to current ones. He decried accusations levelled against the industry as "not supported by medical evidence." His is the only voice in the article, which quotes no critics of asbestos mining or alternative viewpoints.[30]

McDonald's critics have accused him of using flawed and outdated techniques and have questioned why his data wasn't made available to outside researchers. They also claimed he was not always transparent about funding from the asbestos industry, which totalled more than one million dollars over the years. Despite the criticisms, McGill's research was used by the asbestos industry to continue producing and exporting its products. It also influenced Canadian politicians to repeat the industry talking points. As late as 2011, Canada's energy minister insisted that chrysotile fibres could be used safely in controlled environments. In the years leading up to Ottawa's eventual ban on asbestos, Health Canada's website maintained that chrysotile was safer than other types of asbestos and that it only posed a risk when fibres were airborne and significant quantities were inhaled.

In 2012 CBC broadcast an exposé of McGill's research methods,[31] triggering twenty activists and scientists to call on the university to undertake an independent investigation of McDonald's program. Instead, the university conducted its own internal review, eventually concluding that there was no evidence of research misconduct. The review also rejected allegations that McGill colluded with the industry to promote asbestos.[32] That outcome did not satisfy the critics, who pointed to the overwhelming body of opinion that took issue with the university's findings over the years. The World Health Organization, for example, has explicitly said that exposure to all forms of asbestos, including chrysotile, causes lung, larynx, and ovarian cancer, mesothelioma, and asbestosis.

At the same time that McGill and the Canadian government were defending research showing chrysotile could be safe in controlled conditions, the WHO was stating the opposite. "Bearing in mind that there is no evidence for a threshold for the carcinogenic effect of asbestos, including chrysotile, and that increased cancer risks have been observed in populations exposed to very low levels, the most efficient way to eliminate asbestos-related diseases is to stop using all types of asbestos," said a WHO report in 2014.[33]

Does industry funding automatically taint academic research? Opinion is divided on the subject, but as public funds for universities and research teams decrease, institutions inevitably look to private industry for money. The scientific method relies on rigorous independence and open-mindedness, and even the smallest influences that might push outcomes in one direction are dangerous. "Even under the best of circumstances, there's some understanding that future funding depends at least in part on the results you find this time," according to Anthony Robbins, a former director of the National Institute for Occupational Safety and Health in the United States. Then there is the question of how results will be treated once they are analyzed. "There's a systematic failure to publish positive findings when they happen to conflict with the sponsor's interest," according to Sander Greenland, a U.S. epidemiology professor.[34]

As in the tobacco experience, asbestos industry players succeeded in delaying governmental regulatory actions for a long time. This delay has had a deadly impact. The World Health Organization estimates about 100,000 people die annually from asbestos. Because health effects only show up decades after exposure in many cases, countries that have only recently halted the use of asbestos will continue to see diseases and deaths for many years.

After surveying the many ways science has been bent over the years, McGarity and Wagner consider the role of the media and come to a harsh conclusion.

> In keeping with their impressive contributions in raising public awareness of serious social problems, one might expect the mainstream media to be hard at work exposing the manipulations of science, manufactured disputes, and biased, self-serving research studies. Unfortunately, when advocates employ the strategies detailed in this book to bend science to predetermined ends, the media seem to reinforce the carefully crafted message as often as they expose the manipulation. Apparently reporters and their editors rarely have the capacity or the will to challenge the bona fides of the scientific arguments in these technical debates.[35]

• • •

As I will detail in the final chapter, there are strategies the media can use to overcome these deficiencies. One journalist already employing many of them is André Picard of the *Globe and Mail*. His coverage of the Covid pandemic cut through much of the rampant disinformation, misinformation, and confusion. He insists one of the most critical things reporters can do, especially in the health field, is to avoid writing certain articles. "Just don't give attention to total nonsense or jump on something without thinking it through. Give it a more balanced approach," he says. Picard says he avoids preprints, or preliminary drafts of reports before peer review, almost at all costs. But even peer-reviewed papers need to be examined critically, because reviewers sometimes rubber-stamp reports as they want their own articles to be published later. He also believes it's getting harder to distinguish predatory journals from real ones, and even the traditional ones must be scrutinized for their influences. His most important advice to daily journalists is to resist the need for instant reporting and focus more on analyzing the content than on being first with the story.[36]

Most scientific studies remain obscurely tucked away in laboratories and universities, while some are published in specialized journals few people read. That's why media coverage is essential to the researchers and the funders of the studies. But as we have seen in this chapter, flawed methodology, conflicts of interest, and exaggerated claims are rampant. Most media outlets don't have the specialized expertise necessary to evaluate all the claims, and there is increasing reliance on press releases rather than underlying data. The need to file stories quickly and to keep up with the competition means journalists are frequently misled. This is also true in the social scientific field of polling, which is the subject of the following chapter.

Chapter 9

The Power of Polls

PIONEERING POLLSTER GEORGE GALLUP OFTEN POINTED TO a bowl of soup to explain how his new discipline worked. You can get a good idea of what the entire bowl tastes like if you mix it well and sample a teaspoonful. Similarly, a doctor can deduce from just a tiny vial of blood from your arm what's going on with your body. The pollster does the same thing when trying to figure out public opinion. By sampling as few as one thousand people, pollsters can derive a generally reliable picture of what millions or even tens of millions of people might think.

Polling has grown in sophistication over the years. Despite spectacular and well-publicized missteps in predicting some elections, it has proven to be an accurate way of capturing voter intentions and public opinion. Polls can also be a powerful tool in the hands of government, industry, lobby groups, and activists. If you can establish that the public agrees with your policy or point of view, you can leverage even more people to come on board. But as with scientific research, polling is subject to outside influence and manipulation. Various factors can determine whether a poll is reliable or a thinly veiled piece of disinformation. Therefore, the media should engage in a significant amount of due diligence before acting as a megaphone for polling results. But this does not always happen.

An instructive example occurred several years ago in Winnipeg, a city proud of its iconic intersection of Portage Avenue and Main Street. More than forty years ago, the city decided to close the corner to pedestrian traffic, urging people to use an underground concourse instead. People have passionately argued the merits of reopening the street to foot traffic ever since. City councillors, business owners, activist groups, and just about everyone else in town had an opinion on the topic. So CAA (Canadian Automobile Association) Manitoba decided in 2016 to survey its membership on the issue, and when the results were tabulated, the automobile association sent the media a press release.

"Don't Open Up Portage and Main" was the slant in most news headlines that day. Every media outlet essentially rewrote the press release and amplified the association's message that the intersection needed to remain shut. The release said that an "overwhelming majority" didn't want pedestrians on the roads, noting that people felt it would cause traffic congestion and endanger safety. Not a single media outlet initially bothered to ask whether this was a scientific poll that attempted to find a representative sample of the population. One newspaper even reported in its lead sentence that "a large percentage of Winnipeggers" were opposed to the reopening, even though only CAA members were surveyed.[1] Another outlet reprinted two pages of anonymous comments from survey respondents, all of them critical of the reopening idea.[2]

I was the managing editor of the CBC Manitoba newsroom at the time, and I sheepishly admit that we followed the herd by amplifying the association's message. With program lineups to fill and websites that needed constant updating, this story seemed like a no-brainer to produce as quickly as possible.

But more critical thinking was required in dealing with the story. Luckily, our newsroom had some perceptive skeptics who wondered if there was more to the survey. After all, it seemed natural that an association representing drivers would oppose any measure that made driving through the intersection more challenging. We asked for a copy of the detailed survey results, which had not been included in the press package offered to the media. Our data journalist, Jacques Marcoux, wrote a follow-up story entitled "The Perils of Taking Information at Face Value." He found the association had misrepresented some survey results to reinforce the message that the intersection should stay shut. For instance, the press release said three-quarters of the respondents believed traffic congestion would be a significant problem if there were a reopening. But only 56.5 percent said it would be a serious problem, while another 21.9 percent thought it would be a "moderate problem." The association lumped the two categories together. The original release also said more than 70 percent of respondents felt opening the intersection shouldn't be a priority for the city, even though only 45 percent said that. It included others who responded that it should be a low priority.[3]

Taking information at face value is what daily news reporters do routinely, especially when deadlines are looming, and the sources appear to be reliable. But when a story purports to represent the opinion of a large group of people, it's important to subject the details to greater scrutiny. The CAA eventually acknowledged it wasn't a scientific or representative poll. But the vast majority of journalists didn't pause long enough to even ask that question. Winnipeg temporarily settled its perennial Portage and Main controversy by voting in a referendum to keep the intersection shut. Meanwhile, the debate about how to treat polls and surveys is continuing.

• • •

Public opinion polls have been around for at least two centuries. During the 1824 U.S. presidential election, different methods of straw-polling were used to determine support for the candidates. People were canvassed at Fourth of July celebrations, while others stated their preferences at militia meetings.[4] Newspapers began reporting on these polls and initiating their own, often by printing coupons and inviting readers to fill them out. The *Literary Digest* created the idea of a national poll when it sent out eleven million postcards in 1916 to gauge opinion on the next election. Over the years, it correctly forecast the winner in five presidential elections. But in the 1936 vote, it predicted a landslide win for Republican Alf Landon over incumbent Franklin Delano Roosevelt. This was based on more than two million returns from its mailing of ten million surveys. The magazine had to swallow its pride when the results came in — a landslide win for Roosevelt, not Landon.[5]

Pre-election polls are a risky and unforgiving exercise for pollsters. The actual election results provide an immediate scorecard on how well they managed to forecast the vote. When polls radically miss the mark, there is considerable hand-wringing, and the media inevitably raise questions about the reliability of polling altogether. Pollsters saw the 2016 U.S. presidential election as a shoo-in for Hillary Clinton. Of course, Donald Trump won that election. They also underestimated Trump's support four years later. Polls similarly underestimated Conservative David Cameron's support in the 2015 U.K. election, mostly putting him in a neck-and-neck race, though he won easily. There have been similar misses in some Canadian provincial elections over the years. For the most part, however, polls have been reliable. In 2018 researchers from the United Kingdom and Texas analyzed more than thirty thousand national polls conducted in forty-five countries between 1942 and 2017. They looked at polls conducted on the eve of elections, including more than two thousand surveys from Canada. They concluded that the mean difference between the poll predictions and the election results has been remarkably similar over the decades — approximately two percentage points.[6]

While the *Literary Digest* had misjudged the 1936 U.S. election, George Gallup called it correctly. He realized that it wasn't just how many people you polled that mattered but how representative a sample it was. The *Literary Digest* sent its surveys to available lists of people who owned telephones and cars, which skewed the results to wealthier voters. At the height of the Depression, that didn't represent an accurate population profile. Just as a survey of car association members couldn't adequately capture what "Winnipeggers" thought of an issue, the magazine's methodology was faulty. Modern pollsters rely on random sampling to find the most representative slice of the population they seek to survey. Then they will use a technique of weighting results to adjust for any anomalies that might otherwise produce an unrepresentative outcome. Though polling relies on statistical science, it also incorporates subjective techniques to ensure samples are random and representative.

The subjective nature of poll reporting came into sharp focus for me one day when I was involved in organizing coverage of a poll the CBC had commissioned. After the results came in, and before we had begun preparing stories, the pollster looked at me and said, "Do you want to include the 'don't knows'?" In any survey that asks people for an opinion, say about which party or candidate they will support, a percentage of the population will answer that they don't know. Some surveys include that number in the result, while others don't. Now the pollster was asking me to make that decision. The problem is that the choice made will produce different results, which can significantly affect the subsequent headline. A candidate with 60 percent support among decided voters looks like they are winning handily. But if 40 percent of respondents expressed no preference, the story could read very differently. This is where considerable manipulation can happen in press releases from organizations with vested interests. A headline that eliminates the undecided voters might read that the candidate has a 60–40 lead. A headline that includes the "don't knows" could say the leading candidate only got 36 percent approval from people who were canvassed. I learned then that no matter what decision you take on the "don't knows," it has to be fully and transparently explained in the coverage.

Polling came to Canada in a serious way in the early 1940s, when Gallup set up his Canadian Institute of Public Opinion. Its first national poll on voter intentions was before the 1942 plebiscite on conscription. Gallup held a dominant position in the industry for decades. As polling matured and more companies entered the field, pollsters refined their methodology as they went along. They learned through experience that the order in which you list candidate names on a survey questionnaire matters. When gauging opinions on policy, they discovered the phenomenon of "acquiescence bias." People tend to agree with statements presented to them, even when they are in doubt or don't have specific knowledge about the topic.

Perhaps the biggest challenge facing pollsters, and the area that can produce significantly misleading information for the media and the public, is the wording of questions. Exactly how a question is phrased can often influence how a respondent will react, allowing either overt or unintentional bias to creep in. One of America's pioneering pollsters and a contemporary of George Gallup, Elmo Roper, was well aware of the pitfalls when he remarked, "You can ask a question in such a way as to get any answer you want."[7] The problem is less pronounced in political preference polls, which are usually straightforward and ask respondents whom they will support in an election. But when it comes to soliciting opinions on policy questions, the task for pollsters becomes complex. It is also an area the media must be vigilant about scrutinizing, as it can produce results that are not truly reflective of public opinion.

Leading questions can be advantageous in courtroom cross-examinations, but they deliver notoriously unreliable results in polls. An example from the 1970s involved a survey about Britain's intention to join the European Economic Community (EEC). The polling company asked half the respondents the first question and half the second:

> Version 1: France, Germany, Italy, Holland, Belgium and Luxembourg approved their membership of the EEC by a vote of their national parliaments. Do you think Britain should do the same?

> Version 2: Ireland, Denmark and Norway are voting in a referendum to decide whether to join the EEC. Do you think Britain should do the same?

The factual context provided in each version was accurate. Respondents overwhelmingly supported both propositions, even though they recommend different courses of action.[8] The rationale for this polling exercise may seem puzzling. The explanation is simple. Pollsters will sometimes deliberately create a split sample by designing two different versions of the same question and assign each to half the respondents to see whether the wording of the question introduces bias or otherwise influences an answer. A subtle example comes from a 2015 poll conducted by Ipsos MORI in Britain. Here are the two versions randomly assigned to survey respondents:

> Version 1: Do you support or oppose reducing the voting age from 18 to 16 in the referendum on Britain's membership of the European Union?

Version 2: Do you support or oppose giving 16- and 17-year-olds the right to vote in the referendum on Britain's membership of the European Union?

Most people who got the first question didn't want to reduce the voting age. For those answering the second one, the majority said the younger people should be enfranchised.[9] Could it be more desirable to support extending "the right to vote" than endorsing a legislative change to a long-standing law? The polling company reported results for both questions, and it was left to pundits to decide how to interpret the results.

Sometimes questions can be so leading and biased that respondents are almost invited to provide a preferred answer. An extreme example dates back to 2003, when a prestigious golf club in the United States was locked in a battle with a women's rights advocate over who could become a club member. Martha Burk, who represented the National Council of Women's Organizations, wrote to the Augusta National Golf Club, decrying the absence of female members. Augusta, which hosts the annual Masters tournament, was defiant. It hired a crisis management team and launched a public relations campaign to support its sexist policy. Then it commissioned an organization called the Polling Company to conduct a survey on the issue. The media widely reported the results, which showed that 74 percent of respondents wanted the golf club to remain all-male. It's no wonder, given the way pollsters constructed the questions. People were asked to agree or disagree with a series of statements, including the following:

> Martha Burk did not really care if the Augusta National Golf Club began allowing women members, she was more concerned with attracting media attention for herself and her organization.

> In a way, Ms. Burk's actions are insulting to women, because it makes it seem that getting admitted to a golf club is a big priority to all women.

"It is enormously gratifying to see that a majority of Americans feel as we do," the chairman of the golf club said in a statement following the poll.[10] The president of the Polling Company at the time was Kellyanne Conway, who would later become Donald Trump's senior counsellor. She famously proclaimed the existence of "alternative facts" to counter fact-checks on the U.S. president's statements. As for the Augusta Golf Club, it quietly began allowing female members in 2012.

There are other techniques that can be used to encourage respondents to answer questions in a way that is favourable to the poll's sponsors. A U.S. construction association once conducted a poll that produced support for tax increases to improve American highways. An analysis of the survey showed that its questions motivated respondents to see highways as essential to national security and the country's infrastructure. After twenty questions along those lines, pollsters asked whether those surveyed would support a two-cent increase in the gas tax to allow for more roads, bridges, and mass transit. Respondents voted 64–34 percent in favour.[11]

Another example of how poll questions can be manipulated to manufacture support for a sponsoring organization's objectives came in the wake of the Black Lives Matter protests of 2020. Following George Floyd's murder, a wave of demonstrations swept different parts of the world. A central slogan in many protests was "Defund the Police." In July 2020, Global News commissioned a polling company to gauge public opinion in Canada on the issue. A slim majority of people surveyed said they favoured defunding the police and shifting money to social services like housing and mental health. When people under the age of thirty-eight were asked the question, the percentage favouring defunding rose significantly.[12]

Alarmed by the results, the federal government decided to commission a poll of its own. It spent nearly $115,000 on an Environics survey that canvassed more than 2,500 people nationwide. Results were leaked to an Ottawa news outlet in 2021, and soon several media reports were saying that the poll showed Canadians wanted more police funding, not less. That prompted Concordia University professor Ted Rutland to file an Access to Information request, asking to see Public Safety Canada's records on the poll. After reviewing the documents, he concluded that the government deliberately tried to skew public opinion against defunding the police.

On the online site The Breach, Rutland said the internal documents revealed that Environics had drafted a series of polling questions and submitted them to Public Safety Canada for review. The department then consulted with its "policing partners," including the RCMP, about the wording. That resulted in eliminating some questions and altering the language of others. For instance, one of the drafted questions asked whether current police spending was too much, too little, or the right amount. One of the police commentators complained, "This is challenging as some respondents may feel the money being spent isn't being spent in the right areas (i.e. salary vs. equipment)." Another commentator said the same sentiment was captured in another part of the survey. The question was ultimately dropped from the survey.[13]

The department's consultants also took issue with another Environics question, which attempted to capture opinions on three different types of "defund" scenarios. The question was redrafted to include two additional scenarios: one that maintained police budgets and one that increased funds. But "protecting public safety" was only mentioned in the options that maintained or enhanced police funding. Though defunding options were also included, they didn't explain how public safety would be maintained. When shown the poll's wording, author Robyn Maynard, who wrote *Policing Black Lives*, commented, "The only way people can choose safety [in the poll] is to choose the police. The vision of community safety advanced by the defund the police movement appears nowhere." Political scientist Tari Ajadi agreed: "The survey reframes the debate about defunding the police as either we can have safety and police, or no police and no safety."[14]

The City of Winnipeg engaged in similar tactics when it began a public consultation on police funding in early 2022. Critics had increasingly pointed to the escalating police budgets in the city, which accounted for more than one-quarter of spending. Part of the consultation process was a public opinion survey of six hundred residents. Respondents could choose between five different scenarios:

- maintain the status quo, which gives council discretion over each year's budget;
- allow for automatic increases based on inflation;
- increase all budget items by inflation except for wages, which would be determined by collective agreements;
- use a levy on property taxes to increase wages; or
- use money the city gets from property taxes on new projects to increase all city departments proportionately.

Despite the illusion of choice offered by the different scenarios, none included options for ensuring police funding would be frozen or reduced. This was odd, given a finding in the same poll that showed a third of Winnipeggers felt the police were receiving too much money every year. "They're not really offering Winnipeggers a choice," according to Louise Simbandumwe, who represents a group calling for greater police accountability. "Basically the choice is 'how much do you want the police budget to be increased by?'"[15] The polling company acknowledged that while it offered advice, the survey questionnaire had been crafted primarily by the City of Winnipeg.[16] Not surprisingly, many of the comments respondents left on the survey complained about the lack of a "defund" option on the question. One respondent summed up the frustration: "This survey is a farce. The five options presented remind me of the old trick you use with kids: 'Do you want the pink toothbrush or the blue toothbrush?' There's no real choice. The alternatives to the status quo are varying versions of increases to funding while removing city hall's discretion. I'm in favour of huge cuts, a smaller police force focused on law and order and using the diverted funds to improve social services or to cut taxes."[17]

PFIZER AND OVER-THE-COUNTER DRUGS

Analyzing a poll carefully takes time and considerable critical thinking. Companies, governments, and organizations realize that many newsrooms won't invest that kind of time. Public relations agencies package polls and survey results with easily digestible press releases and key findings, stressing results they want journalists to highlight while ignoring others that might be less favourable to their clients' interests. Sometimes the missing information that doesn't get reported provides crucial context to the survey results.

Put yourself in the shoes of a newsroom assignment editor when a press release lands on your desk with the following headline: "Ten Million Canadians at Risk for Serious Side Effects from Over-the-Counter Pain Medications." That's a blockbuster story by anyone's standards. But does it tell the whole story? The press release began this way: "The results of a national Ipsos Reid survey released today suggest that as many as ten million people may be at risk for potentially serious side effects because they ignore label directions, misuse, overuse or combine these powerful drugs." The assignment editor would undoubtedly spot the name of a credible source, a nationally recognized polling company, and begin to pay even more serious attention. At issue were OTC (over-the-counter) drugs that offered pain relief. The third paragraph of the press release quotes an expert, McMaster University rheumatologist Dr. William Bensen: "OTC pain relievers are serious drugs. According to this survey, many patients are not reading the product labels, nor are they discussing appropriate use and potential side effects of these medications with their physician or pharmacist. This is putting Canadians at risk for serious complications."[18]

A diligent reader of the press release would have had to go fifteen paragraphs deep to discover that Pfizer Canada sponsored the survey. Many news organizations either didn't see that or chose not to delve into it. The survey received extensive media coverage, reaching national broadcasts, newspapers, and websites. Some television stations took advantage of the offer in the press release to use the supplied video footage of Dr. Bensen warning about the dangers of the drugs. The *Hamilton Spectator*'s story was typical of the media coverage:

> Got a headache? Think twice before grabbing the most colourful bottle off the pharmacy shelf and gulping down three pills without so much as a glance at the fine print on the side of the box.
>
> An Ipsos Reid survey shows as many as 10 million Canadians are at risk of severe side effects including death

because they take too much over-the-counter pain medication too often.[19]

On the surface, this was a straightforward press release reporting the results of a reputable survey, picked up and magnified across the country by the media. But as with much surface news, there is more than meets the eye. Surveys can only ask people questions about their actions, knowledge, and opinions. It's open to anyone to interpret the results, but here the press release's authors invited the media to conclude that as many as ten million Canadians could be at serious risk by taking over-the-counter pain relievers. In the initial coverage, I found no evidence of news outlets asking why Pfizer would be interested in sponsoring such a survey. Could it be that Pfizer was also in the business of producing pain relievers, but mainly of the prescription variety?

It's helpful to analyze the timeline of events in the months before the release was distributed at the beginning of February 2006. In April of 2005, the Food and Drug Administration in the United States asked Pfizer to remove Bextra from the market. The prescription pain reliever was in the class of drugs called COX-2 inhibitors, which came under scrutiny in the mid-2000s. The agency said Bextra increased the risk of heart attack and stroke, and also led to life-threatening skin reactions in some patients. It also asked drug makers to include the strongest possible warnings about heart attack and stroke on all COX-2 drugs, including Pfizer's Celebrex. Given the U.S. action, Health Canada also asked Pfizer to pull Bextra from the market, as had been done by European regulators. Despite appeals from Pfizer in the following months, the Canadian government concluded in December 2005 that it wouldn't allow any further sales of Bextra.[20]

Less than two months later, the Pfizer-sponsored survey warning about non-prescription pain relievers hit the headlines. Nowhere in the press release or the initial news coverage was it mentioned that Dr. William Bensen, whose quotes and video statements were supplied to the media, was a Pfizer consultant. In fact, he had been the lead investigator for clinical trials of Bextra in Canada, and also led trials for Celebrex. He published several articles pointing to positive results for the drugs. Yet media reports presented him as a university expert without providing context about a potential conflict of interest. Soon after the FDA and Health Canada decision, Bensen lamented the withdrawal of Bextra from the market. "People have suffered enormously from the withdrawal of Bextra. The people with chronic severe arthritis have had the rug pulled out from under them. We get 20 calls a day now from Bextra people who are desperate," he said in mid-2005.[21] Still, the adverse effects from Bextra continued to pile up. In 2008 Pfizer agreed to set aside US$894 million to settle lawsuits related to Bextra and Celebrex. That came a year after Merck agreed to a nearly US$5 billion settlement over its painkiller, Vioxx. Celebrex was allowed to remain on the market.[22]

Perhaps the most glaring omission from the original press release was that an earlier Health Canada study in 2003 showed 31 percent of people said they had experienced an adverse reaction to a prescription drug in their lifetimes, while only 3 percent reported such a reaction to an over-the-counter medication. In other words, while the danger does exist of taking too many pills or not reading the label instructions carefully, actual adverse effects are more commonly reported with prescription drugs. The Pfizer-funded study itself showed that 41 percent of doctors surveyed had concerns about prescription drug side effects, far greater than those who worried about non-prescription drugs. That wasn't included in the press release.

In February 2006, the same month it was distributing the Ipsos Reid survey results, Pfizer announced it was selling its over-the-counter healthcare division, which produced products like decongestants and eye drops. It eventually sold the division to Johnson & Johnson for more than US$16 billion.[23] As for concerns about how its survey was framed, Pfizer said it believed "in providing information to help Canadians make informed decisions about their health and treatment options."[24]

CBC Manitoba was one of the media outlets that created a straightforward and superficial report of the press release when it was first released. A few weeks later, though, our enterprise reporting team took a deeper look at the situation and noted some of the context around the Pfizer study. But large corporations and public relations agencies know that kind of scrutiny will be the exception and not the norm. The quick and easy headline, gleaned from a well-packaged release, will often go unchallenged.

Failing to disclose a doctor's or researcher's connection to a drug company is not uncommon. This is true whether the doctor is commenting on a poll, a scientific study, or any other kind of research. Gary Schwitzer was the publisher of HealthNewsReview, a U.S. website that scrutinized health-care press releases for conflicts of interest, inflated claims, and unsubstantiated statements. In 2016 he noted that 48 percent of the 224 press releases he had reviewed didn't identify funding sources or disclose conflicts of interest.[25] Academics have come up with similar findings. Studies show that as many as 69 percent of reports fail to include disclosures of conflicts of interest. Even when a scientific paper reports a conflict, it rarely finds its way into a newspaper report. In 2013 a study found just three of 425 newspaper articles about the H1N1 pandemic of 2009 mentioned the conflicts of interest in the research they were quoting. Some researchers argue that being on the payroll of companies shouldn't disqualify their participation in studies on those firms' products. But academic research shows that bias can creep in without transparency on those connections. As one study summarizes: "Researchers with conflicts of interest were found to be more likely to choose comparators that would produce favourable results, selectively include only certain outcomes in published reports, publish conclusions that are inconsistent with the study results, or complete a clinical trial without subsequent publication of the results."[26]

Recognizing that polls and surveys can significantly influence public opinion, many news organizations have created guidelines around how they should be reported. The BBC enforces some of the most detailed and cautious rules regarding polls. It warns editors not to lead news broadcasts or programs with the results of a poll unless the survey has prompted a story that itself merits being a headline. Even then, references to the poll are only permitted if they are deemed necessary to understand the situation. It also advises journalists not to give polls greater credibility than they deserve and urges them to say polls "suggest" or "indicate" rather than "prove" or "show." The broadcaster provides a comprehensive review of how polling methodology needs to be judged but suggests even scientific polls should be treated with skepticism:

When reporting surveys — and opinion polls — we should remember that even with comparatively robust methodology, they can be wrong or contradicted by other evidence. It is always worth applying a "common sense" test: if the results seem odd or surprising, or conflict with other evidence, or even with "gut instinct" — do not ignore those doubts. For instance: double-check the timing, the framing of the questions, the spread of locations, ages, social background, or any other relevant variables. When the nature and subject of the survey is known to respondents in advance, that may have an influence on those choosing to take part and thus impact on the results. If possible, factor in the element of doubt, or possible explanations, to the way the survey is reported.[27]

Such a rigorous scrutiny of methodology takes time, and that can run up against the need to keep up with the competition and match a rival outlet's breaking story. If a poll suddenly indicates a surprise turnaround in fortunes for a politician, the natural instinct of any editor will be to rush to publication. Similarly, if a journalist is pressed for time, they will rely on an accompanying news release to summarize a poll's findings rather than delve into the detailed tables themselves. But that's exactly what produced much of the coverage of the CAA Manitoba and Ipsos Reid news release stories. In this respect, the BBC also has another useful piece of advice: "We should not normally rely on the interpretation given to a poll's results by the organization or publication which commissioned it."[28]

Media organizations can also go astray when they attempt to enhance audience engagement with tools that look and sound like polls but have no scientific validity. Asking viewers or readers to go online and express an opinion about something cannot guarantee a representative sample. Such tools are also subject to manipulation. Michael Cohen, President Donald Trump's former lawyer, admitted that he paid a company to manipulate an online poll to boost his client's standing. He said he paid a company to write a computer script that would repeatedly vote for Trump in a 2015

Drudge Report website poll on potential Republican candidates. The effort put Trump fifth in the online poll. He said he did the same for a CNBC online poll, though with less success.[29]

The desire to enhance audience engagement landed the CBC in some controversy in 2014. The corporation's former director of research, Barry Kiefl, complained to the CBC ombudsman that several features on the *Power and Politics* program violated the broadcaster's standards and practices. Like the BBC, the CBC also urges programmers to consult with its research department before reporting on polls from outside organizations. It also warns against presenting online surveys as credible, representative polls. While the CBC doesn't prohibit such surveys, it adds an important caveat: "We report the results by giving the number of votes cast for each option. We do not give the results as a percentage, as we normally do with bona fide polls."[30] Kiefl argued that the CBC wasn't enforcing its own policies.

The CBC's ombudsman at the time, Esther Enkin, substantiated some of Kiefl's complaints. She criticized the broadcaster for presenting its "Ballot Box" survey results in percentage terms. She also noted that other polling results hadn't been vetted by the company's research department, as the policy required. "Overall, there seems to be inconsistent application of the policies on polling. I urge CBC News management to review its practices and provide practical guidelines for abiding by those policies," she said. CBC management didn't dispute the findings. Jennifer McGuire, then chief editor for the CBC, responded: "The Ombudsman review reminds us that new ways of storytelling can't come at the expense of our journalistic standards. You can be sure we'll re-examine and tighten up our processes where necessary."[31]

Even if a poll adheres to acceptable norms of methodology, there are still questions that can be raised about the wisdom of undertaking the survey in the first place. Governments routinely commission polls to gauge the public's mood and formulate their policies accordingly. But changing policy or introducing legislation simply on the basis of public opinion polling can be a risky and dangerous venture. In 2017 a poll surveyed Canadians on their opinions about women in politics. Women rarely occupy more than 30 percent of the seats in the House of Commons. Yet 58 percent of respondents said they felt there were either too many, or just the right number of women in politics. That led Indigenous rights activist Pam Palmater to question the tyranny of public opinion:

> It's a galling dissonance, but the premise of the question also feels frankly immaterial to how change is made. How relevant is it that Canadians think this dismal representation of women in government is either enough or too much female representation, when laws and policies in Canada specifically advocate for gender equality and protect against gender discrimination? How much should public opinion matter about whether Canadians agree with gender equality, when it is in fact the law? After all, if women had to wait for all men in Canada to agree with or like women's equality, we might still be waiting.[32]

Palmater used the same argument with respect to polls on Indigenous rights. She noted that an Angus Reid poll found most Canadians felt the country spends too much time apologizing for residential schools and believe Indigenous people should have no special status. Palmater's argument in *Maclean's* revealed an important truth about polling. As refined and scientific as the methodology might be, it is still the pollsters and the people who hire them who subjectively decide which topics are surveyed and which questions are asked. The ability to frame the debate, which is routinely amplified by media coverage, is a powerful tool in the hands of those who have the resources to pay for it.

Palmater said the government had already apologized for its role in forcing Indigenous children to attend residential schools, and successive administrations have pledged themselves to reconciliation. "It's long past time that pollsters stop asking Canadians if they like Indigenous peoples or agree with our rights — and start asking them whether they feel like they've put Canada's apology into action."[33]

Chapter 10

The Age of Influencers

EDWARD BERNAYS AND THE OTHER PUBLIC RELATIONS PI-
oneers would be dumbfounded by the possibilities offered in the internet
age. The ability to reach masses of people with a single click and in an
instant would have been inconceivable to the early peddlers of influence.
Governments, corporations, and interest groups have perfected methods of
disseminating propaganda on a massive scale. With each new and exciting
online development that promises to improve people's lives comes a dark
reminder that fraud and fakery are now weaponized in cyberspace.

First Draft, a non-profit coalition established in 2015 to debunk online
disinformation and misinformation, described the current landscape as an
"age of information disorder." There is a continuing campaign to publish
misleading, false, and malicious messages for various purposes. First Draft
says that "disinformation" involves a deliberate intention to mislead; ordinary people, on the other hand, can often spread "misinformation" without
even realizing it. Those seeking to spread disinformation exploit the unique
power of the internet to effortlessly share content online. By sharing content
that they haven't scrutinized, people can innocently misinform their friends
and colleagues. The founders of the coalition, who are now working with
the Brown School of Public Health, delineated seven types of mis- and
disinformation:

- satire or parody, which often is distorted as it is shared;
- false connection — when a headline, visual or lead sentence doesn't support the actual content;
- misleading content, including using techniques that deliberately frame statistics, facts, or images deceptively;
- false context — when genuine content is accompanied by false contextual information, such as the time and place a photo was taken;
- imposter content — a deliberate impersonation of genuine sources or people;
- manipulated content, which includes the range of audio and visual trickery to distort reality; and
- fabricated content — where things are just made up to deceive or cause harm.[1]

Artificial intelligence and machine-learning techniques have only ramped up the possibilities of spreading propaganda. Since its founding in 2015, the U.S. laboratory OpenAI has created a series of applications that allow users to generate all kinds of content by using natural language and other simple inputs. ChatGPT, for example, can turn a prompt of a few words into an essay, a report, or even a poem. The company's DALL-E product does the same thing with digital images, while MuseNet and Jukebox generate songs and vocals in different styles. "Our mission is to ensure that artificial general intelligence benefits all of humanity," declares the company.[2] But once a technique is unleashed in the world, it can be used both for benefit and harm.

Sock puppets, or false online identities, can be automated to spew out disinformation without needing constant human oversight. Bot farms are mobilized to carry out repetitive online tasks, boosting traffic to some websites or flooding others with denigrating comments. Fake reviews for products or professional services can be bought en masse and used to populate a site instantly. Sophisticated software can create phony images and videos or manipulate existing ones to tell misleading stories. More routine applications of artificial intelligence involve serving up videos, articles, and content for users to consume, all of which can be manipulated in the hands of the algorithm creators. Some analysts believe we have entered an era of computational propaganda, where algorithms and bots alter our perceptions and convince us to buy specific products or subscribe to particular ideologies.

A revealing example of how online sentiment can be manipulated came in July 2019, when then U.S. president Donald Trump told four congresswomen of diverse backgrounds to "go back" to their countries of origin. Trump's statement drew widespread condemnation. Prime Minister Justin Trudeau stopped short of calling him a racist, but he did say, "That's not how we do things in Canada."[3] Before long, the hashtag #TrudeauMustGo went nearly to the top of Twitter's trending list in Canada. Was the prime minister courting a public backlash by critiquing, albeit as mildly as possible, the president? The National Observer analyzed more than thirty-one thousand tweets that used the hashtag over two days. It found more than two dozen accounts had been created in the previous two days, "many of which tweeted at non-human rates."[4] Some tweeted more than two hundred times per day, leading critics to charge that automated bots were aiding the campaign to criticize Trudeau.

This might amount to yet another field of mischief for journalists to investigate if it weren't for one pertinent fact: many reporters rely on the web for story ideas and their understanding of the world. Journalists have been trying to divine what the public thinks for centuries. Letters to the editor have been seen as a gauge of the public mood. Newspapers would occasionally send out questionnaires, asking readers what was on their minds and what kinds of stories they'd like to see. More recently, media outlets have turned to polls and focus groups to take the temperature of their audiences. But all of these techniques have their pitfalls. For several years, the CBC used U.S.-based consultants to survey public opinion and advise on how to adjust the broadcaster's programming. That led to some controversial decisions. Some local outlets, for instance, increased crime coverage significantly because audiences appeared to prefer those kinds of stories. The problem was that more crime coverage created more fear of crime, even when overall offence rates had declined. The challenge became interpreting what the public was really concerned about and converting that into responsible coverage.

Many journalists today feel they don't even have to leave their offices to know what the public is thinking. Instead, they rely on social media. The Pew Research Center surveys U.S.-based journalists every year. In 2022 the vast majority reported using social media for their work. Twitter was the most popular site among journalists, followed by Facebook. Sites like Instagram, LinkedIn, and YouTube were also in the journalist toolbox, although to a lesser degree. Significantly, Pew found that three-quarters of the journalists surveyed who used social media found it helpful in identifying stories to cover. The lesson for online propagandists is clear: if you can manufacture or manipulate a message online, it has a good chance of migrating to media reports.

A team of researchers in France designed a study to find out exactly how the transfer of ideas from social media to major outlets works. They built a database that included 70 percent of all the tweets produced in French between August 2018 and July 2019. That amounted to nearly two billion tweets. Then they compared the tweets to the content published online by more than two hundred media outlets in the same period. The conclusion? The popularity of a story on social media significantly increased the coverage of the same story by the news media.[5] Those who believe governments and corporations bypass traditional media gatekeepers to get their messages directly before the public are half right. They have another objective: to generate online buzz, which persuades reporters to run with the story. Many media outlets publish regular features on viral trends and topics they believe are getting attention online. When academics did a content analysis of two national newspapers in India, they found journalists got most of their news sources from Twitter and didn't hesitate to use them as primary and stand-alone sources.[6] While Twitter has been undergoing upheaval and a rebranding to X since billionaire Elon Musk assumed ownership, there are plenty of other social media alternatives waiting in the wings should it falter.

Journalists, of course, are not oblivious to the fake news circulating online. In the last decade, and especially in the Donald Trump era, fact-checking has proliferated. Some outlets have set up units or commissioned reporters to track online disinformation and attempt to debunk it. This can sometimes backfire. Some propagandists are delighted to have their material "debunked" by a mainstream media outlet since it guarantees the kind of attention the original content could never command. Researchers have shown that audiences often hear about fake content first from media organizations who are attempting to set the record straight.[7] But even as one arm of a media organization earnestly tries to discredit an egregious act of disinformation, a colleague at the other end of the newsroom is being duped by what they're reading online.

Buying influence online comes in many forms, some more direct than others. During the run-up to a municipal election in Winnipeg, one candidate seemed to have built a significant social media following quickly. His Twitter account grew to forty-four thousand in a few months.[8] But this was someone who was a relative unknown to the CBC newsroom. We used one of the many available Twitter analytics and found giant unexplained spikes in his account. In just one month, for instance, his followers jumped from 243 to 23,000. The analysis showed that most of his followers were fake. Confronted with the evidence, he blamed a marketing company for the deception.

Purchasing social media followers is a common tactic not just for political candidates but for actors, musicians, and anyone seeking to appear influential online. Followers can cost pennies apiece, but the more you pay, the more authentic they will appear. If it's Facebook "likes" you're after, they are also available for sale. So are views on YouTube and plays on SoundCloud. In 2018 the *New York Times* published an exposé of a company called Devumi, that had sold more than two hundred million Twitter followers to that point.[9] The U.S. Federal Trade Commission investigated the company and eventually banned it from selling social media influence, imposing a US$2.5 million judgment against its owner.[10]

But enforcement action has been unable to stop the spread of influence buying online. A Google search will produce dozens of outfits willing to sell any type of follower or social media influence. Facebook, Twitter, and other platforms repeatedly purge their systems of fake accounts, but they return in short order. Before he bought Twitter in 2022, Musk often complained about the fake accounts on the platform. He should know, since half of his own followers on Twitter were shown to be fake.[11]

Local journalists who try to gauge the credibility of businesses or professionals based on their online reviews are also being misled. A study in 2021 analyzed four million reviews on Google, Facebook, Yelp, and Tripadvisor. It used artificial intelligence and natural language processing to see whether the content was authentic or fake. Google had the highest rate of counterfeit reviews at 10.7 percent, though all the websites had substantial amounts of deceptive material.[12] As with the phony-follower industry, fake reviews are commodities that can be bought and sold. Companies churn them out en masse with false profile pictures and language that can fool many consumers.

Kathryn Dean, a former federal fraud investigator in the United States, has developed a substantial following by exposing the companies that sell fake reviews. She found the same reviewers who raved about a dental office in Toronto had also left positive reviews for cleaning companies in Florida and locksmiths in Texas and Maryland. Then there were the reviewers who simultaneously liked a pizza restaurant in Toronto, a tutoring club in Delaware, and a counselling centre in Michigan. Dean is critical of Google and other big tech companies for not taking the issue seriously. When Google removes fake reviews following one of her investigations, she says, it doesn't provide an explanation to consumers about what has occurred.[13]

Even employees at one of Canada's largest corporations gamed the system to produce positive reviews. Bell Canada launched its Bell and Virgin mobile apps in November 2014 and immediately started getting five-star reviews in online app shops. Scott Stratten, who wrote a blog about dodgy marketing practices, thought the reviews were suspicious. He double-checked the names of the reviewers on LinkedIn and found many were employees of Bell, sometimes in senior positions of authority.[14] He wrote about it in his blog, and soon bigger media outlets picked up the story. The Competition Bureau investigated, finding that Bell employees were encouraged to post positive reviews without disclosing that they worked for the company. Bell paid a $1.25 million penalty and promised not to encourage or incentivize its employees to do the same again.

Wikipedia — treasured by students, journalists, and the general public — is frequently gamed and manipulated. Since its creation in 2001, it has tried to design methods to prevent and fix faked content. But as with any system dependent on user-generated content, it is frequently targeted by propagandists. A disturbing example emerged in 2021 when an investigation by the Wikimedia Foundation determined that a network of administrators overseeing the Croatian-language version of the site was deliberately skewing content to promote radical right-wing causes. Auschwitz, for example, was described merely as a "collection camp," while crimes of Croatian Nazi collaborators during the Second World War were whitewashed. According to the investigation, the propaganda campaign had been going on for a long time. "A group of Croatian language Wikipedia admins held undue de-facto control over the project at least from 2011 to 2020," Wikimedia said. "During that time, the group intentionally distorted the content presented in Croatian language Wikipedia articles in a way that matched the narratives of political organizations and groups that can broadly be defined as the Croatian radical right. The group systematically produced and edited articles containing unencyclopaedic content and overt historical revisionism. The content became so pervasive and remained online for so long that it created a web of deception to influence the reader's moral or value judgement in a way that corresponded to the group's ideological views."[15]

Croatians had been complaining about the content for years, but the self-correcting structure of the site was unable to respond quickly. Wikimedia exposed an even longer-running scam in 2022 when it found a contributor had written several million words of fake Russian history over ten years. She had created more than two hundred articles and contributed to hundreds more without being detected, inventing scholarly citations and creating bogus maps and faked images.[16] In its report on the Croatian scandal, Wikimedia concedes that there could be similar attempts to introduce disinformation into the site: "A more resourced and better-organized attempt to do so could be harder to detect and protect against."[17]

. . .

It's no surprise that governments are significant players in buying influence, massaging public opinion, and pushing outright propaganda online. The ability to cause mischief in foreign countries without involving operatives on the ground is a compelling option for intelligence agencies. It also helps that lies tend to spread faster than the truth online. A research report published in the journal *Science* confirmed that bleak finding: "Falsehood diffused significantly farther, faster, deeper, and more broadly than the truth in all categories of information, and the effects were more pronounced for false political news than for false news about terrorism, natural disasters, science, urban legends, or financial information."[18]

Networks of fake websites routinely sprout in Russia, China, Eastern Europe, and the Western world. In September 2022, Meta, the parent company of Facebook and Instagram, announced it had taken down dozens of websites it said were part of coordinated inauthentic behaviour emanating from China and Russia. The Russian operation impersonated legitimate news organizations in Europe, posting pro-Russian articles and amplifying them on social media. For social media companies, it's a constant problem and a never-ending game of Whac-A-Mole. "Throughout our investigation, as we blocked this operation's domains, they attempted to set up new websites, suggesting persistence and continuous investment in this activity," Meta said.[19]

Most governments do an excellent job of obscuring where the influence factory is based, but a surprising disclosure of public documents in China provided insight into how the game works. In May 2021, a branch of the Shanghai police invited bids for contractors to supply a "public opinion management" system, according to the *New York Times*. The job involved maintaining and disguising hundreds of overseas accounts on Facebook, Twitter, and other platforms in an effort to shape public opinion. The winning bidder had to guarantee an increase in fans every month and quickly fix suspended accounts.[20]

Disguising the identities of websites and social media users is also routine in the United States and Western countries. In 2011 testimony at a Senate hearing revealed the U.S. military was developing software that would create fake online identities, influence social media debates, and spread pro-U.S. propaganda. Officials hired a California company to create a system that allowed the U.S. military to control fake identities worldwide "without fear of being discovered by sophisticated adversaries." The contract also called for "traffic mixing," which would intermingle the fake personas' posts with those of real people in a way that would offer "excellent cover and powerful deniability."[21]

In the political world, it has become standard operating procedure for both Republican and Democratic supporters to unleash armies of bots to influence public opinion in the lead-up to elections. Researchers at Oxford University determined that the bots supporting Donald Trump over-whelmed similar automated cheerleaders for Hillary Clinton by five to one in the lead-up to the 2016 presidential election. Their central purpose was to confuse people about facts and muddy the waters, and their use was deliber-ate and strategic during the campaign, the researchers found.[22]

The newest frontier in online public relations and propaganda is influen-cer marketing. So-called influencers have built an online following through their websites or social media platforms. The popularity of video content on sites like YouTube and TikTok has enhanced the standing of influencers, particularly among young people. The Influencer Marketing Hub says the market has grown from US$1.7 billion in 2016 to more than US$16 billion in 2022, with about twenty thousand companies now involved in the indus-try.[23] The lack of human contact during the pandemic boosted the growth of online influence, and companies have been quick to take advantage of the possibilities. While celebrity endorsements have been around forever, influencers promise to be more authentic and relatable to their followers.

Advertising agencies didn't take long to see the value of influencers in designing public relations campaigns. Unlike with billboards or television commercials, there are often little or no production costs in getting an in-fluencer to boost a product. While celebrities and sports stars like Cristiano Ronaldo can command $2 million or more per post, most influencers charge far more modest fees. Micro- or nano-influencers, who typically have fewer than ten thousand followers, are highly valued. While the reach of such influencers is small, companies count on the close connection these social media personalities have with each of their fans. A recommendation from this kind of influencer is similar to one from a family member or friend. Companies can hire a micro-influencer to issue a post for as little as one hun-dred dollars. The exponential growth of the industry prompted the Canada

Revenue Agency to warn influencers in 2022 that any endorsements triggered an obligation to report income, even when the reward involved perks like products, clothes, trips, or other gifts.[24]

Advertising agencies initially recruited influencers in consumer lifestyle fields like beauty, fashion, and travel. They soon realized they could buy influence in other realms, intending to create buzz around a product or event. With luck, media outlets would pick up the message and produce some "earned media" for the sponsoring company. While the results of these efforts could be benign, there was also the danger that the influencers could be foot soldiers for deception and propaganda. That's what happened with the infamous Fyre Festival in 2017.

THE FYRE FESTIVAL

"Move over Coachella, there's a new festival that all the models will party at in 2017," gushed the headline in *Harper's Bazaar* at the beginning of 2017. "Once upon a time, it used to be that Coachella attracted the world's most stylish to its gates ... Well this year ... there could be a new frontrunner for the world's most fashionable festival; Fyre Festival."[25]

The phrase "Move over Coachella" made the media rounds extensively that year, from music magazines to the *Los Angeles Times*. But the publicity surrounding the newest entry on the music festival scene was filled with lies. It was manufactured by soon-to-be-convicted fraud artist Billy McFarland, and he used social media influencers extensively to dupe the media, fans, and his own investors.

McFarland partnered with rapper Ja Rule to organize the festival on the Bahamian island of Great Exuma in April and May 2017. They promised world-class music acts, luxury accommodations, gourmet food, and a chance to party with famous and beautiful celebrities. Fans paid up to US$12,500 for tickets, with some packages exceeding US$100,000. But when guests arrived for the festival's first weekend, they were greeted by disorganized and dangerous conditions. The luxury sleeping arrangements turned out to be disaster-relief tents, and food consisted of plastic-wrapped cheese sandwiches in foam containers. No proper arrangements had been made for security, transportation, and sanitation. The festival was promptly cancelled, and McFarland was eventually convicted of two counts of wire fraud and sentenced to six years in prison. Documentaries on Netflix and Hulu have ensured that people will remember the Fyre Festival as one of the music industry's biggest fails.

But as a case study in duping media, investors, and ticket buyers, the festival is instructive. *Vanity Fair* obtained an investor slide presentation that exposed the carefully orchestrated influence campaign. Organizers recruited more than four hundred people with big social media followings, dubbing them "Fyre Starters." They included supermodels and celebrities like Kendall Jenner, Bella Hadid, Emily Ratajkowski, and Nick Bateman. Some were flown to the Bahamas to spend a week frolicking on beaches and Jet Skis, generating suspense among their followers about what they were doing. Finally, at 5:00 p.m. on December 12, 2016, all influencer accounts posted an orange tile to their sites promoting the festival. Organizers boasted the campaign drew three hundred million social media impressions in forty-eight hours. They also noted 1.5 million media mentions, from *Sports Illustrated*, *Vogue*, *Cosmopolitan*, and *Esquire* to *Playboy* and Fox News.[26]

Kendall Jenner was reportedly paid US$275,000 for a single Instagram post in which she hyped the festival and provided a special code for fans to buy tickets. She suggested anyone using the code would get on a list for the artist and talent "after party." In their investor slide presentation, organizers crowed that the post received six million impressions within five days, "leading to an exponential leap in website views and ticket purchases." Many influencers failed to disclose they had been paid to promote the festival. Jenner was sued in U.S. Bankruptcy Court in 2019 by attorneys looking to recover money lost by investors. She agreed to pay US$90,000 for her part in promoting the festival.[27] The entire episode was seen as a stain on the influencer marketing industry.

• • •

Undeterred by previous controversies, the industry continues to expand rapidly every year. Sara Koonar, president and founder of Platform Media and Management in Toronto, works with about sixty influencers who generate a total of five to six million dollars in business yearly. Interest increased during the pandemic because companies and ad agencies realized influencers could continue to create content cheaply from their homes. She says the key to the company's success is working with people who feel like friends to their followers. Such influencers are inherently more trustworthy than celebrities, who might have no connection to the product they're promoting. Koonar says companies will sometimes dictate a script for an influencer, but she tries to make the promotions sound authentic and fit in naturally with the lifestyle the person is already living. Some of her influencers are routinely used as experts on radio and television programs, and it's always advantageous when they can prompt media to amplify a message, she says.[28]

Internationally, influencer campaigns promote every conceivable product, event, or institution. A case study on the website of NeoReach, a major U.S. marketing firm, showed how influencers can highlight the sunny side of problematic and even toxic controversies. "With the 2022 World Cup approaching quickly and skepticism spreading amongst soccer lovers across the globe, FIFA knew they needed to spark enthusiasm and draw attention to all the wonderful things the host city Doha, Qatar has to offer," the NeoReach case study said. "FIFA needed our help to launch an international campaign that proved Doha was more than worthy of hosting in 2022." As soon as Qatar won the right to host the championship, it began to face controversy. Amnesty International, Human Rights Watch, and other agencies criticized the systematic abuse of workers who built the event's infrastructure. Many athletes called for a boycott of the competition because Qatar's laws criminalized same-sex relationships.

NeoReach hired seventeen influencers in five countries, focusing on soccer hubs, and flew them all to Doha. "Our influencers spent the entire week staying in 5-star hotels, attending excursions like [dune buggying] in the desert, exploring the city, attending matches, going to concerts, and touring stadiums. During the course of these events, they were capturing their experiences and love for Doha on film to share with their followers on YouTube and Instagram."[29] In a subsequent post, one of the influencers wrote, "Has anyone been to Qatar? I was pleasantly surprised at how it was as a place, it reminded me of a sort of mini Dubai. Both places are the perfect locations for a break if you're flying further east as they generally have sun all year round, good food and good shopping." There was no indication anywhere in the post that it was sponsored. NeoReach touted the campaign as a success, with 1.4 million video views and a total reach of ten million.

Just as the Fyre Festival debacle was playing out, the U.S. Federal Trade Commission issued ninety warning letters to companies advising them to always disclose paid sponsorships and endorsements in influencer content. It said the disclosures had to be unambiguous and not relegated to a hashtag buried in a list at the end of a post that few people would read. The commission has continued to beat the drum of transparency since then. It issued seven hundred "notice of penalty offence" letters in October 2021 to many of the country's largest companies, advertisers, and ad agencies. The letters warned of significant civil penalties for disregarding rules around disclosure. Despite the threats, studies continue to show repeated violations.

In 2020 the United Kingdom's Advertising Standards Authority conducted a three-week monitoring exercise to review the Instagram accounts of 122 influencers. It wanted to see if influencers were properly labelling advertising content. Researchers looked at twenty-four thousand individual stories, posts, and videos. The compliance rates were "far below what we would expect," according to the authority's report. The regulatory body categorized one in four posts as marketing, but only 35 percent of them were clearly labelled and identifiable as advertising. The regulator said it wrote to all the influencers, as well as some of the brands featured in the undisclosed ads, putting them on notice they would be subject to enforcement action if future monitoring revealed an infraction.[30]

The Competition Bureau in Canada followed in the footsteps of its United States and U.K. counterparts by sending letters to about one hundred brands and marketing agencies in December 2019, telling them to comply with the law. It warned influencers of the duty to disclose their relationships with the companies or products they promote, whether that involved receiving money or perks, or even if there was a business or family connection to the brand. It reminded them that laws governing deceptive marketing also applied to influencers. There is no evidence the bureau is continuing to monitor the industry or has taken any enforcement action since then.

While the traditional realm for online influencers is in the beauty, fashion, travel, and lifestyle industries, many are now also embracing the world of politics. Governments and political parties are recognizing the value of influencer marketing in their campaigns. Both Republicans and Democrats made use of influencers in the last few midterm and presidential elections. In 2020 presidential hopeful Mike Bloomberg offered US$150 to individual micro-influencers for posts touting him as the best candidate. The agency organizing the campaign, Tribe, was careful to tell influencers not to publish the content themselves in order to stay within federal regulations. Instead, it used the posts on its own channels. When news of the campaign hit the mainstream media, Tribe was delighted. Stories by the Daily Beast, CBS, *Vanity Fair*, and the *Guardian* only drew more attention to the Bloomberg campaign. What started as a modest effort to pay small amounts to micro-influencers suddenly became a bonanza of "earned media." When one headline accused the billionaire candidate of "paying influencers to make him seem cool," Tribe saw a further marketing opening: "The Bloomberg team seizes an opportunity, owning their actions and capitalizing on the coverage surrounding this non-traditional approach to the campaign. They transform the seemingly embarrassing headline into one of the most unique Influencer Marketing strategies the political stage has seen. Bloomberg's team proceeds to pay larger social influencers to create and publish memes of Mike awkwardly trying to be cool."[31]

Legions of influencers took part in the 2022 midterm U.S. elections, operating at state and national levels. An agency called People First said it worked with about ten thousand influencers in seven congressional races and state-level campaigns. The Democratic Majority Action committee said it paid influencers between US$300 and US$500 to support candidates in Wisconsin and Pennsylvania.[32] Another Democratic political action committee, NextGen America, organized a campaign called Hot Girls Vote. It worked with more than seventy influencers to act as "messengers and validators" of its message.[33] Some platforms, like Twitter and TikTok, have tried banning political ads. But posts from influencers are in a grey category, and it's sometimes hard to differentiate a sponsorship from someone's genuine opinion. It can be challenging for journalists to distinguish between real viral trends and campaigns of sponsored statements.

In the summer of 2020, for example, thousands of social media posts began circulating in the accounts of young people in Arizona, amplifying Donald Trump's re-election talking points. There was no indication the posts were coordinated or paid for by any organization. However, an investigation by the *Washington Post* showed the teenagers had been recruited and paid by Turning Point Action, a branch of a conservative youth organization in Phoenix. When the newspaper checked with some of the social media companies, Twitter suspended about twenty accounts for "platform manipulation and spam," while Facebook also removed accounts.[34] In response, the group said the campaign was sincere political activism conducted by real people.

Turning Point USA isn't shy about explaining its mission: "The Turning Point USA Media Department exists to saturate social and traditional media markets with the message of freedom and limited government through influencer-based and digital marketing initiatives. The TPUSA Influencer Media Program identifies current and potential thought leaders and personalities who will advance this mission and equips contributors and ambassadors with every available tool to successfully spread these ideas on college campuses and beyond."[35] As of early 2023, Turning Point said it had 254 "ambassadors" with an average following of 275,644 people.

In Canada, parties looking to increase their profile among young people are beginning to pay attention to influencers. The federal Liberals acquired the Greenfly app before the 2021 election, hoping to capitalize on an online sharing system that has worked for the U.S. Democrats. In addition to rapid dissemination across many channels of party posts, the app promised novel approaches. "As 'official' social media channels have less and less organic reach, Greenfly enables you to amplify your campaign's message by harnessing the power of your surrogates to tell your story authentically to their own networks."[36] Elections Canada, meanwhile, warns parties that influencer content must be labelled as advertising.

Governments recognize the power of social media influencers as well. In 2021 the White House recruited more than fifty Twitch streamers, YouTubers and TikTokers, and pop star Olivia Rodrigo to promote Covid-19 vaccines. State governments did the same, paying some micro-influencers up to US$1,000 a month.[37] When the war in Ukraine erupted, the White House organized a Zoom call with thirty top TikTok stars to give them the U.S. position on the war. The influencers reiterated the administration's talking points in their videos almost immediately.

The Canadian government has done much the same. It has been engaging social media influencers for the last decade, promoting various government programs and initiatives. CTV analyzed documents tabled in the House of Commons to estimate that more than a dozen government departments spent $600,000 on influencers in 2021. A big chunk went to promoting vaccine uptake, but many other programs and events were boosted in the campaigns. In one case, the Canada Deposit Insurance Corporation spent $95,000 on influencers to promote confidence in the Canadian financial system. While some posts contained detailed explanations of who paid for the initiative, others look like casual posts with the addition of a "#sponsored" in the list of hashtags at the bottom. The reader might be left to wonder who the sponsor was.

However, as in all cases of buying influence, these campaigns are not without risk. Individual influencers need to be vetted, as do their claims about how many authentic followers they have. In 2019 Elections Canada budgeted $650,000 for a campaign that would have seen thirteen social media influencers produce a video to encourage young people to vote in the upcoming election. Voter registration among people aged eighteen to twenty-four lags significantly behind that of the general population, so the agency thought it would try to reach young people where they live. Conservative Party politicians immediately attacked the plan, pointing out that influencers might be partisan. They also weren't thrilled at the prospect of more young people voting, since they have traditionally been weak at attracting that demographic.

After spending most of the budget, Elections Canada did a final vetting of the Olympic athletes, Instagram personalities, and other influencers. That's when they decided to pull the plug on the project. "This final vetting revealed that some past activities of influencers that were not captured previously, could be perceived as partisan," the agency said. "The video therefore posed an unacceptable risk to the agency's core pillars of non-partisanship and neutrality, and the chief electoral officer decided to remove it from the pre-election campaign."[38] Though Elections Canada declined to specify its exact concerns, the *Globe and Mail* found one of the influencers had previously called on Conservative prime minister Stephen Harper to be voted out of office. Another referred to Justin Trudeau as "really dreamy."[39]

As more and more people rely on their social media feeds for news, friendships, and information on how to understand the world, the growth of online influence threatens to overwhelm even the most literate of consumers. Everyone is influenced by what they see online, even journalists, and the boundaries between truth and hype become blurrier every day. It doesn't help when media organizations themselves muddy the distinctions by embracing sponsored content. Getting paid to write content dictated by vested interests has an inevitably corrupting effect. Musing about recent developments, Canadian marketing expert Mary Charleson speculated about a future that focuses directly on journalists: "Where this all gets interesting is the traditional journalist who, in addition to publishing on established media has also developed their own following on social media as well as their own blog, video or podcast channels that they own and control fully. These JOURNALISTS WITH INFLUENCE are a powerful hybrid, and they are likely where the future of influencer marketing will lie."[40]

If Charleson's prediction comes true, the implications for journalism are troubling. Journalists who have built up a substantial social media following will become valuable targets for the influence machine. As they move from job to job, their media organizations will take a back seat in importance to the number of followers they command. They will have to become ever more vigilant about being captured by money, flattery, promises of access, or the allure of being offered exclusive information for undisclosed considerations.

Chapter 11

Fighting Back

IT WOULD BE EASY TO GET DESPONDENT ABOUT THE INFLU-
ence of the rampant propaganda and disinformation we confront at every
turn. If you have relied on the media to help you make sense of the world,
the realization that journalists themselves are being systematically misled
will only add to the feeling of despair. What can be done?

Quite a bit, in my estimation. The media can improve the situation
and blunt the force of the barrage of misleading messages directed at them.
In addition, there are things ordinary people — any concerned citizen or
grassroots organization — can do to determine the truth of matters vital to
them. I don't pretend to have all the answers to this complex problem, but I
will offer some suggestions in this chapter.

Everyone should try to enhance their media literacy skills as a first
step. Exercising deliberate thinking when consuming media and pausing
before reflexively sharing content can go a long way. In addition, anyone
who exercises skepticism and critical thinking can learn to spot misleading
information in news reports. It's always useful to ask questions like these:
Who created the content, and when did they create it? Is any evidence
offered for the claims in the story? Does the evidence support the story's
thesis or conclusions? Does the story support the article's headline and
lead paragraph? Whose interests are being served by the article? Are the

sources in a conflict of interest, or do they have a vested interest in offering a skewed perspective?

When it comes to stories involving numbers, polls, or science, additional questions must be posed. When confronted with scientific studies, it's necessary to determine if the results have been misinterpreted, innocently or deliberately. Has the study been peer-reviewed? How big was the sample size and control group? Has causation been confused with correlation? When reading stories about polls, it's crucial to ask: How many people were surveyed, and is it a representative sample of the population? How were people chosen to participate? What is the margin of error? Has the pollster released the wording of the questions? Who is the sponsor of the poll? When was it taken?

Anyone — journalist or ordinary citizen — who hopes to avoid being misled should sharpen their numeracy skills. It helps to know the difference between a percent increase and a percentage point increase. For example, when inflation rises from four to five percent, it has increased by one percentage point but 25 percent in total. In the hands of propagandists and masters of manipulation, creating confusion around numbers is a deliberate tactic.

We should all also become familiar with the scientific method, which has been the primary tool for establishing truth in science and social science since the Enlightenment. Scientists look for truth by developing hypotheses and rigorously testing them through proven trials and techniques. The pandemic has starkly reinforced the lesson that we need the scientific method to guide our thinking.

As someone who has taught students and journalists investigative journalism techniques for nearly thirty years, I have a secret to reveal. The methods are straightforward, easy to learn, and accessible to anyone with a computer. If you're reading a news article and wondering about someone's credentials, connections, or history, you can research much of it from your home. For example, it's possible to determine who owns any parcel of land in the country and how much property tax they pay. You can discover whether the person in question owns a boat or a plane or owes debt on a car or other property. You can access their court involvements, bankruptcies, and professional discipline histories. You can see who contributes to politicians and how much candidates spend. You can build detailed profiles of anyone's online and social media activity.

In short, people can take an active role in cutting through the spin and finding information on their own. But we all lead busy lives, and it's the job of professional journalists to report on news and help us understand the world.

To that end, it would be valuable if people insisted that journalists improve some of their practices to reduce the risk of being misled. Ordinary citizens have every right to make such demands. Most media outlets insist they serve the public, yet it's unclear how the public can play a role in demanding they exercise a high level of professionalism. With an increasing number of outlets now drawing financial support from the federal government, it's more appropriate than ever for the public to voice their opinions on what changes need to be made so that media coverage of issues and events is fact-based. Here are some suggestions on how the media could improve the current state of affairs.

STOP RELYING ON PRESS RELEASES AS A BASIS FOR NEWS REPORTS

Allan Thompson spent seventeen years as a reporter at the *Toronto Star* before joining Carleton University's journalism faculty, becoming head of the department in 2020. He is disturbed by the increasing reliance on press releases as a primary source of information for journalists. After all, the release is designed to present a politician, a company, or an institution in the best possible light. While not all releases can be categorized as outright propaganda, they are deliberately crafted to highlight specific facts and omit others. With shrinking resources and time-strapped reporters, it's easy for news organizations to cut and paste supplied material into articles.

Now that he is guiding a new generation of students, Thompson insists on issuing a clear warning: "People just have to be constantly reminded of being critical of this information that is pushed at us. Because, of course, those who are pushing at us are going to be trying to spin and manipulate and contrive the message. I did that as a political candidate."[1]

Thompson is referring to his two unsuccessful bids to become a Liberal member of Parliament in a southwestern Ontario riding. When no reporters came to cover some of his meetings, he would write up a report in the form of a news story and send it to the media. "I was just flabbergasted that a daily newspaper would run a press release issued by a candidate and present it as a news story," he says. "No one should ever run a press release issued by a political candidate."[2]

Press releases attempt to dictate the news agenda to journalists, eroding the ability of news organizations to decide on their own what is important to cover. I saw this phenomenon play out daily in my years as the editorial leader in a large newsroom. We had morning brainstorming meetings in which reporters were encouraged to pitch original ideas. Some days there were lots of great suggestions, while on others there were practically none. But it didn't matter as far as filling our newscasts was concerned, since we had plenty of stories to choose from based on the multitude of press releases that had rolled in that day. The press release stories were typically easier to get, while it was always uncertain whether the original ideas would pan out. You can guess which stories were preferred by the lineup editors who needed to quickly and reliably fill their television, radio, and online slots.

It's bad enough when reporters act as megaphones for politicians, governments, corporations, and other special interests, but press release journalism can be downright dangerous when it comes to stories involving people's health and well-being. "An abundance of news articles on Covid-19 therapies and clinical trials that rely solely or almost exclusively on press releases has been one of the biggest journalistic malpractices of pandemic reporting," according to Tara Haelle of the Association of Health Care Journalists in the United States.[3] After citing stories that touted breakthrough treatments for critically ill patients based on little more than anecdotes, she concluded, "If journalists do decide to report on press releases (I'd argue that they shouldn't most of the time), it's irresponsible to do so without consulting outside experts and getting multiple clinical and/or research perspectives."

Public relations professionals are aware of the power of press releases and how journalists have come to depend on them. Cision, the communications platform that sends out statements on behalf of more than one hundred thousand PR and marketing professionals worldwide, said reporters need the releases now more than ever. "Journalists want PR pros to help make their jobs easier," Cision contended in its 2021 Global State of the Media report. "With journalists covering several beats and stories per week, they're looking for press releases that are chock full of original research, graphics and invites to interview experts or attend events."[4] Cision naturally has a vested interest in promoting the value of its service, but this statement also reveals a salient fact: journalists who are short of time are more likely to rely on press releases to meet their deadlines.

There will always be a need for press releases that announce important events, emergencies, and safety alerts. There will always be value in gleaning information from them as a basis for further interviews and investigation. But in most cases, journalists need to wean themselves off press releases and begin independently finding the stories that matter most to their audience.

CHALLENGE CONVENTIONAL NARRATIVES MORE FREQUENTLY

Trusted and so-called reliable sources continue to hold sway over much of the Canadian journalistic landscape. A relatively small number of people are called upon to comment on and define the day's issues. Breaking into that circle can be difficult, and journalists who try to widen the range of sources risk criticism and condemnation. The sources — from political parties, government departments, universities, think tanks, the police, the military, or other fields — often reinforce mainstream narratives and the status quo. At different moments in time, those narratives turn into conventional wisdom: budgets must balance at all costs; wage increases fuel inflation; the mining and use of asbestos can be safe in controlled conditions; Iraq possesses weapons of mass destruction; our military allies always tell the truth, and our adversaries always lie.

Conventional wisdom can be manufactured for ulterior purposes. For example, military analysts inhabit U.S. networks and cable stations, usually affirming the narrative that a strong and well-armed America needs to make its presence felt worldwide. Despite repeated exposés showing how many commentators have direct and often undisclosed ties to military suppliers or political parties, these pundits are routinely considered reliable sources of information on world affairs. Whether it was to stress the importance of the war on terror following 9/11, to decry the U.S. withdrawal from Afghanistan in 2021, or to advocate for maximum armaments for Ukraine in its war with Russia, the message may be a strong America, but the commercial result is more weapons sales. When the *New York Times* did a major investigation into this process in 2008, it pointed to internal Pentagon documents that referred to military analysts as "message force multipliers" and "surrogates" who delivered administration themes "in the form of their own opinions."[5] In Canada, defence reporter David Pugliese of the *Ottawa Citizen* says he constantly warns other journalists to be wary of people who claim expertise in military matters and represent themselves as unaligned. "In the world of defence and intelligence and security, 99 percent of them are compromised by their connections with government and military," he says.[6]

Investigative journalists have successfully challenged conventional narratives over the years, but they face obstacles and risks whenever they do. In the United States, journalists who scrutinize U.S. military involvements around the world often have their loyalty questioned. Pugliese has had to incur the wrath of the defence department every time he explodes one of their mythologies. Every Canadian journalist who has attempted to investigate a suspected wrongful conviction has come up against the weight of an intransigent justice system. Meanwhile, most daily journalists struggle to find the time or resources to delve deeper into why everyone seems to believe one message or another. It's helpful, therefore, to look into the investigative process and see how it can be more widely applied.

When investigative journalist Harvey Cashore went on a four-month leave to Cortes Island in British Columbia a few years ago, his kids rode a bus to classes every day. It got him wondering: "Why are there no seat belts on school buses?" The conventional wisdom for decades has been that seat belts don't do any good on these vehicles and may even be harmful. It's been repeated incessantly by school administrators, politicians, and even safety experts. Cashore admitted that he is not immune to the pressure of conventional narratives and is always open to the possibility that they are true. But with time on his hands to think critically about the situation, he decided to pose a question that guides all of his investigations: How did this come to happen?

It turns out that Transport Canada did a seminal test in 1984, sending buses headlong into a wall to see how crash test dummies would be impacted. The department concluded that the compartmentalization of seats lessened injuries, while seat belts might result in whiplash or more damage. The study was sent across North America and became the basis for the argument that seat belts don't work. Cashore and his team at CBC's *Fifth Estate* found significant flaws with the study, pointing out that it didn't consider side impacts or rollovers where children would be ejected from their seats and sent flying. They produced a documentary in 2018 showing the extensive incidence of injuries and deaths in school bus accidents where passengers didn't use seat belts. The documentary also questioned why another Transport Canada report from 2010, which affirmed the effectiveness of seat belts, had never been publicized. Suddenly a piece of conventional wisdom didn't seem so wise anymore.[7]

It wasn't the first time Cashore's guiding question had exploded an entrenched belief. In 2002 the Canadian Hockey Association decided to allow nine-year-old players to bodycheck, a decision based on a Lakehead University study that concluded it wouldn't increase injury rates. Hockey administrators used the research to convince parents and coaches that physical contact was best for the kids. That reaffirmed the long-standing narrative that hard-hitting hockey was essential to the Canadian fabric. But Cashore was skeptical of the findings and discovered a flaw in the university's research. In reality, bodychecking resulted in three times the number of injuries. The results appeared on a *CBC News: Disclosure* program in 2003. The professor who conducted the research conceded there was an error in his conclusions.[8]

Journalists need to be constantly challenging conventional wisdom and asking how things come to happen. As in any field of inquiry, they shouldn't prejudge where their research will take them. But the first step is to ask the question.

RECOGNIZE AND REJECT COLONIAL STEREOTYPES AND RACIST AND SEXIST PREJUDICES

In his book *Decolonizing Journalism*, Duncan McCue says an elder once told him that the only way an Indigenous person would make it into the news was if they were one of the four *D*s: *drumming, dancing, drunk*, or *dead*. To that, McCue added a fifth *D*, *defiant*, and proceeded to show how negative stereotypes remain pervasive in Canadian media reports. Citing decades of research into news coverage, he showed how Indigenous people are routinely depicted as being morally depraved, inherently racially inferior, and resistant to progress.[9] As European powers colonized North America, they proceeded to oppress Indigenous peoples, swindle them of their land and resources, suppress their languages and culture, and, in different ways, eliminate them. Media were part of the apparatus to aid the process.

In 2015 the Truth and Reconciliation Commission said the media have continued to play this role. "To ensure that the colonial press truly becomes a thing of the past in twenty-first-century Canada, the media must engage in its own acts of reconciliation with Aboriginal peoples," the commission said.[10] Has journalism been misled into being an accomplice to colonialism by powerful institutions that try to retain control of Indigenous people's land and resources, or are the media themselves knowingly complicit? Whatever individual journalists might believe, McCue argues an urgent change is needed. "I define 'decolonizing journalism' as the process of deconstructing and dismantling the structures and practices in the media that perpetuate colonial ideals and privilege Western ways of doing. Decolonization means addressing power imbalances in newsrooms and news organizations, by valuing Indigenous knowledge and weeding out Western biases that impact Indigenous ways of being."[11]

Not many Canadian media organizations have acknowledged their colonial biases and apologized for past behaviour, but the *Winnipeg Free Press* is an exception. In a 2020 article, editor Paul Samyn said it was partly the newspaper's fault that people of colour in the community were denied the same rights, advantages, and opportunities as others. He says one of the newspaper's early owners, one-time federal immigration minister

Clifford Sifton, had a plan to open up the Canadian West that was "rooted in racism." As for legendary *Free Press* editor John Dafoe, his idea during the 1919 Winnipeg General Strike was "to clean the aliens out of this community and ship them back to their happy homes in Europe which vomited them forth a decade ago." Samyn also detailed the demonization of Métis people in the newspaper's pages when civic officials evicted them from their Winnipeg neighbourhood in the 1950s, and the outlet's silence when Jews and people of colour were banned from beaches, golf courses, and private clubs. "That's why on behalf of the *Free Press*, I am apologizing for the times when our coverage has fallen short, for being blind to those marginalized by the colour of their skin, and yes, for a history that shows we have, at times, been part of the problem, not the solution."[12]

The murder of George Floyd led many journalists to reassess how Black and dispossessed people are treated in society. Were "wellness checks" really the humanitarian actions police forces claimed, or were too many people dying as a result? Was the overrepresentation of Indigenous people in prisons the result of a smoothly functioning justice system, or was racism at play? Do the names and mascots adopted by sports teams represent a harmless tradition, or do they perpetuate hatred? While journalistic methodology has to remain objective, deciding what stories need covering is entirely subjective. More stories need to be assigned and written about systemic racism and the oppression of poor and disadvantaged people. Waiting for those stories to appear in press releases or on the daily news agenda is tantamount to complicity in maintaining the status quo.

For decades, Black, Indigenous, and all people of colour were largely shut out of mainstream Canadian newsrooms as they were from many other institutions. Despite recent efforts to diversify workforces, newsrooms continue to be overwhelmingly white. Research by the Canadian Association of Journalists shows that about 83 percent of newsroom supervisors are white, while eight in ten newsrooms employ no Indigenous, Black, Middle Eastern, or Latin journalists. Women and racially diverse employees tend to be overrepresented in junior and precarious roles.[13] If media organizations don't represent the populations they purport to serve, it's unlikely they will choose pertinent stories to tell or report on others accurately and sensitively. It's also far more likely they will be misled by police forces, government institutions, and corporations when dealing with different population strata.

When I started in journalism, newspapers still had a "women's section" where editors placed stories they thought would be of interest primarily to women. The people making those decisions were mostly men. While strides have been made in recruiting more women into journalism, sexist attitudes, practices, and stereotypes persist. Research continues to show that women don't appear nearly as frequently as men in news stories, a reflection of who is considered an official source in society. Newsrooms have also been slow to recognize that diversity requires paying more attention to a broad range of people, groups, and organizations that have alternative views and are normally shut out of media discourse.

Journalism organizations should not only have greater diversity of people and opinions, they should also consult more frequently with the groups they are covering. It's the height of conceit to believe they can understand the complexities of all the communities they cover without speaking directly to those groups. In their "Calls to Action" published in 2020, the Canadian Association of Black Journalists and the Canadian Journalists of Colour called on news outlets to increase representation and coverage of racialized communities by hiring more editors and reporters of colour. They also recommended formally consulting with racialized communities about news coverage and establishing community advisory boards so that journalists could learn from people in diverse groups.[14] Education is also crucial to rooting out colonial vestiges. Echoing one of the Truth and Reconciliation Commission's calls to action, McCue said: "To not provide journalism students with a cultural competency when it comes to Indigenous issues and to send them off to newsrooms with a diploma is a little bit akin to not teaching them how to write a lede or how to white balance a camera."[15]

ENGAGE IN MORE SELF-CRITICISM

In 2021 Ricochet Media and *Jacobin Magazine* turned their investigative attention to a topic news organizations don't often scrutinize — the media industry itself. In this case, the focus was political talk shows on television. They analyzed programs across CBC, CTV, and Global over six weeks, compiling a list of all 860 guests and then using lobbyist registries to find out more about them. They concluded that lobbyists for banks, oil companies, arms manufacturers, and other corporations routinely appear on the shows without fully disclosing their connections on air. "More than one in every 10 guests analyzing the news worked for firms paid to influence the government and the public," according to their report. "Despite their vested interests, networks often described these panellists as 'strategists.'" The percentage of people paid to peddle influence was even higher on critical issues. One in every five guests commenting on climate change and the federal budget was active in the PR industry, as was one in every three who spoke about national politics.[16]

It wasn't the first time someone revealed the lack of transparency on such shows. Earlier in 2021, CBC's ombudsman made similar observations in responding to a viewer complaint about partisan analysts on a talk show. "These commentators are all intelligent people with interesting insights to share," wrote ombudsman Jack Nagler. "But if one of the reasons they're on the air is because they have ties to one of Canada's political parties, then the audience deserves to know that." He suggested the CBC needed to do better in this area. And while he stopped short of finding the corporation had breached its ethical obligations, he said it had failed its responsibility to communicate clearly with the audience. "I strongly encourage programmers to reconsider how they introduce and describe the commentators on this panel, and elsewhere in their programs," he said.[17] Viewers might also be left wondering why so many people employed by public relations and crisis management firms, who are paid handsomely to burnish the reputation of their clients, are privileged guests so frequently on television.

Media organizations in Canada are notoriously reluctant to criticize themselves or their competitors. Jesse Brown, the publisher of Canadaland, thinks he knows why. "We are a small, insular, incestuous community," he says. "There are a limited number of newsrooms we can work in, so there's not much to be gained from embarrassing our competitors. It really is about protecting ourselves from journalism." When he first came up with the idea of doing regular media criticism under the name of Canadaland, the reaction from established news outlets was less than enthusiastic. "I tried to do it as a newspaper column and was rejected by editors who had always welcomed my pitches in the past. I tried to get it as a CBC show and was rejected. Nobody would hire me to do it. So, I did it independently."[18]

Brown thinks the stated reasons for the lack of interest were smoke-screens. Editors told him it was too "inside baseball" and that no one was interested in how the sausage was made in the news factory. Established in 2013, Canadaland began producing podcasts and web articles that questioned media practices and the actions of news personalities. Brown reported on oil lobbyists paying high-profile CBC personalities to speak at their conferences. He did stories about the predatory behaviour of CBC radio host Jian Ghomeshi. He published a leaked memo showing how *Globe and Mail* management wanted its staff to work on branded and sponsored content. While mainstream journalists sometimes decried Brown's ap-proach, the stories often led to internal reviews and vigorous debate in the journalism community.

Canadaland has broadened its coverage, though it continues to monitor media practices. Brown doesn't see too many competitors in the space. "It remains a really underserved beat," he says. Compared to the United States, which has many journalism critics, a weekly media show on National Public Radio, and regular satiric news criticism on late-night talk shows, among other places, Canada lags behind.

In an era when people unfairly fling the "fake news" label at journalists, it's understandable that media outlets are shy about opening their practices to public debate. To ensure they earn and retain public trust, however, news organizations must be continuously self-critical. A handful of media groups in Canada employ an ombudsman or public editor to respond to audience complaints. Notes from editors outlining news policies are also helpful, es-pecially when they explain how and why specific topics are covered. After all, it's entirely subjective which stories a news organization chooses to cover. Bias can be present not only in the stories that are reported, but in the de-cisions to ignore certain subjects altogether. The *New York Times* famously coined its mission as providing "All the News That's Fit to Print" without ever defining what it actually meant. Many other newsrooms have followed suit, making decisions on where to allocate resources and where to cut them without consulting its audiences or telling them why. Media organizations need to explain their reasoning and motivations for everything they do, and never hesitate to admit when they have taken the wrong course of action.

DON'T USE UNNAMED SOURCES, EXCEPT WHEN CRITICALLY NECESSARY

In a remarkable column in 2004, *New York Times* public editor Daniel Okrent scathingly denounced his newspaper's coverage of the lead-up to the Iraq war that had begun in March 2003. United States officials had accused Saddam Hussein of having weapons of mass destruction, and journalists repeated the assertion daily. Senior editors offered a *mea culpa* a week before his column, but Okrent said it hadn't gone far enough. He talked about flawed journalism and institutional failure, and pointed to some practices that gave rise to the problem. That included an incessant hunger for scoops and "front page syndrome." He referred to the newsroom maxim that you could "write it onto [page] 1" by hyping the story. "Whispering is for wimps, and shouting is for the tabloids, but a terrifying assertion that may be the tactical disinformation of a self-interested source does the trick." Okrent reserved his most significant criticism for false reports that were attributed to unnamed sources, resulting in stories that "pushed Pentagon assertions so aggressively you could almost sense epaulets sprouting on the shoulders of editors."[19]

It's a common tactic for governments, the police, the military, and many other institutions to demand confidentiality before sharing information with reporters. Journalists are often happy to comply, especially when it produces a scoop. The problem is that when information turns out to be incomplete, misleading, or downright false, there is no one to hold accountable. It's no exaggeration to say this phenomenon happens multiple times a day. Just Google "sources say" or "on condition of anonymity" to get a sense of how much information the media disseminates without naming a source.

In Canada, the mischief perpetrated by the government and other powerful institutions in extracting promises of confidentiality often doesn't come to light until a public inquiry reveals it. Allan Thompson learned he was being duped into granting confidentiality to a senior government official to smear a whistle-blower only when all the facts emerged at the Somalia Inquiry in 1996. It also took a commission of inquiry to discover the truth about what happened to Maher Arar, the engineer falsely accused of being a terrorist and ultimately tortured in Syria. The commissioner concluded Arar was the victim of a government smear campaign that recruited journalists to amplify false messages. "There were at least eight media stories containing leaked information about Mr. Arar and/or the investigation that involved him. Typically, the leaked information was attributed to an unnamed government official, an official closely involved in the case, or some similar source," the commissioner said.[20]

The devotion to official and supposedly reliable sources is part of the problem. Arar has been critical of journalists for giving powerful interests the benefit of the doubt while treating those without power differently. According to Australian investigative journalist John Pilger, many journalists who rely on such sources are part of a propaganda apparatus without consciously realizing it. "Power rewards their collusion with faint recognition: a place at the table, perhaps even a Companion of the British Empire. At their most supine, they are spokesmen of the spokesmen, de-briefers of the briefers, what the French call *functionnaires* [*sic*]."[21]

I am not suggesting a ban on using unnamed sources. Some of investigative journalism's biggest revelations originated with sources who feared going public. Victims of sexual assault need to have their identities protected, as do people who risk losing their jobs, liberty, or lives if they blow the whistle on illegal or unethical practices. When the *Globe and Mail* allowed an unnamed national security official to write an editorial claiming that China was interfering in Canadian elections, it asked its readers to trust its judgment. Readers have no way of knowing how thoroughly the newspaper corroborated the source's claims to make sure the information was valid. In effect, the newspaper is staking its reputation on its decision to provide confidentiality. Sometimes it takes years before the truth of such revelations becomes clear, as it did in the case of Bob Woodward and Carl Bernstein's Watergate-era source they dubbed "Deep Throat." That is why camouflaging identities needs to be done judiciously and sparingly. Some news organizations set down rules for when it's justified to grant confidentiality, but enforcement is often lax. Anytime you see a news organization grant confidentiality for no reason other than the sources "aren't authorized to speak publicly" on a subject, you should take everything they say with a large grain of salt. It is often code for a government or institution trying to manipulate news coverage.

Okrent summarized the issue's nuances elegantly in his column:

> There is nothing more toxic to responsible journalism than an anonymous source. There is often nothing more necessary, too; crucial stories might never see print if a name had to be attached to every piece of information. But a newspaper has an obligation to convince readers why it believes the sources it does not identify are telling the truth. That automatic editor defence, "We're not confirming what he says, we're just reporting it," may apply to the statements of people speaking on the record. For anonymous sources, it's worse than no defence. It's a license granted to liars.

Journalists need to be on especially high alert during times of war, when all sides try their best to control public opinion. In November 2022, the Associated Press reported, "A senior U.S. intelligence official says Russian missiles crossed into NATO member Poland, killing two people." The report was false, and AP later corrected it but didn't explain who their source was or why they granted confidentiality.[22] Far more problematic are the stories backed by unnamed sources that are never exposed or corrected.

INVEST IN MODERN TOOLS OF INQUIRY

Malachy Browne of the *New York Times* was at home one Sunday evening, in the early days of the war between Russia and Ukraine, when his phone rang. His editor wanted him to look at some pictures showing bodies lying on the road in Bucha, a suburb of Kyiv. Russia had occupied Bucha through most of March, then withdrawn its troops. Ukraine accused Russia of killing civilians, while the Russians denied responsibility and said the bodies must have appeared after they left town. Who was telling the truth? Could

Browne, a producer with the newspaper's visual investigations team, help to figure this out?

"The pictures were shocking, horrifying," Browne says. "I actually went downstairs to have dinner with my family and my wife said, What's wrong? Because I was pale and couldn't talk to my kids. But then I was thinking: satellite imagery can tell us how long those bodies were there."[23]

Browne returned to his computer and checked his account with Maxar Technologies, a satellite image provider. There was too much cloud in the first few days of March 2022 to make anything out, but later, pictures revealed human-sized shapes on the streets. The satellite company provided higher resolution versions, and the *New York Times* also compared them with locally shot video from the scene. The newspaper quickly published a story showing convincingly that at least eleven bodies were present in the streets since March 11, when Russia was still in control of the town. Instead of just printing competing statements from the two sides, Browne used objective evidence to determine the truth of what happened.[24]

The visual investigations team uses forensic analysis of photos and video to guide its journalism. "It's the collection, analysis and layering of evidence that's buried within that visual evidence that's useful to us," Browne says. In another investigation, the team analyzed videos, photos, and satellite images of Israeli air strikes in Gaza that destroyed three apartment buildings in May 2021. Team members visited the bombing sites and conducted interviews on the ground. While the Israeli military said the strikes were carefully targeted, the investigation showed how Israel "dropped some of its heaviest bombs in its arsenal without warning on a densely packed neighbourhood and with limited intelligence about what they were attacking." Experts told the newspaper that kind of bombing can easily be catastrophic and may constitute a war crime.[25]

Browne's team uses the tools and techniques of a burgeoning field called open-source intelligence, or OSINT, which taps openly accessible evidence to establish what's true and what's spin. The vast amount of data that is publicly available provides investigators with the ability to find facts like never before: ships and aircraft can be tracked, artificial intelligence can detect hidden patterns in blocks of text, facial recognition tools can isolate people of interest, and dozens of software programs can be harnessed for investigative work. Even if governments or private institutions are reluctant to release data, journalists can use techniques to scrape the web and collect raw sources of information.

U.S. journalist Philip Meyer pioneered the science of harnessing computers to help with reporting projects. He used mainframe computers to analyze a survey of Detroit residents during riots in 1967 and later employed similar techniques to examine sentencing patterns in the court system. When personal computers became widespread in the 1980s, more news organizations practised what was then called computer-assisted reporting. It involved collecting and analyzing data to identify trends rather than relying on anecdotal evidence. With more sophisticated tools and practitioners, the field is now called data or computational journalism. Some of the most impactful pieces of investigative journalism over the last decade have used data analysis.

The International Consortium of Investigative Journalists specializes in tackling projects that involve journalists from many countries. Whether looking at offshore tax avoidance, the dangers of medical implants, or worldwide money laundering, the consortium has used sophisticated data analysis to produce its reports. The series of stories entitled The Implant Files, which tracked the dangers of medical devices implanted into human bodies, showed how products withdrawn or banned in one country remained in use in others. By banding together, journalists could share information and databases across many countries, combatting the spin efforts by multinational corporations.

Data analysis, advanced visual investigation techniques, and using artificial intelligence for journalistic purposes require significant time, resources, and specialized expertise. Canadian news organizations have been slow to embrace these methods on a large scale. While there are several good examples of Canadian projects that have used data journalism with significant impact, they are far fewer than those produced in the United States and throughout Europe.

Every serious news organization should hire reporters competent in computational journalism and open-source intelligence–gathering techniques.

This needs to be the most significant growth area in investigative work. It can be achieved, in many cases, by shifting resources away from covering daily, agenda-driven stories and investing in training or hiring people with the right skills. Using a scientific and statistically sound method of analysis is crucial in preventing vested interests from distorting reports and using random anecdotes to mislead reporters.

LET NEW START-UPS PROLIFERATE AND FLOURISH

"Freedom of the press is guaranteed only to those who own one," American media critic A.J. Liebling famously said in 1960. Newspapers still held a stranglehold on news dissemination at the time, and the barriers to entry for new industry players were enormous. More than sixty years later, the media environment has changed considerably. Though wealth still holds huge and often decisive sway, it's easier today to publish a message and begin to build a following.

As some local media outlets have shut down, various hyper-local online start-ups have replaced them. Sites devoted to niche topics and narrowly defined locations are finding an interested audience. If corporate pressure, or public relations influence, or lack of resources has prevented mainstream media from providing adequate coverage in areas like climate change, poverty, social inequality, or labour issues, these new sites offer an alternative. Organizations like Canada's National Observer, The Tyee, IndigiNews, The Breach, The Sprawl, The Maple, New Canadian Media, Ricochet, The Coast, and dozens more are covering stories that typically don't get sustained attention in legacy media outlets. Some were started by individuals, while motivated investors funded others. They use various organizational structures, and many rely on subscribers and members for their continued existence. One of the most successful recent ventures is The Narwhal, which focuses on the environment. By the end of 2022, it claimed support from 4,600 members. "As a non-profit online magazine, our goal isn't to sell advertising or to please corporate bigwigs — it's to bring evidence-based news and analysis to the surface for our readers."[26]

Canada already had a strong history of alternative magazines before the internet era. Starting in the late 1960s and continuing for a decade, the *Last*

Post produced muckraking reports that covered national and international stories the mainstream media were too timid to touch. *Canadian Dimension* began publishing its alternative magazine and challenging conventional narratives in 1963. It continues in online form to this day. Publications like *Briarpatch*, *This Magazine*, and others have also survived through the years. But many new start-ups blend daily reporting with longer features and analysis and can be more nimble in addressing issues as soon as they arise. With the combined power of their social media channels, they can play a more significant role in shaping daily conversations.

"I think the simple answer to making journalism better is having more of it," says Carleton's Allan Thompson. "So I think the presence of these new organizations is enormously valuable because more journalism that is original is a good thing, rather than fewer people literally trying to all do the same stories."[27] Narwhal co-founder Emma Gilchrist is also the chair of Press Forward, a group representing independent journalism organizations in Canada. According to her, the start-ups aren't burdened by legacy operating costs, so they can spend substantially more of their budgets on the actual journalism. But the key aim is to "reinvigorate relationships with readers by publishing journalism people are willing to pay for."[28]

Just how sustainable such a model is remains uncertain. The federal government has begun funding journalism ventures, but it hasn't been without criticism about who gets the money and how much they get. One of the perennial questions that's hard to resolve is: Precisely who qualifies as a journalist? If most of the government money goes to legacy news organizations, with no corresponding obligation to provide maximum accountability and transparency, the fundamental structural problems aren't being addressed. Thompson thinks the government should continue its funding and suggests that part of the federal bureaucracy's enormous communications budget could be shifted to shore up independent journalism. On the other hand, Jesse Brown isn't a fan of government support, fearing it poisons the relationship between journalists and their audiences. Some other start-ups worry that relying on government support too heavily would decimate an organization if the flow of dollars suddenly stops, whether for budgetary or political reasons.

One way to defeat the constant pressure to mislead journalists into perpetuating the narratives of vested interests is to help new organizations build capacity to cover the news in diverse ways. If charities can qualify for favourable tax treatment, why shouldn't journalism outlets? The public can and should play a role in paying directly for ethical and responsible journalism. And if the government recognizes journalism to be at least as important as culture, education, and fixing potholes, it will figure out how to support the new start-up ventures in ways that don't compromise their independence and integrity. Denying public money to journalists will only mean handing the greatest degree of control and influence to those with the deepest pockets.

· · ·

Here is one final thought. I have spent the bulk of my career doing investigative journalism. I admire the work of those Canadian journalists who have dedicated their careers to this genre. But too many newsrooms see it as an optional exercise, to be used when budgets allow and only after all the news releases, press conferences, and events of the day have been covered. I sincerely hope all news organizations, from legacy media outlets to one-person start-ups, recognize the importance of investigative work and its mission to cut through the barrage of hype. Seeking the truth, holding powerful interests to account, and doing so with a sound methodology are the keys to not ending up as someone's dupe.

Acknowledgements

A BOOK OF THIS SORT WOULD NOT HAVE BEEN POSSIBLE without a lifetime of lessons learned in the trenches of journalism. Every story, every editorial conversation, and every ethical debate about what should or should not be reported has given me a greater understanding of the role journalism plays. From that point of view, I can't possibly begin to acknowledge the contributions hundreds of people have made to my development as a journalist.

I do want to mention some people I have worked directly with over the years who have done important work to untangle manipulated messages and hold powerful forces to account. Some of them are investigative journalists, some are very good reporters and producers, and others have worked hard in different ways to ensure truthful stories get told. They include Melanie Verhaeghe, Diana Swain, Reg Sherren, Ross Rutherford, Carl Karp, Christian Cote, Harvey Cashore, Timothy Sawa, Sig Gerber, Vera-Lynn Kubinec, Joanne Levasseur, Chris Armstrong, Joni Nikolou, Andy Blicq, Morris Karp, David Roberts, Katie Nicholson, Caroline Barghout, Jacques Marcoux, Kristin Annable, Alex Freedman, Ryszard Hunka, Curt Petrovich, Gosia Sawicka, Alison Crawford, Conway Fraser, Holly Moore, Coleen Rajotte, Brian Cole, Steve Pona, Bob McKeown, Catherine Clark, Mark Kelley, David Studer, Judy Trinh, Emmanuel Marchand, Rachel Ward, Kimberly Ivany, Lisa Mayor, Lisa Ellenwood, Scott Anderson, Joseph Loiero, Dave Seglins, Enza Uda, Erica Johnson, Rosa Marchitelli, Jim Williamson, Jane Mingay, Linda Guerriero, Virginia Smart, Ronna

Syed, Nazim Baksh, Andrew Culbert, Lynette Fortune, Katie Pedersen, Kate McKenna, Saman Malik, Catherine Mitchell, Gillian Findlay, Martha Troian, Paisley Woodward, Declan Hill, Peter Walsh, Krista Barnes, Frédéric Zalac, Tara Carman, Valérie Ouellet, Roberto Rocha, Marie Caloz, Jack Nagler, Paul Hambleton, Dan Henry, Michael Hughes, Danielle Stone, Dustin Milligan, Katarina Germani, Ève St-Laurent, Sean Moreman, and the entire talented teams at CBC Manitoba, *CBC News: Disclosure*, CBC regions, and the *Fifth Estate,* which I had the privilege of working alongside.

It's important for journalists to engage in continuous discussion about what they do and how they do it. Professional associations are useful vehicles for these conversations. I have learned a great deal from participating in conferences organized by the Canadian Association of Journalists, Investigative Reporters and Editors, and the Global Investigative Journalism Network. I have also benefitted tremendously by teaching journalists both at the CBC and the University of Winnipeg. It's a rare class where I do not learn something new or gain fresh insights through interacting with students.

Hope Kamin, a skilled editor and a good friend, provided valuable suggestions for improving the book. Christopher Adams and Donald Gutstein gave me important feedback to think about. I am grateful to Rob Firing of the Transatlantic Agency for supporting this project, to Kathryn Lane and her entire team at Dundurn Press for embracing it, and to Dominic Farrell for helping to refine the manuscript. I also want to acknowledge and thank the Canada Council for the Arts and the Manitoba Arts Council for believing this book was important and supporting it.

I am indebted to my brother and my three kids for their encouragement and suggestions. None of them are terribly shy about telling me what they think. They are all usually right. Usually. Most importantly, I could not have done this or pretty much anything else in life without the steadfast support of my life partner and award-winning fellow writer, Harriet Zaidman. I hope we keep typing away in our house forever. Thank you.

Select Bibliography

Adams, Samuel Hopkins. *The Great American Fraud*. Gutenberg. 2013. gutenberg.org/files/44325/44325-h/44325-h.htm.

Bernays, Edward. *Propaganda*. New York: Liveright Publishing, 1928. archive .org/details/bernays-edward-l.-propaganda-1928-1936_202107/page/9/mode /2up.

Bernstein, Carl. "The CIA and the Media." *Rolling Stone*, October 20, 1977. carlbernstein.com/the-cia-and-the-media-rolling-stone-10-20-1977.

Bethlehem, Jelke G. *Understanding Public Opinion Polls*. Boca Raton, FL: CRC Press, 2018.

Bok, Sissela. *Secrets: On the Ethics of Concealment and Revelation*. New York: Vintage, 1989.

Bowker, Michael. *Fatal Deception: The Terrifying True Story of How Asbestos Is Killing America*. New York: Simon & Schuster, 2003.

Boyko, John. *The Devil's Trick: How Canada Fought the Vietnam War*. Toronto: Vintage Canada, 2022.

Bryden, John. *Deadly Allies: Canada's Secret War, 1937–1947*. Toronto: McClelland & Stewart, 1989.

Burton, Bob. *Inside Spin: The Dark Underbelly of the PR Industry*. Crows Nest, AU: Allen & Unwin, 2007.

Campbell, W. Joseph. *Lost in a Gallup: Polling Failure in U.S. Presidential Elections*. Oakland: University of California Press, 2020.

Carlson, Matt. "Dueling, Dancing, or Dominating? Journalists and Their Sources." *Sociology Compass* 3, no. 4 (July 2009): 526–42. doi.org/10.1111/j.1751-9020 .2009.00219.x.

Cunningham, Stanley B. *The Idea of Propaganda: A Reconstruction*. Westport, CT: Praeger, 2005.

Davies, Nick. *Flat Earth News: An Award-Winning Reporter Exposes Falsehood, Distortion and Propaganda in the Global Media*. London: Vintage, 2009.

Dick, Philip K. *Lies, Inc.* New York: Vintage, 2004.

Dion, Mario. *Trudeau II Report.* Ottawa: Office of the Conflict of Interest and Ethics Commissioner, 2019. ciec-ccie.parl.gc.ca/en/publications/Documents/InvestigationReports/Trudeau%20II%20Report.pdf.

Emms, Merle. "The Origins of Public Relations as an Occupation in Canada." M.A. thesis, Concordia University, 1995.

Engler, Yves. *Lester Pearson's Peacekeeping: The Truth May Hurt.* Halifax: Fernwood, 2012.

_____. *A Propaganda System: How Canada's Government, Corporations, Media and Academia Sell War and Exploitation.* Vancouver: RED Publishing, 2016.

Ericson, Richard V. "Patrolling the Facts: Secrecy and Publicity in Police Work." *British Journal of Sociology* 40, no. 2 (June 1989): 205. doi.org/10.2307/590269.

Ericson, Richard, Patricia M. Baranek, and Janet B.L. Chan. *Negotiating Control: A Study of News Sources.* Milton Keynes, U.K.: Open University Press, 1989.

Ewen, Stuart. *PR!: A Social History of Spin.* New York: Basic Books, 1996. "Fatal Deception." CBC, 2019. cbc.ca/player/play/2196289159.

Gutstein, Donald. *Harperism: How Stephen Harper and His Think Tank Colleagues Have Transformed Canada.* Toronto: James Lorimer, 2014.

_____. *Not a Conspiracy Theory: How Business Propaganda Hijacks Democracy.* Toronto: Key Porter, 2009.

Guttenplan, D.D. *American Radical: The Life and Times of I.F. Stone.* Evanston, IL: Northwestern University Press, 2012.

Herman, Edward S., and Noam Chomsky. *Manufacturing Consent: The Political Economy of the Mass Media.* New York: Pantheon Books, 1988.

Holiday, Ryan. *Trust Me, I'm Lying: Confessions of a Media Manipulator.* Rev. ed. New York: Portfolio / Penguin, 2017. Apple Books.

Knightley, Phillip. *The First Casualty: The War Correspondent as Hero, Propagandist, and Myth-Maker from the Crimea to Vietnam.* New York: Harcourt Brace Jovanovich, 1975.

Kumari, Niky. "Citing Social Media as a News Source in Mainstream Media: An Analysis of Indian Newspapers." *International Journal of Communication and Media Studies* 9, no. 3 (June 2019): 37–50.

Lachapelle, Guy. *Polls and the Media in Canadian Elections.* Toronto: Dundurn Press, 1991. publications.gc.ca/collections/collection_2020/bcp-pco/Z1-1989-2-41/Z1-1989-2-41-16-eng.pdf.

Lindgren, April. *Aiding and Abetting: How Police Media-Information Units Shape Local News Coverage.* Toronto: University of Toronto Press, 2016.

Loomis, Burdett. "From Hootie to Harry (and Louise): Polling and Interest Groups." *Brookings Review* 21, no. 3 (2003): 45. doi.org/10.2307/20081120.

Manvell, Roger, and Heinrich Fraenkel. *Doctor Goebbels: His Life and Death.* Barnsley, U.K.: Frontline, 2010.

Martin, David C. *Wilderness of Mirrors.* New York: Simon and Schuster, 2018.

Martino-Taylor, Lisa. *Behind the Fog: How the U.S. Cold War Radiological Weapons Program Exposed Innocent Americans.* New York: Routledge, 2018.

Mayer, Jane. *Dark Money: The Hidden History of the Billionaires Behind the Rise of the Radical Right.* New York: Anchor, 2017.

McCoy, Alfred W. *Torture and Impunity.* Madison: University of Wisconsin Press, 2012.

McCue, Duncan. *Decolonizing Journalism: A Guide to Reporting in Indigenous Communities.* Toronto: Oxford University Press, 2022.

————. "On Reconciliation and the Canadian Media." Reporting in Indigenous Communities, December 18, 2020. riic.ca/on-reconciliation-and-the -canadian-media/.

McCulloch, Jock, and Geoffrey Tweedale. *Defending the Indefensible: The Global Asbestos Industry and Its Fight for Survival.* Oxford: Oxford University Press, 2008.

Mitrovica, Andrew. "Hear No Evil, Write No Lies." *Walrus,* December 12, 2006. thewalrus.ca/hear-no-evil-write-no-lies/.

Morris, Trevor, and Simon Goldsworthy. *PR — A Persuasive Industry? Spin, Public Relations, and the Shaping of the Modern Media.* London: Palgrave Macmillan, 2008.

Morrow, Richard L., Barbara Mintzes, Garry Gray, Michael R. Law, Scott Garrison, and Colin R. Dormuth. "Industry Sponsor Influence in Clinical Trial Reporting in Canada: A Qualitative Interview Study." *Clinical Therapeutics* (December 2021). doi.org/10.1016/j.clinthera.2021.11.019.

National Inquiry into Missing and Murdered Indigenous Women and Girls. *Reclaiming Power and Place: The Final Report of the National Inquiry into Missing and Murdered Indigenous Women and Girls.* Volume 1. Ottawa: Government of Canada, 2019. mmiwg-ffada.ca/wp-content/uploads/2019 /06/Final_Report_Vol_1a-1.pdf.

Pack, Mark. *Polling UnPacked: The History, Uses and Abuses of Political Opinion Polls.* London: Reaktion Books, 2022.

Pilger, John. *Tell Me No Lies: Investigative Journalism and Its Triumphs.* London: Jonathan Cape, 2004.

Ponsonby, Arthur. *Falsehood in War-Time: Propaganda Lies of the First World*

War. Crows Nest, AU: George Allen and Unwin, 1928; WWI Resource Centre, n.d. vlib.us/wwi/resources/archives/texts/t050824i/ponsonby.html.

Rabin-Havt, Ari, and Media Matters. *Lies, Incorporated: The World of Post-Truth Politics.* New York: Anchor Books, 2016. Apple Books.

Rosner, Cecil. *Behind the Headlines: The History of Investigative Journalism in Canada.* Don Mills, ON: Oxford University Press, 2008.

Ruff, Kathleen. "Asbestos: A Continuing Failure of Ethics by McGill University." *International Journal of Occupational and Environmental Health* 20, no. 1 (January 2014): 1–3. doi.org/10.1179/1077352513z.000000000102.

Sawatsky, John. *Men in the Shadows: The RCMP Security Service.* Toronto: Doubleday Canada, 1980.

Silverman, Craig, and European Journalism Centre. *Verification Handbook: An Ultimate Guideline on Digital Age Sourcing for Emergency Coverage.* Maastricht, Netherlands: European Journalism Centre, 2014.

Smith, Doug. *As Many Liars.* Winnipeg: Arbeiter Ring Publishing, 2003.

Stauber, John C., and Sheldon Rampton. *Toxic Sludge Is Good for You: Lies, Damn Lies and the Public Relations Industry.* London: Robinson, 2004.

Stephens, Mitchell. *A History of News.* Belmont, CA: Wadsworth Publishing, 1997.

Thomas, William Nolan. *Perilous Policing: Criminal Justice in Marginalized Communities.* New York: Routledge, 2019.

Thucydides. *History of the Peloponnesian War.* Translated by Rex Warner. Melbourne: Penguin, 1983.

Truth and Reconciliation Commission of Canada, *Canada's Residential Schools: The Final Report of the Truth and Reconciliation Commission of Canada*, vol. 6, *Reconciliation* (Montreal: McGill-Queen's University Press, 2015), 194, publications.gc.ca/collections/collection_2015/trc/IR4-9-6-2015-eng.pdf.

Tye, Larry. *The Father of Spin: Edward L. Bernays & the Birth of Public Relations.* New York: Henry Holt, 1998. Apple Books.

Vigen, Tyler. "15 Insane Things That Correlate with Each Other." Tylervigen.com, 2009. tylervigen.com/spurious-correlations.

Vosoughi, Soroush, Deb Roy, and Sinan Aral. "The Spread of True and False News Online." *Science* 359, no. 6380 (March 9, 2018): 1146–51. doi.org/10.1126/science.aap9559.

Wadman, Meredith. "One in Three Scientists Confesses to Having Sinned." *Nature* 435, no. 7043 (June 2005): 718–19. doi.org/10.1038/435718b.

Wagner, Wendy, and Thomas O. McGarity. *Bending Science: How Special Interests Corrupt Public Health Research.* Cambridge, MA: Harvard University Press, 2008.

Wasilow, Sherry Marie. "Contemporary Canadian Military/Media Relations: Embedded Reporting during the Afghanistan War." Ph.D. Dissertation, Carleton University, 2017.

Willmott, Kyle, and Alec Skillings. "Anti-Indigenous Policy Formation: Settler Colonialism and Neoliberal Political Advocacy." *Canadian Review of Sociology/Revue Canadienne de Sociologie* 58 (October 24, 2021). doi.org/10.1111/cars.12357.

Wilson-Raybould, Jody. *Indian in the Cabinet: Speaking Truth to Power.* Toronto: HarperCollins, 2021.

Zubek, John. John P. Zubek Fonds. University of Manitoba Archives. Accessed October 28, 2022. libguides.lib.umanitoba.ca/c.php?g=547350.

Notes

PREFACE

1   "Public Relations Market Size Worldwide from 2022 to 2027," Statista; January 2023, statista.com/statistics/645836/public-relations-pr-revenue/.

2   Statistics Canada, Government of Canada, "Employment Income Statistics by Occupation, Major Field of Study and Highest Level of Education: Canada," November 30, 2022, www150.statcan.gc.ca/t1/tbl1/en/cv.action ?pid=9810041201.

3   Ben Collins, "Dan Nainan, the Media's Favorite 'Millennial,' Is 55 Years Old," Daily Beast, January 5, 2017, thedailybeast.com/dan-nainan-the -medias-favorite-millennial-is-55-years-old.

4   Nick Davies, *Flat Earth News: An Award-Winning Reporter Exposes Falsehood, Distortion and Propaganda in the Global Media* (London: Vintage, 2009), 51.

5   Justin Lewis et al., "The Quality and Independence of British Journalism: Tracking the Changes Over 20 Years," Cardiff School of Journalism, Media, and Cultural Studies, Cardiff University, n.d., orca.cardiff.ac.uk /id/eprint/18439/1/Quality%20&%20Independence%20of%20British %20Journalism.pdf.

6   Mitchell Stephens, *A History of News* (Belmont, CA: Wadsworth Publishing, 1997), 267.

1   HOW MANIPULATION WORKS

1   Stuart Ewen, *PR!: A Social History of Spin* (New York: Basic Books, 1996), 21–27.

2   Steve Buttry, "Verification Fundamentals: Rules to Live By," in *Verification Handbook: An Ultimate Guideline on Digital Age Sourcing for Emergency Coverage*, ed. Craig Silverman (Maastricht, Netherlands: European Journalism Centre, 2014).

3   Thucydides, *History of the Peloponnesian War*, trans. Rex Warner (Melbourne: Penguin, 1983), 46–48.

4   "It's in the Journal. But This Is Reporting?," *Columbia Journalism Review* 18, no. 6 (March/April 1980), archive.org/details/sim_columbia -journalism-review_march-april-1980_18_6/page/34/mode/2up.

5   Diane Farsetta, "Fake TV News: Widespread and Undisclosed," *PR Watch*, March 16, 2006, prwatch.org/fakenews/execsummary.

6   Richard Carufel, "Strained Media Relations: Why Some Journalists Feel Duped by PR Professionals," Agility PR Solutions, June 9, 2015, agilitypr .com/pr-news/social-media/strained-media-relations-why-some-journalists -feel-duped-by-pr-professionals/.

7   Agility PR Solutions, "How to Get Journalists to Open, Click, and Love Your Email Pitch," cdn2.hubspot.net/hubfs/469676/AgilityPRSolutions -whitepaper-emailpitches.pdf.

8   Eric Sparling, "Confessions of a Former Spin Doctor," *Toronto Star*, June 21, 2000, A25.

9   Sarah Jones, "Professional Counters Spin Doctor's Tales," *Toronto Star*, June 28, 2000, A27.

10   Alex Kuczynski, "Media Talk; in Public Relations, 25% Admit Lying," *New York Times*, May 8, 2000.

11   Cecil Rosner, "Knowles Accuses Lang of Conflict of Interest," *Winnipeg Free Press*, July 14, 1979.

12   Matt Carlson, "Dueling, Dancing, or Dominating? Journalists and Their Sources," *Sociology Compass* 3, no. 4 (July 2009): 527, doi.org /10.1111/j.1751-9020.2009.00219.x.

13   Carlson, "Dueling, Dancing, or Dominating?," 532.

14   Davies, *Flat Earth News*, 121.

15   Jeremy Scahill, "The Disturbing Groupthink over the War in Ukraine," The Intercept, March 3, 2023, theintercept.com/2023/03/03/russia -ukraine-war-weapons/.

16   Cecil Rosner, *Behind the Headlines: The History of Investigative Journalism in Canada* (Don Mills, ON: Oxford University Press, 2008), 30.

17   "The First Press Release," NewsMuseum, April 10, 2016, newsmuseum.pt /en/spin-wall/first-press-release.

18   Ewen, *PR!*, 78–79.

19   Edward Bernays, *Propaganda* (New York: Liveright Publishing, 1928), 28, archive.org/details/bernays-edward-l.-propaganda-1928-1936_202107/page /9/mode/2up.

20   Bernays, *Propaganda*, 9–10.

21   "Group of Girls Puff at Cigarettes as a Gesture of 'Freedom,'" *New York Times*, April 1, 1929.

22 Larry Tye, *The Father of Spin: Edward L. Bernays & the Birth of Public Relations* (New York: Henry Holt, 1998), 67–73, Apple Books.

23 Edward S. Herman and Noam Chomsky, *Manufacturing Consent: The Political Economy of the Mass Media* (New York: Pantheon Books, 1988), xi.

24 Merle Emms, "The Origins of Public Relations as an Occupation in Canada" (MA thesis, Concordia University, 1995), 98.

25 Emms, "Origins of Public Relations," 116–23.

26 Emms, "Origins of Public Relations," 158.

27 Statistics Canada, "2001 Census Topic-Based Tabulations," accessed March 16, 2023, www12.statcan.gc.ca/English/census01/products /standard/themes/index-eng.cfm.

28 Statistics Canada, "Employment Income Statistics by Occupation, Major Field of Study and Highest Level of Education: Canada," accessed November 30, 2022, www150.statcan.gc.ca/t1/tbl1/en/tv.action?pid =9810041201.

29 Employment and Social Development Canada, "Public Relations Specialist in Canada," Job Bank, Government of Canada, accessed April 28, 2023, jobbank.gc.ca/marketreport/outlook-occupation/20976/ca.

30 "Removing Coordinated Inauthentic Behavior from Israel," Meta, May 16, 2019, about.fb.com/news/2019/05/removing-coordinated-inauthentic -behavior-from-israel/.

31 Ryan Holiday, *Trust Me, I'm Lying: Confessions of a Media Manipulator*, rev. ed. (2012; New York: Portfolio / Penguin, 2017), 15, Apple Books.

32 Holiday, *Trust Me*, 2.

33 Daniel Schorn, "Meet Rick Berman, A.K.A. 'Dr. Evil,'" CBS News, February 25, 2011, cbsnews.com/news/meet-rick-berman-aka-dr-evil/.

34 Ari Rabin-Havt and Media Matters, *Lies, Incorporated: The World of Post-Truth Politics* (New York: Anchor Books, 2016), 15, Apple Books.

35 Eric Lipton, "Fight over Minimum Wage Illustrates Web of Industry Ties," *New York Times*, February 10, 2014, nytimes.com/2014/02/10/us/politics /fight-over-minimum-wage-illustrates-web-of-industry-ties.html.

36 Schorn, "Meet Rick Berman."

37 Tye, *The Father of Spin*, 124.

38 Tye, *The Father of Spin*, 324.

39 Roger Manvell and Heinrich Fraenkel, *Doctor Goebbels: His Life and Death* (Barnsley, U.K.: Frontline, 2010), 152.

40 "Ivy Lee, as Adviser to Nazis, Paid $25,000 by Dye Trust," *New York Times*, July 12, 1934.

41 Manvell and Fraenkel, *Doctor Goebbels*, 264.

42 "Edward Bernays on Letterman, April 4, 1985," accessed June 26, 2022, youtube.com/watch?v=y-4AulOuCPI.

2 CORPORATE PROPAGANDA

1 Stanley B. Cunningham, *The Idea of Propaganda: A Reconstruction* (Westport, CT: Praeger, 2005), 13.

2 "The Evolution of Carbon Footprint Measurement," ClimateTrade, August 18, 2022, climatetrade.com/the-evolution-of-carbon-footprint-measurement/.

3 Chantal Beck et al., "The Future of Oil and Gas Is Now: How Companies Can Decarbonize | McKinsey," McKinsey & Company, January 7, 2020, mckinsey.com/industries/oil-and-gas/our-insights/the-future-is-now -how-oil-and-gas-companies-can-decarbonize.

4 Samuel Hopkins Adams, *The Great American Fraud*, Gutenberg, 2013, gutenberg.org/files/44325/44325-h/44325-h.htm.

5 Public Prosecution Service of Canada, "Volkswagen AG Sentenced to Pay Environmental Fines Totalling $196.5 Million," January 22, 2020, ppsc -sppc.gc.ca/eng/nws-nvs/2020/22_01_20.html?wbdisable=true.

6 Government of Canada, "Deceptive Marketing Practices — Cases and Outcomes," Competition Bureau, February 24, 2020, competitionbureau .gc.ca/eic/site/cb-bc.nsf/eng/h_04443.html.

7 Michael Oliveira, "Netflix Apologizes for Using Actors to Meet Press at Canadian Launch," *Globe and Mail*, September 22, 2010, theglobeandmail .com/technology/netflix-apologizes-for-using-actors-to-meet-press-at -canadian-launch/article4326706/.

8 CBC Manitoba, "Winnipeg Media Chided for Taking IKEA Freebies," CBC, November 28, 2012, cbc.ca/news/canada/manitoba /winnipeg-media-chided-for-taking-ikea-freebies-1.1183866.

9 Murray McNeill, "Toyota Tests New Retailing Concept," *Winnipeg Free Press*, February 2, 2000.

10 Toyota Canada, "Advertisement," *Winnipeg Free Press*, March 2, 2000.

11 "CBC News: Disclosure, Program Archives, Access Toyota," CBC News, February 20, 2003, web.archive.org/web/20030220134413/www.cbc.ca /disclosure/archives/030211_notebook.html.

12 "Federal Court of Canada — Information to Obtain Search Warrants," CBC, accessed July 30, 2022, web.archive.org/web/20040720172341 /www.cbc.ca/disclosure/archives/documents/030211_access_courtfile.pdf.

13 Greg Keenan, "Competition Bureau Orders Toyota Canada to Revamp Pricing," *Globe and Mail*, March 29, 2003, theglobeandmail.com/report-on-business/competition-bureau-orders-toyota-canada-to-revamp-pricing/article18285123/.

14 Jim Bender, "Plan for Tallest Building in Winnipeg Unveiled," *Winnipeg Sun*, May 22, 2013, winnipegsun.com/2013/05/22/massive-downtown-development-to-be-announced-today.

15 Murray McNeill, "Sky's Still the Limit," *Winnipeg Free Press*, March 27, 2015.

16 Todd Lewys, "Luxury Living Among the Clouds," *Winnipeg Free Press*, May 27, 2017.

17 Kenneth E. Warner, "Tobacco Industry Scientific Advisors: Serving Society or Selling Cigarettes?," *American Journal of Public Health* 81, no. 7 (July 1991): 839–42, doi.org/10.2105/ajph.81.7.839.

18 Clark Hoyt, "The Doctors Are In. The Jury Is Out," *New York Times*, February 17, 2008, nytimes.com/2008/02/17/opinion/17pubed.html?searchResultPosition=2.

19 John H. Cushman, "Industrial Group Plans to Battle Climate Reality," *New York Times*, April 26, 1998, nytimes.com/1998/04/26/us/industrial-group-plans-to-battle-climate-treaty.html.

20 Intergovernmental Panel on Climate Change, "Climate Change 2022," IPCC, 2022, ipcc.ch/report/ar6/wg2/downloads/report/IPCC_AR6_WGII_FinalDraft_FullReport.pdf.

21 Maxwell T. Boykoff and Jules M. Boykoff, "Climate Change and Journalistic Norms: A Case-Study of US Mass-Media Coverage," *Geoforum* 38, no. 6 (November 2007): 1190–204.

22 Timothy Sawa, Lynette Fortune, and Bob McKeown, "Breaking Their Silence," CBC, 2020, newsinteractives.cbc.ca/longform/peter-nygard-1.

23 Caroline Barghout, "Law Society Charges Jay Prober over Public Comments He Made About Peter Nygard's Alleged Victims," CBC, August 26, 2021, cbc.ca/news/canada/manitoba/law-society-charges-jay-prober-over-public-comments-he-made-about-peter-nygard-s-alleged-victims-1.6151631.

24 Sawa, Fortune, and McKeown, "Breaking Their Silence."

25 Julian Borger, "The Guardian Profile: Ralph Nader," *Guardian*, October 21, 2004, theguardian.com/world/2004/oct/22/uselections2004.usa.

26 Julia Carrie Wong, "Facebook Policy Chief Admits Hiring PR Firm to Attack George Soros," *Guardian*, November 22, 2018, theguardian.com

/technology/2018/nov/21/facebook-admits-definers-pr-george-soros
-critics-sandberg-zuckerberg.

27 Glenn Greenwald, "The Personal Side of Taking on the NSA: Emerging
    Smears," *Guardian*, June 26, 2013, theguardian.com/commentisfree/2013
    /jun/26/nsa-revelations-response-to-smears.

28 "Brand Management," School of Continuing Studies, University of
    Toronto, accessed August 1, 2022, learn.utoronto.ca/programs-courses
    /certificates/brand-management.

29 Competition and Markets Authority, "Global Sweep Finds 40% of Firms'
    Green Claims Could Be Misleading," GOV.UK, January 28, 2021, gov
    .uk/government/news/global-sweep-finds-40-of-firms-green-claims-could
    -be-misleading.

30 Automobile Journalists Association of Canada, "Code of Ethics," AJAC,
    October 2018, ajac.ca/ethics.asp.

31 Connie Thiessen, "CBC/Radio-Canada Media Solutions Launches
    Dedicated Branded Content Service," *Broadcast Dialogue*, September 17,
    2020, broadcastdialogue.com/cbc-radio-canada-media-solutions-launches
    -dedicated-branded-content-service/.

32 Simon Houpt, "Hundreds of CBC Staff Sign Open Letter against
    Broadcaster's Paid-Content Plans," *Globe and Mail*, December 9, 2020,
    theglobeandmail.com/arts/article-hundreds-of-cbc-staff-sign-open
    -letter-against-broadcasters-paid/.

33 Rosie DiManno, "Shame on the *Globe and Mail* for Running Chinese
    Government Propaganda," *Toronto Star*, September 24, 2020, thestar.com
    /opinion/star-columnists/2020/09/24/shame-on-the-globe-and-mail-for
    -running-chinese-government-propaganda.html.

34 *Last Week Tonight*, season 8, episode 13, "Sponsored Content," aired May
    23, 2021, on HBO, youtube.com/watch?v=sIi_QS1tdFM.

3   THINK TANKS OR SPIN FACTORIES?

1 Neil Brooks, *Tax Freedom Day: A Flawed, Incoherent, and Pernicious
   Concept* (Ottawa: Canadian Centre for Policy Alternatives, 2005)
   policyalternatives.ca/sites/default/files/uploads/publications/National
   _Office_Pubs/2005/tax_freedom_day.pdf.

2 Mark Gollom, "Critics Question Tax Freedom Day Concept," CBC, April
   20, 2012, cbc.ca/news/business/taxes/critics-question-tax-freedom
   -day-concept-1.1180687.

3   Fraser Institute, *2021 Annual Report*, 2022, 14, fraserinstitute.org/sites
    /default/files/uploaded/2022/2021-annual-report.pdf.
4   Fraser Institute, *35 Big Ideas: How the Fraser Institute Is Changing the World*,
    2009, fraserinstitute.org/sites/default/files/35th-anniversary-book.pdf.
5   Fraser Institute, *The Fraser Institute Annual Report 2020*, 2021, 3,
    fraserinstitute.org/sites/default/files/uploaded/annual-report-2020.pdf.
6   Doug Ward and Tiffany Crawford, "First NDP Premier of B.C., Dave
    Barrett, Dead at 87," *Vancouver Sun*, February 6, 2018, vancouversun.com
    /news/local-news/first-ndp-premier-of-b-c-dave-barrett-dead-at-87.
7   Donald Gutstein, *Harperism: How Stephen Harper and His Think Tank
    Colleagues Have Transformed Canada* (Toronto: Lorimer, 2014), 50.
8   "Who We Are," Atlas Network, accessed July 21, 2022, atlasnetwork.org
    /who-we-are.
9   Donald Gutstein, *Not a Conspiracy Theory: How Business Propaganda
    Hijacks Democracy* (Toronto: Key Porter, 2009), 123.
10 Gutstein, *Not a Conspiracy Theory*, 124.
11 Gutstein, *Not a Conspiracy Theory*, 127.
12 "Fraser Institute Invitation," accessed March 16, 2023, edprograms
    .forwardtomyfriend.com/t-jrkrkrihii-47666999-quyhdud-l-v.
13 Fraser Institute, *2021 Annual Report*, 20.
14 Ryan Kelpin and Benjamin Johnson, "Munk, Hayek and the Fraser
    Institute: Tracing the Insurgent Pedagogy of the Canadian Right," Canadian
    Dimension, April 8, 2021, canadiandimension.com/articles
    /view/munk-hayek-and-the-fraser-institute-insurgent-pedagogies-of-the
    -canadian-right.
15 "Who We Are," Atlas Network.
16 Lee Fang, "Sphere of Influence: How American Libertarians Are
    Remaking Latin American Politics," The Intercept, August 9, 2017,
    theintercept.com/2017/08/09/atlas-network-alejandro-chafuen-libertarian
    -think-tank-latin-america-brazil/.
17 Fang, "Sphere of Influence."
18 Atlas Network, *Atlas Network Annual Report 2021*, admin.atlasnetwork.org
    /assets/documents/financials/AtNet-2021AnnualReport_Digital_sprd.pdf.
19 Brett Skinner and Nigel Rawson, "Extreme Regulations to Lower Drug
    Prices Mean Canada Will Get Fewer New Drugs," *Financial Post*, February
    7, 2020, financialpost.com/opinion/extreme-regulations-to-lower-drug-prices
    -mean-canada-will-get-fewer-new-drugs.

20 Thomas Walkom, "Right-Wing Causes Find a Rich and Ready Paymaster," *Toronto Star*, October 25, 1997.

21 Allison Lampert, "Many Parents Take Note of School Rankings," *Montreal Gazette*, November 1, 2003.

22 Gutstein, *Not a Conspiracy Theory*, 161–62.

23 "Donner Canadian Foundation 2022 Grants," web.archive.org/web /20230205072506/https://donnerfoundation.org/dcf/documents/Donner _Canadian_Foundation_2022_Grants_List.pdf.

24 *Making History — Making an Impact: The 2020 Annual Report of the Canadian Centre for Policy Alternatives* (Ottawa: Canadian Centre for Policy Alternatives, 2021), policyalternatives.ca/sites/default/files/uploads /publications/National%20Office/2021/10/2020%20annual%20report.pdf.

25 Tonda MacCharles, "Think-Tank Says It Was Targeted with Tax Audit Because of Its Politics," *Toronto Star*, September 5, 2014, thestar.com/news /canada/2014/09/05/thinktank_says_it_was_targeted_with_tax_audit _because_of_its_politics.html.

26 Gutstein, *Harperism*, 75.

27 Brent Stafford, "Think Tanks in the News," *NewsWatch Monitor* (April 1997), sfu.ca/content/dam/sfu/cmns/research/projects/newswatchcanada /publications/Brent-Stafford-April-1997-Think-tanks-in-the-news. -NewsWatch-Monitor-Issue-13.pdf

28 "A Conversation with Brian Lee Crowley," Frontier Centre for Public Policy, December 1, 1997, fcpp.org/1997/12/01/a-conversation-with -brian-lee-crowley/.

29 "Brian Lee Crowley," Atlantic Institute for Market Studies, March 10, 2016, aims.ca/people/brian-lee-crowley/.

30 Patricia Best, "Flaherty a Big Fan of a New Think Tank," *Globe and Mail*, June 18, 2009.

31 Scott Newark, *Why Canadian Crime Statistics Don't Add Up* (Ottawa: Macdonald-Laurier Institute, 2011), macdonaldlaurier.ca/files/pdf/MLI -Crime_Statistics_Review-Web.pdf.

32 Ken Coates and Brian Lee Crowley, *New Beginnings: How Canada's Natural Resource Wealth Could Re-Shape Relations with Aboriginal People* (Ottawa: Macdonald-Laurier Institute, 2013), macdonaldlaurier.ca/files /pdf/2013.01.05-MLI-New_Beginnings_Coates_vWEB.pdf.

33 Geoff Dembicki, "First Nations Are 'the Magic Sauce' for Getting Gas Projects Built, Says LNG Insider," DeSmog, June 17, 2022, desmog.com /2022/06/17/first-nations-magic-sauce-gas-lng-nikolejsin/.

34 Deborah Jaremko, "Mark Ruffalo Is Wrong (Again) About Coastal GasLink," Troy Media, September 22, 2022, troymedia.com/business /mark-ruffalo-is-wrong-again-about-coastal-gaslink/.

35 Macdonald-Laurier Institute, *Aboriginal Canada and the Natural Resource Economy Project* (Arlington, VA: Atlas Network, 2018), web.archive.org /web/20190331220550/www.atlasnetwork.org/assets/uploads/misc/MLI _Aboriginal_Canada_Case_Study_Final.pdf.

36 Macdonald-Laurier Institute, *Aboriginal Canada*, 7.

37 Jeff Kucharski, "Line 5 and Colonial Reveal Much about Politicians and Pipelines," *Inside Policy*, June 2021, 4, macdonaldlaurier.ca/files/pdf /202106_JUNE_Inside_Policy_FWeb.pdf.

38 "Macdonald-Laurier Institute," DeSmog, accessed July 23, 2022, desmog .com/macdonald-laurier-institute/

39 Troy Lanigan, "Influence Driven from 'the Outside,'" taxpayer.com, October 3, 2009, web.archive.org/web/20091013231201/www.taxpayer .com/blog/03-10-2009/influence-driven-outside.

40 Neil Desai, LinkedIn, n.d., linkedin.com/in/neil-desai-ca/details /experience/.

41 Canadian Taxpayers Federation, *2020 Annual Report*, taxpayer.com/media /CTF-2020_Annual_Report.pdf

42 Canadian Taxpayers Federation, *2020 Annual Report*.

43 David J. Climenhaga, "What Does the Canadian Taxpayers Federation Get from Its Right-Wing US Partner?," *The Tyee*, July 5, 2018, thetyee.ca /Opinion/2018/07/05/Canadian-Taxpayers-Federation-Get/.

44 David J. Climenhaga, "Minuscule Canadian Taxpayers Federation in Running for 'Turfy Award,'" rabble.ca, March 13, 2013, rabble.ca/politics /canadian-politics/minuscule-canadian-taxpayers-federation-running-turfy -award/.

45 Scott Hennig, "Setting the Record Straight: How the CTF Is Governed," Canadian Taxpayers Association, August 22, 2014, taxpayer.com /newsroom/Setting%20the%20record%20straight:%20How%20the%20 CTF%20is%20governed.

46 Scott Hennig, "Setting the Record Straight: Why the CTF Protects the Privacy of Its Donors," Canadian Taxpayers Association, August 22, 2014, taxpayer .com/newsroom/Setting%20the%20record%20straight:%20Why%20the%20 CTF%20protects%20the%20privacy%20of%20its%20donors?id=9536.

47 Kyle Willmott and Alec Skillings, "Anti-Indigenous Policy Formation: Settler Colonialism and Neoliberal Political Advocacy," *Canadian Review*

of Sociology/Revue Canadienne de Sociologie 58, no. 4 (October 24, 2021), doi.org/10.1111/cars.12357.

48 Eric Lipton, Nicholas Confessore, and Brooke Williams, "How Think Tanks Amplify Corporate America's Influence," *New York Times*, August 7, 2016, nytimes.com/2016/08/08/us/politics/think-tanks-research-and -corporate-lobbying.html.

49 Eric Lipton, Nicholas Confessore, and Brooke Williams, "Think Tank Scholar or Corporate Consultant? It Depends on the Day," *New York Times*, August 8, 2016, nytimes.com/2016/08/09/us/politics/think-tank -scholars-corporate-consultants.html.

50 Gutstein, *Harperism*, 75–76.

4 POLITICAL LIES

1 In 2014 an Access to Information request revealed the federal government had 3,325 communications people, at a cost of $263 million. This excludes RCMP, military, CRA, and Crown corporations. See Gregory Thomas, "Ottawa's Spin Doctor Payroll Rivals That of the Commons," *Toronto Star*, August 3, 2014, thestar.com/opinion/commentary/2014/08/03/ottawas _spin_doctor_payroll_rivals_that_of_the_commons.html.

2 For one of the best biographies of Stone, see D.D. Guttenplan, *American Radical: The Life and Times of I.F. Stone* (Evanston, IL: Northwestern University Press, 2012).

3 "Doctors Are the Most Trusted Profession in Canada and Across the World," Ipsos, October 12, 2021, ipsos.com/en-ca/news-polls/ doctors-most-trusted-profession-in-canada.

4 Andrew Mitrovica, "Hear No Evil, Write No Lies," *Walrus*, December 12, 2006, thewalrus.ca/hear-no-evil-write-no-lies/.

5 Mitrovica, "Hear No Evil."

6 PolitiFact, s.v. "Donald Trump," politifact.com/personalities/donald-trump/.

7 Glenn Kessler, Salvador Rizzo, and Meg Kelly, "Trump's False or Misleading Claims Total 30,573 over 4 Years," *Washington Post*, January 24, 2021, washingtonpost.com/politics/2021/01/24/trumps-false-or -misleading-claims-total-30573-over-four-years/.

8 Daniel Dale, "The 15 Most Notable Lies of Donald Trump's Presidency," CNN, January 16, 2021, cnn.com/2021/01/16/politics/fact-check-dale-top -15-donald-trump-lies/index.html.

9 Tucker Carlson, "Tucker Carlson: Yes, the Election Was Rigged for Joe Biden. Here's How," Fox News, November 23, 2020, foxnews.com

/opinion/tucker-carlson-2020-presidential-election-rigged-big-tech
-mainstream-media.

10 Maya Yang, "More than 40% in US Do Not Believe Biden Legitimately
Won Election – Poll," *Guardian,* January 5, 2022, theguardian.com
/us-news/2022/jan/05/america-biden-election-2020-poll-victory.

11 For the most comprehensive account of the whole affair, see Doug Smith,
As Many Liars (Winnipeg: Arbeiter Ring Publishing, 2003).

12 "Meet the Man Who Broke the SNC-Lavalin Story | P&P Power Lunch,"
CBC News, May 3, 2019, youtube.com/watch?v=kz9uP0_8gOA.

13 Jody Wilson-Raybould, *Indian in the Cabinet: Speaking Truth to Power*
(Toronto: HarperCollins, 2021), 23–24.

14 Damon van der Linde, "SNC-Lavalin Group Inc Targets Canadian
Public with Major Publicity Campaign," *Financial Post*, June 3, 2015,
financialpost.com/news/fp-street/snc-lavalin-group-inc-targets-canadian-
public-with-major-publicity-campaign.

15 Kathryn Blaze Baum and Sean Fine, "A Deal Denied: How SNC-Lavalin
Spent Years Fighting for a Deferred Prosecution Law, but Then Lost the
Battle to Use It," *Globe and Mail*, July 24, 2019, theglobeandmail.com
/politics/article-a-deal-denied-how-snc-lavalin-spent-years-fighting-for
-a-deferred/.

16 "Finding the Right Balance: Policies to Combat White-Collar Crime in
Canada and Maintain the Integrity of Public Procurement," IRPP, March
10, 2016, irpp.org/research-studies/finding-the-right-balance/.

17 Mario Dion, *Trudeau II Report* (Ottawa: Office of the Conflict of Interest
and Ethics Commissioner, 2019), 2, ciec-ccie.parl.gc.ca/en/publications
/Documents/InvestigationReports/Trudeau%20II%20Report.pdf, 57.

18 Global News, "Unpacking the Politics of the SNC-Lavalin Affair," YouTube,
February 24, 2019, youtube.com/watch?v=5nGJ-95ElyM.

19 "Rob Ford's Crack Use — in His Own Words," CBC, November 5, 2013, cbc
.ca/news/canada/toronto/rob-ford-s-crack-use-in-his-own-words-1.2415605.

20 Alex Ballingall, "Trudeau's Trip to Aga Khan's Private Island Kept Secret
to Protect Privacy, PMO Says," *Toronto Star*, January 6, 2017, thestar.com
/news/canada/2017/01/06/trudeaus-trip-to-aga-khans-private-island-kept
-secret-to-protect-privacy-pmo-says.html.

21 "PMO Tried to Keep Trudeau's Vacation Details Secret," CTV News,
January 2, 2017, ctvnews.ca/politics/pmo-tried-to-keep-trudeau-s
-vacation-details-secret-1.3225061.

22   Elizabeth Thompson, "RCMP Owe the Aga Khan's Island More than $56,000 for Trudeau Vacation," CBC, December 4, 2019, cbc.ca/news /politics/trudeau-aga-khan-bahamas-rcmp-1.5382374.

23   Mercedes Stephenson and Rachel Gilmore, "Trudeau Spends 1st Truth and Reconciliation Day in Tofino on Vacation, Contradicting Itinerary," Global News, September 30, 2021, globalnews.ca/news/8234246 /trudeau-vacation-indigenous-tofino-truth-and-reconciliation/.

24   Chris Glover et al., "Brian Pallister Spends Nearly 1 in 5 Days of His Time in Costa Rica, Travel Logs Show," CBC, April 14, 2016, cbc.ca/1.3535782.

25   Larry Kusch, "In Conversation with Brian Pallister," *Winnipeg Free Press*, December 27, 2014, winnipegfreepress.com/local/in-conversation-with --brian-pallister-286915541.html.

26   Dan Lett, "Biden Charade Latest Pallister Lie to Manitobans," *Winnipeg Free Press*, May 24, 2021, winnipegfreepress.com/breakingnews /2021/05/24/biden-charade-latest-pallister-lie-to-manitobanss.

27   "November 28, 1984," *House of Commons Debates: First Session — Thirty-Third Parliament* (Ottawa: House of Commons, 1984), 676, parl.canadiana.ca/view/oop.debates_HOC3301_01/678?r=0&s=3.

28   Cecil Rosner, "Lessons That Should Have Been Learned," CBC, June 10, 2009, cbc.ca/news/canada/lessons-that-should-have-been-learned-1.792427.

29   Stephanie Ebbs, "'Mr. President, the Media Is Not Fake News,' Bob Woodward Says at White House Correspondents' Dinner," ABC News, April 29, 2017, abcnews.go.com/Politics/mr-president-media-fake-news -bob-woodward-white/story?id=47109367.

5   THIN BLUE LIES

1   Richard V. Ericson, Patricia M. Baranek, and Janet B.L. Chan, *Negotiating Control: A Study of News Sources* (Milton Keynes, U.K.: Open University Press, 1989), 91.

2   Minneapolis Police Department, "Investigative Update on Critical Incident — Minneapolis Police," Internet Archive, March 31, 2021, web.archive .org/web/20210331182901/https://www.insidempd.com/2020/05/26/man -dies-after-medical-incident-during-police-interaction/.

3   Aboriginal Justice Implementation Commission, *Report of the Aboriginal Justice Inquiry of Manitoba* (Winnipeg: Government of Manitoba, 1991), ajic.mb.ca/volume.html.

4   Thomas William Nolan, *Perilous Policing: Criminal Justice in Marginalized Communities* (New York: Routledge, 2019), 59–60.

5 David Bruser and Jesse McLean, "Police Who Lie: How Officers Thwart Justice with False Testimony," *Toronto Star*, April 26, 2012, thestar.com /news/canada/2012/04/26/police_who_lie_how_officers_thwart_justice _with_false_testimony.html.

6 Jesse McLean and David Bruser, "Police Who Lie: False Testimony Often Goes Unpunished," *Toronto Star*, April 26, 2012, thestar.com/news/canada /2012/04/26/police_who_lie_false_testimony_often_goes_unpunished.html.

7 Joe Sexton, "New York Police Often Lie Under Oath, Report Says," *New York Times*, April 22, 1994, nytimes.com/1994/04/22/us/new-york-police -often-lie-under-oath-report-says.html?pagewanted=all.

8 John Kelly and Mark Nichols, "We Found 85,000 Cops Who've Been Investigated for Misconduct. Now You Can Read Their Records," *USA Today*, May 23, 2019, usatoday.com/in-depth/news/investigations/2019/04/24/usa -today-revealing-misconduct-records-police-cops/3223984002/.

9 Reid Rusonik, "Police, Lies and Higher Standards," *Toronto Star*, May 4, 2012.

10 Randy Boswell, "Police Shouldn't Deceive the News Media — Even to Catch a Killer," *Ottawa Citizen*, July 20, 2016, ottawacitizen.com/opinion/columnists /boswell-police-shouldnt-deceive-the-news-media-even-to-catch-a-killer.

11 Jacques Marcoux, "Deadly Force: How CBC Analyzed Details of Hundreds of Fatal Encounters Between Canadians, Police," CBC, June 5, 2018, cbc.ca /news/canada/manitoba/iteam/deadly-force-cbc-analysis-1.4603696.

12 Nolan, *Perilous Policing*, 54.

13 Jacques Marcoux and Katie Nicholson, "Deadly Force: Fatal Encounters with Police in Canada: 2000–2017," CBC News, 2017, newsinteractives .cbc.ca/longform-custom/deadly-force

14 Ericson et. al., *Negotiating Control*, 105.

15 Clyde Haberman, "For Shame: A Brief History of the Perp Walk," *New York Times*, December 2, 2018, nytimes.com/2018/12/02/us/perp-walk.html.

16 John Daniszewski, "Why We're No Longer Naming Suspects in Minor Crime Stories," AP Definitive Source, June 15, 2021, blog.ap.org/behind-the-news /why-were-no-longer-naming-suspects-in-minor-crime-stories.

17 Canadian Association of Journalists, "Ethics," CAJ, n.d., caj.ca/ethics/.

18 "Policeman Fined on Driving Charges," *Winnipeg Free Press*, January 25, 1977.

19 April Lindgren, *Aiding and Abetting: How Police Media-Information Units Shape Local News Coverage* (Toronto: University of Toronto Press, 2016), 193.

20 April Lindgren, "Interpreting the City: Portrayals of Place in a Toronto-Area Ethnic Newspaper," *Aether: The Journal of Media Geography* 8 (Fall 2011):

85, academia.edu/9528590/Interpreting_the_City_Portrayals_of_place_in
_a_Toronto_ethnic_newspaper.

21 Lindgren, *Aiding and Abetting*, 211–12.

22 National Inquiry into Missing and Murdered Indigenous Women and
Girls, *Reclaiming Power and Place: The Final Report of the National Inquiry
into Missing and Murdered Indigenous Women and Girls*, Volume 1a
(Ottawa: Government of Canada, 2019), 388, mmiwg-ffada.ca/wp-content
/uploads/2019/06/Final_Report_Vol_1a-1.pdf.

23 *Reclaiming Power and Place*, 388.

24 "Families of Missing and Murdered Indigenous Women Give Police a
Failing Grade," CBC, April 8, 2015, cbc.ca/news/canada/manitoba
/families-of-missing-and-murdered-indigenous-women-give-police-a
-failing-grade-1.3022709.

25 Human Rights Watch, *Submission to the House of Commons Standing
Committee on Public Safety and National Security: Systemic Racism
in Policing in Canada* (New York: Human Rights Watch, 2020),
ourcommons.ca/Content/Committee/432/SECU/Brief/BR11055572/br
-external/HumanRightsWatch-e.pdf.

26 Jim Rankin et al., "Singled Out," *Toronto Star*, October 19, 2002, thestar
.com/news/gta/knowntopolice/2002/10/19/singled-out.html.

27 "'We Do Not Accept Your Apology,' Activist Tells Toronto's Police Chief
After Race-Based Data Released," CBC, June 16, 2022, cbc.ca/news
/canada/toronto/toronto-police-race-based-data-use-force-strip-searches
-1.6489151.

28 Amber Bracken, "'I Felt Kidnapped': A Journalist's View of Being Arrested
by the RCMP," The Narwhal, December 16, 2021, thenarwhal.ca/opinion
-amber-bracken-rcmp-arrest/.

29 Tom Cardoso and Molly Hayes, "Canadian Cities' Police Spending Ranges
from One-10th to Nearly a Third of Total Budgets, Globe Analysis Finds,"
Globe and Mail, August 16, 2020, theglobeandmail.com/canada/article
-canadian-cities-police-spending-ranges-from-one-10th-to-nearly-a/.

30 Sam Levin, "These US Cities Defunded Police: 'We're Transferring Money
to the Community,'" *Guardian*, March 7, 2021, theguardian.com/us
-news/2021/mar/07/us-cities-defund-police-transferring-money-community.

31 ShotSpotter, Webinar on Demand, "Media Relations in the Time of
Defund the Police," accessed August 8, 2022, go.soundthinking.com
/webinar-on-demand-media-relations-in-the-time-of-defund-the
-police?submissionGuid=577dccf8-ffec-4439-8330-b85170d6c28a.

32 John Rieti and Shawn Jeffords, "Toronto Police Spending $337K on a Podcast to Avoid Perception They're Making 'Copaganda,'" CBC, March 30, 2023, cbc.ca/news/canada/toronto/tps-podcast-costs-revealed-1.6746905.

33 Chris Cillizza, "Analysis: Even Democrats Are Now Admitting 'Defund the Police' Was a Massive Mistake," CNN, November 5, 2021, cnn.com/2021/11/05/politics/defund-the-police-democrats/index.html.

34 "'We Do Not Accept Your Apology.'"

6 MILITARY LIES

1 Elizabeth McMillan, "Military Personnel in Proud Boys Incident Return to Regular Duty," CBC News, August 31, 2017, cbc.ca/news/canada/nova-scotia/military-personnel-proud-boy-s-incident-jobs-1.4269952.

2 David Pugliese, "DND Planned PR Campaign to Counter Concerns About Racists in the Ranks but Scuttled Plan After High-Profile Incidents," *Ottawa Citizen*, October 20, 2020, ottawacitizen.com/news/national/defence-watch/dnd-planned-pr-campaign-to-counter-concerns-about-racists-in-the-ranks-but-scuttled-plan-after-high-profile-incidents.

3 Jacques Gallant, "Too White and Too Male, Canadian Armed Forces Are Rethinking Recruiting as Staffing Slides, Senior Officers Say," *Toronto Star*, March 23, 2022, thestar.com/politics/federal/2022/03/23/too-white-and-too-male-canadian-armed-forces-are-rethinking-recruiting-as-staffing-slides-senior-officers-say.html.

4 "Systemic Racism in the Canadian Forces Detailed in New Report | Full," Global News, April 25, 2022, youtube.com/watch?v=vqiNRU0I7z8.

5 David Pugliese, "Chief of the Defence Staff Gen. Jon Vance and the 'Weaponization of Public Affairs,'" *Ottawa Citizen*, September 21, 2015, ottawacitizen.com/news/national/defence-watch/chief-of-the-defence-staff-gen-jon-vance-and-the-weaponization-of-public-affairs.

6 David Pugliese, "Military Propaganda Exercise That Caused Panic About Wolves on the Loose," *Ottawa Citizen*, October 14, 2020, ottawacitizen.com/news/national/defence-watch/military-propaganda-exercise-that-caused-panic-about-wolves-on-the-loose-lacked-oversight-investigation-finds.

7 Brett Boudreau, "The Rise and Fall of Military Strategic Communications at National Defence 2015–2021: A Cautionary Tale for Canada and NATO, and a Roadmap for Reform," *Canadian Global Affairs Institute*, May 2022, cgai.ca/the_rise_and_fall_of_military_strategic_communications_at_national_defence_2015_2021#_ftnref149.

8 Boudreau, "The Rise and Fall of Military Strategic Communications."

9 David Pugliese, "Veteran DND Public Affairs Staff Quitting over Interference: Report," *National Post*, September 25, 2011, nationalpost .com/news/canada/veteran-dnd-public-affairs-staff-quitting-over -interference-report.

10 Chief Review Services, *Evaluation of Security and Defence Forum (SDF) Class Grant Program* (Ottawa: Department of National Defence, 2010), canada.ca/content/dam/dnd-mdn/migration/assets/FORCES_Internet /docs/en/about-reports-pubs-audit-eval/150p0921.pdf.

11 "Centre for Defence and Security Studies," University of Manitoba, accessed August 16, 2022, umanitoba.ca/arts/centre-defence-and-security-studies.

12 Amir Attaran, "When Think Tanks Produce Propaganda," *Globe and Mail*, February 21, 2008, theglobeandmail.com/opinion/when-think -tanks-produce-propaganda/article718255/.

13 Chief Review Services, *Evaluation of Security and Defence Forum*.

14 Assistant Deputy Minister, Review Services, *Evaluation of the Defence Engagement Program (DEP)* (Ottawa: Department of National Defence, 2017), canada.ca/en/department-national-defence/corporate/reports- publications/audit-evaluation/evaluation-defence-engagement- program.html.

15 Jane Kirby, "Military Ties at Dalhousie's Centre for Foreign Policy Studies," Halifax Media Co-op, September 7, 2009, halifax.mediacoop.ca/story/1874.

16 Rob Huebert, "Canada Must Do Its Part to Defend the Arctic. That Requires F-35 Purchases and NORAD Modernization," *Globe and Mail*, December 28, 2021, theglobeandmail.com/opinion/article-canada-must -do-its-part-to-defend-the-arctic-that-requires-f-35/.

17 Thomas Juneau, "Canada and Saudi Arabia: A Deeply Flawed but Necessary Partnership," Canadian Global Affairs Institute, July 2016, www.cgai.ca/canada_and_saudi_arabia.

18 "Military Journalism Course," Canadian Global Affairs Institute, accessed August 16, 2022, cgai.ca/military_journalism_course.

19 Attaran, "When Think Tanks Produce Propaganda."

20 John Geddes, "This Op-Ed Is Brought to You By ..." *Maclean's*, November 26, 2007.

21 David Pugliese, interview with the author, August 18, 2022.

22 John Scott Cowan, "War and National Interest," *On Track* 13, no. 2 (Summer 2008): 11, cdainstitute.ca/wp-content/uploads/2022/11 /ontrack13n2.pdf.

23 Kathleen Harris, "960 Regular Force Military Members Reported Sexual Assault in the Past Year, StatsCan Survey Finds," CBC, November 28, 2016, cbc.ca/news/politics/sexual-misconduct-military-survey-1.3868377.

24 Rachel Ward, "Commanding Officers Interfered in Sexual Assault Investigations, Retired Military Police Officer Says," CBC News, March 11, 2021, cbc.ca/news/canada/fifth-estate-military-justice-1.5943931.

25 Ward, "Commanding Officers Interfered in Sexual Assault Investigations."

26 Ken Dilanian et al., "In a Break with the Past, U.S. Is Using Intel to Fight an Info War with Russia, Even When the Intel Isn't Rock Solid," NBC News, April 6, 2022, nbcnews.com/politics/national-security/us-using -declassified-intel-fight-info-war-russia-even-intel-isnt-rock-rcna23014.

27 Julian Borger, "Colin Powell's UN Speech: A Decisive Moment in Undermining US Credibility," *Guardian*, October 18, 2021, theguardian .com/us-news/2021/oct/18/colin-powell-un-security-council-iraq.

28 Craig Whitlock, "At War with the Truth," *Washington Post*, December 9, 2019, washingtonpost.com/graphics/2019/investigations/afghanistan -papers/afghanistan-war-confidential-documents/.

29 Arthur Ponsonby, *Falsehood in War-Time: Propaganda Lies of the First World War* (Crows Nest, AU: George Allen and Unwin, 1928; WWI Resource Centre, n.d.), vlib.us/wwi/resources/archives/texts/t050824i/ponsonby.html.

30 Phillip Knightley, *The First Casualty: The War Correspondent as Hero, Propagandist, and Myth Maker from the Crimea to Vietnam* (New York: Harcourt Brace Jovanovich, 1975), 872–73, Apple Books.

31 John Boyko, *The Devil's Trick: How Canada Fought the Vietnam War* (Toronto: Vintage Canada, 2022), 98.

32 Yves Engler, *Lester Pearson's Peacekeeping: The Truth May Hurt* (Halifax: Fernwood, 2012), 128.

33 Greg Weston, "Canada Offered to Aid Iraq Invasion: WikiLeaks," CBC, May 16, 2011, cbc.ca/news/politics/weston-canada-offered-to-aid-iraq -invasion-wikileaks-1.1062501.

34 Mallory Schwartz, "War on the Air: CBC-TV and Canada's Military, 1952–1992" (Ph.D. diss., University of Ottawa, 2014), 18, ruor.uottawa.ca /bitstream/10393/30345/3/Schwartz_Mallory_2014_thesis.pdf.

35 Sherry Marie Wasilow, "Contemporary Canadian Military/Media Relations: Embedded Reporting during the Afghanistan War" (Ph.D. diss., Carleton University, 2017), 205.

36 Wasilow, "Contemporary Canadian Military/Media Relations," 183.

37 Wasilow, "Contemporary Canadian Military/Media Relations," 147.

38 Steven Chase, "PM's Office Sought 'a Positive Spin' from Reporters," *Globe and Mail*, June 4, 2008, theglobeandmail.com/news/national/pms-office -sought-a-positive-spin-from-reporters/article959572/.

39 Pugliese, interview with the author.

7 SPIES AND THEIR LIES

1 Dailymotion/Newsweek, "Mike Pompeo Says 'We Lied, We Cheated, We Stole' in CIA," Dailymotion, July 23, 2019, dailymotion.com/video/x7e2tr9.

2 Catharine Tunney and Peter Zimonjic, "'Intelligence Is Not Truth': Why Prosecuting Foreign Election Interference Is Rare," CBC News, March 2, 2023, cbc.ca/news/politics/fadden-vigneault-intelligence-bar-evidence -1.6765673.

3 Senate Select Committee on Intelligence, *Committee Study of the Central Intelligence Agency's Detention and Interrogation Program* (Washington, D.C.: United States Senate, 2012, 2014), 8–9, upload.wikimedia.org /wikipedia/commons/a/a2/US_Senate_Report_on_CIA_Detention _Interrogation_Program.pdf.

4 Alfred W. McCoy, *Torture and Impunity* (Madison: University of Wisconsin Press, 2012), 55.

5 McCoy, *Torture and Impunity*, 63.

6 J. Scott, "See, Hear, Feel Nothing Research Shows Bored Brain Acts Queerly," *Montreal Gazette*, January 14, 1954.

7 Memo from George C. Sisler to Zubek, November 6, 1961, Zubek Fonds, box 5, folder 2, University of Manitoba Archives.

8 Ross Henderson, "10 Days of Sheer Monotony," *Winnipeg Tribune*, October 5, 1959.

9 "Brainwashing 'Not Object of Research,'" *Winnipeg Free Press*, March 9, 1972.

10 McCoy, *Torture and Impunity*, 6.

11 Nicholas Horrock, "80 Institutions Used in CIA Mind Study," *New York Times*, August 4, 1977, timesmachine.nytimes.com/timesmachine/1977 /08/04/75678321.html?pageNumber=17.

12 "Report to the Chairman DRB on 1963 activities of the Human Resources Research Advisory Committee by Dr. C.R. Myers, Chair of the Committee, March 6, 1964," Zubek Fonds, box 6, folder 9, University of Manitoba Archives.

13 John Crewdson, "Worldwide Propaganda Network Built by the CIA," *New York Times*, December 26, 1977, timesmachine.nytimes.com /timesmachine/1977/12/26/issue.html.

14 Crewdson, "Worldwide Propaganda Network Built by the CIA."

15 Carl Bernstein, "The CIA and the Media," *Rolling Stone*, October 20, 1977, carlbernstein.com/the-cia-and-the-media-rolling-stone-10-20-1977.

16 John Sawatsky, *Men in the Shadows: The RCMP Security Service* (Toronto: Doubleday Canada, 1980).

17 Sawatsky, *Men in the Shadows*, ix.

18 John Bryden, *Deadly Allies: Canada's Secret War, 1937–1947* (Toronto: McClelland & Stewart, 1989).

19 Dave O'Brien, "North Was Offered for N-Tests," *Winnipeg Free Press*, February 9, 2003, winnipegfreepress.com/historic/2003/02/09/north-was -offered-for-n-tests.

20 O'Brien, "North Was Offered for N-Tests."

21 O'Brien, "North Was Offered for N-Tests."

22 Sissela Bok, *Secrets: On the Ethics of Concealment and Revelation* (New York: Vintage, 1989), 166.

23 Barton Gellman and Ellen Nakashima, "U.S. Spy Agencies Mounted 231 Offensive Cyber-Operations in 2011, Documents Show," *Washington Post*, August 30, 2013, washingtonpost.com/world/national-security/us-spy -agencies-mounted-231-offensive-cyber-operations-in-2011-documents -show/2013/08/30/d090a6ae-119e-11e3-b4cb-fd7ce041d814_story.html.

24 Glenn Greenwald, "How Covert Agents Infiltrate the Internet to Manipulate, Deceive, and Destroy Reputations," The Intercept, February 24, 2014, theintercept.com/2014/02/24/jtrig-manipulation/.

25 Mandeep K. Dhami, "Behavioural Science Support for JTRIG'S Effects and Online HUMINT Operations," The Intercept, June 22, 2015, theintercept.com/document/2015/06/22/behavioural-science-support-jtrig.

26 "JTRIG Tools and Techniques," The Intercept, July 14, 2014, theintercept .com/document/2014/07/14/jtrig-tools-techniques/.

8 SCIENCE OR JUNK?

1 Institute of Diet and Health, "International Press Release: Slim by Chocolate," news release, December 12, 2015, web.archive.org/web /20151212010740/instituteofdiet.com/2015/03/29/international-press -release-slim-by-chocolate/.

2   John Bohannon, "I Fooled Millions into Thinking Chocolate Helps Weight Loss. Here's How," Gizmodo, May 27, 2015, gizmodo.com /i-fooled-millions-into-thinking-chocolate-helps-weight-1707251800.

3   Ann G. Wylie et al., *Final Report* (College Park: University of Maryland, 2016), web.archive.org/web/20160418111821/umdrightnow.umd.edu/sites /umdrightnow.umd.edu/files/16-03-24-report-final.pdf.

4   Jim Waterson, "UK Media Outlets Told Not to Promote Baseless 5G Coronavirus Theories," *Guardian,* April 2, 2020, theguardian.com /media/2020/apr/02/uk-media-outlets-told-not-to-promote-baseless -5g-coronavirus-theories.

5   Catalina Jaramillo, "No Credible Evidence COVID-19 mRNA Vaccines 'Dramatically Increase' Heart Attack Risk, Contrary to Flawed Abstract," FactCheck.org, December 16, 2021, factcheck.org/2021/12/no-credible -evidence-covid-19-mrna-vaccines-dramatically-increase-heart-attack-risk -contrary-to-flawed-abstract/.

6   Gundry MD, gundrymd.com/.

7   Meredith Wadman, "One in Three Scientists Confesses to Having Sinned," *Nature* 435, no. 7043 (June 2005): 718–19, doi.org/10.1038/435718b.

8   Tyler Vigen, "15 Insane Things That Correlate with Each Other," Tylervigen.com, 2009, tylervigen.com/spurious-correlations.

9   P. Sumner et al., "The Association Between Exaggeration in Health Related Science News and Academic Press Releases: Retrospective Observational Study," *BMJ* 349, no. 7 (December 9, 2014), doi.org/10.1136 /bmj.g7015.

10 Wendy Wagner and Thomas O. McGarity, *Bending Science: How Special Interests Corrupt Public Health Research* (Cambridge, MA: Harvard University Press, 2008), 38–9.

11 Richard L. Morrow et al., "Industry Sponsor Influence in Clinical Trial Reporting in Canada: A Qualitative Interview Study," *Clinical Therapeutics* (December 2021), doi.org/10.1016/j.clinthera.2021.11.019.

12 Wagner and McGarity, *Bending Science*, 107.

13 "EPA Says Air, Water Safe Around Attack Sites," CNN, September 19, 2001, cnn.com/2001/US/09/19/rec.wtc.environment/ (page discontinued).

14 Rick Beusse et al., *EPA's Response to the World Trade Center Collapse: Challenges, Successes, and Areas for Improvement* (Washington, D.C.: United States Environmental Protection Agency, 2003), epa.gov/sites /default/files/2015-12/documents/wtc_report_20030821.pdf.

15 Beusse et al., *EPA's Response to the World Trade Center Collapse*.

16 "World Trade Center Health Registry," NYC, nyc.gov/site/911health
/about/wtc-health-registry.page.

17 Joanne Levasseur and Vera-Lynn Kubinec, "Pesticide Residue Found on
Nearly Half of Organic Produce," CBC, January 9, 2014, cbc.ca/news
/canada/manitoba/pesticide-residue-found-on-nearly-half-of-organic
-produce-1.2487712.

18 Joanne Levasseur and Vera-Lynn Kubinec, "Organic Test Results Not Sent
for Followup, CFIA Admits," CBC, January 23, 2014, cbc.ca/news/canada
/manitoba/organic-test-results-not-sent-for-followup-cfia-admits-1.2507481.

19 "Harper Letter Called Kyoto 'Socialist Scheme,'" *Toronto Star*, January 30,
2007, thestar.com/news/2007/01/30/harper_letter_called_kyoto_socialist
_scheme.html.

20 Carol Linnitt, "Harper's Attack on Science: No Science, No Evidence, No
Truth, No Democracy," *Academic Matters* (May 2013), academicmatters.ca
/harpers-attack-on-science-no-science-no-evidence-no-truth-no-democracy/.

21 Jonathan Gatehouse, "When Science Goes Silent," *Maclean's*, May 3, 2013,
macleans.ca/news/canada/when-science-goes-silent/.

22 Suzanne Legault to Calvin Sandborn, 28 February, 2018, Democracy
Watch, accessed September 18, 2022, democracywatch.ca/wp-content
/uploads/InfoCommMuzzlingRulingFeb282018.pdf.

23 "It's Official — the Harper Government Muzzled Scientists. Some Say It's
Still Happening," CBC, March 22, 2018, cbc.ca/news/health/second
-opinion-scientists-muzzled-1.4588913.

24 Jock McCulloch and Geoffrey Tweedale, *Defending the Indefensible: The
Global Asbestos Industry and Its Fight for Survival* (New York: Oxford
University Press, 2008), 1.

25 Canadian Centre for Occupational Health and Safety, *Health and Safety
Report* 11, no. 8 (August 2013) ccohs.ca/newsletters/hsreport/issues/2013/08
/ezine.html#:~:text=However%2C%20according%20to%20a%20recent.

26 Michael Bowker, *Fatal Deception: The Terrifying True Story of How Asbestos
Is Killing America* (New York: Simon & Schuster, 2003), 99.

27 Bowker, *Fatal Deception*, 217.

28 Kathleen Ruff, "Asbestos: A Continuing Failure of Ethics by McGill
University," *International Journal of Occupational and Environmental
Health* 20, no. 1 (January 2014): 1–3, doi.org/10.1179/107735251
3z.000000000102.

29 "Minutes of the 95th Meeting of the Quebec Asbestos Mining Association"
(Chateau Frontenac, QC, November 29, 1965), contributed by Jim Morris,

Center for Public Integrity, documentcloud.org/documents/3034-qama -minutes.

30 "Health Hazards, Pollution Termed Controlled After Millions Spent by Asbestos Industry," *Globe and Mail*, October 23, 1971.

31 "Fatal Deception," CBC, 2012, cbc.ca/player/play/2196289159.

32 McGill Communications, "Report Finds No Evidence of Research Misconduct," news release, October 17, 2012, mcgill.ca/newsroom/channels /news/report-finds-no-evidence-research-misconduct-218574.

33 World Health Organization, "Elimination of Asbestos-Related Diseases," March 1, 2014.

34 Katrina Arabe, "Does Industry Money Taint Research?," Thomas, August 15, 2005, thomasnet.com/insights/imt/2005/08/15/does_industry_m/.

35 Wagner and McGarity, *Bending Science*, 221–22.

36 André Picard, interview with the author, June 21, 2022.

9 THE POWER OF POLLS

1 David Larkins, "Don't Open Up Portage and Main: CAA," *Winnipeg Sun*, August 25, 2016, winnipegsun.com/2016/08/25/dont-open-up-portage -and-main-caa.

2 "Opening Portage and Main to Pedestrians Not a Priority: Survey," ChrisD.ca, August 25, 2016, chrisd.ca/2016/08/25/portage-main -pedestrians-traffic-survey-winnipeg/.

3 Jacques Marcoux, "The Perils of Taking Information at Face Value," CBC, August 29, 2016, cbc.ca/news/canada/manitoba/perils-of-taking -information-at-face-value-1.3738561.

4 Mark Pack, *Polling UnPacked: The History, Uses and Abuses of Political Opinion Polls* (London: Reaktion Books, 2022), 13.

5 Pack, *Polling UnPacked*, 15–16.

6 Will Jennings and Christopher Wlezien, "Election Polling Errors Across Time and Space," *Nature Human Behaviour* 2, no. 4 (March 12, 2018): 276–83, doi.org/10.1038/s41562-018-0315-6.

7 W. Joseph Campbell, *Lost in a Gallup: Polling Failure in U.S. Presidential Elections* (Oakland: University of California Press, 2020), 37–8.

8 Dick Leonard, "Polls and the Use of Leading Questions," Politico, May 2, 2007, politico.eu/article/polls-and-the-use-of-leading-questions/.

9 Jelke G. Bethlehem, *Understanding Public Opinion Polls* (Boca Raton, FL: CRC Press, 2018), 32–3.

10 Burdett Loomis, "From Hootie to Harry (and Louise): Polling and Interest Groups," *Brookings Review* 21, no. 3 (2003): 45, doi.org/10.2307/20081120.

11 Loomis, "From Hootie to Harry (and Louise)."

12 Andrew Russell, "Defund the Police? Canadians Split Along Generational Lines, Ipsos Poll Suggests," Global News, July 25, 2020, globalnews.ca /news/7213811/defund-the-police-canada-ipsos-poll/

13 Ted Rutland, "Government Poll Tried to Skew Public Opinion Against Defunding the Police," The Breach, April 14, 2022, breachmedia.ca /government-poll-tried-to-skew-public-opinion-against-defunding-the-police/.

14 Rutland, "Government Poll Tried to Skew Public Opinion."

15 Sam Samson, "City of Winnipeg Asks Public for Feedback on Proposed Police Funding Models, but None Include Budget Cut," CBC, January 7, 2022, cbc.ca/news/canada/manitoba/winnipeg-police-budget-models -public-opinion-1.6306762.

16 Mary Agnes Welch, *Police Funding Model Preference* (Winnipeg: City of Winnipeg/Probe Research, 2021), engage.winnipeg.ca/26397/widgets /106994/documents/76888.

17 Welch, *Police Funding Model Preference.*

18 Canada News Wire, "Ten Million Canadians at Risk for Serious Side Effects from Over-the-Counter Pain Medications," February 1, 2006, fdanews.com/articles/84231-ten-million-canadians-at-risk-for-serious-side -effects-from-over-the-counter-pain-medications.

19 Joanna Frketich, "Too Many Popping Pain Pills 'Like Candy': Over-the-Counter Meds Being Abused: Survey," *Hamilton Spectator*, February 2, 2006.

20 "Health Canada Bars Bextra's Return," *Globe and Mail*, December 16, 2005, theglobeandmail.com/amp/life/health-canada-bars-bextras-return /article1132224/.

21 Steve Buist, Luma Muhtadie, and Joan Walters, "Like a Punch in the Gut; Blind Faith — Second of a Five-Part Series," *Hamilton Spectator*, June 27, 2005.

22 Stephanie Saul, "Pfizer to Settle Claims over Bextra and Celebrex," *New York Times*, October 7, 2008.

23 "Pfizer Sells OTC Business to J&J for $16.6 Billion," IndustryWeek, June 26, 2006, industryweek.com/leadership/companies-executives/article/21938645 /pfizer-sells-otc-business-to-jj-for-166-billion.

24 Conway Fraser, "Behind the Headlines — Risky Drugs," CBC Television, Canada Now National, March 17, 2006.

25 Andrew Holtz, "Update: Conflict of Interest/Funding Disclosure Missing from Half of News Releases We've Reviewed — A Case Study on Why That's Important," HealthNewsReview, August 18, 2016, web.archive.org /web/20180324194249/https://www.healthnewsreview.org/2016/08/conflict -of-interest-disclosures-absent-from-half-of-news-releases-weve-reviewed-a -case-study-on-why-thats-important.

26 Adam G. Dunn et al., "Conflict of Interest Disclosure in Biomedical Research: A Review of Current Practices, Biases, and the Role of Public Registries in Improving Transparency," *Research Integrity and Peer Review* 1, no. 1 (May 3, 2016), doi.org/10.1186/s41073-016-0006-7.

27 "Guidance: Opinion Polls, Surveys, Questionnaires, Votes and 'Straw Polls,'" bbc.com, accessed October 5, 2022, bbc.com/editorialguidelines /guidance/surveys#pollsatelectiontimes.

28 "Guidance," BBC.

29 Michael Rothfeld, Rob Barry, and Joe Palazzolo, "Cohen Hired IT Firm to Rig Early CNBC, Drudge Polls to Favor Trump," *Wall Street Journal*, January 17, 2019, wsj.com/articles/poll-rigging-for-trump-and-creating -womenforcohen-one-it-firms-work-order-11547722801.

30 "Journalistic Standards and Practices," CBC, 2020, cbc.radio-canada.ca/en /vision/governance/journalistic-standards-and-practices.

31 Jennifer McGuire, "Responsible Reporting on Polls," Editor's Blog, CBC, February 5, 2014, cbc.ca/newsblogs/community/editorsblog/2014/02 /responsible-reporting-on-polls.html.

32 Pam Palmater, "Indigenous Rights Are Not Conditional on Public Opinion," *Maclean's*, June 8, 2018, macleans.ca/opinion/indigenous -rights-are-not-conditional-on-public-opinion/.

33 Palmater, "Indigenous Rights Are Not Conditional on Public Opinion."

10 THE AGE OF INFLUENCERS

1 Claire Wardle, "Understanding Information Disorder," *First Draft*, September 22, 2020, firstdraftnews.org/long-form-article/understanding-information-disorder/.

2 "About OpenAI," openai.com/about.

3 John Paul Tasker, "'That's Not How We Do Things in Canada': Trudeau Stops Short of Calling Trump's Tweets 'Racist,'" CBC, July 16, 2019, cbc .ca/news/politics/trudeau-trump-tweets-1.5212019.

4 Caroline Orr, "Twitter Bots Boosted the Trending #TrudeauMustGo Hashtag," Canada's National Observer, July 18, 2019, nationalobserver.com /2019/07/18/news/twitter-bots-boosted-trending-trudeaumustgo-hashtag.

5   Julia Cagé, Nicolas Hervé, and Béatrice Mazoyer, "Social Media Influence Mainstream Media: Evidence from Two Billion Tweets" (discussion paper no. 17358, Centre for Economic Policy Research, London, June 5, 2022), cepr.org/publications/dp17358.

6   Niky Kumari, "Citing Social Media as a News Source in Mainstream Media: An Analysis of Indian Newspapers," *International Journal of Communication and Media Studies* 9, no. 3 (June 2019): 37–50.

7   Yariv Tsfati et al., "Causes and Consequences of Mainstream Media Dissemination of Fake News: Literature Review and Synthesis," *Annals of the International Communication Association* 44, no. 2 (April 2, 2020): 157–73, doi.org/10.1080/23808985.2020.1759443.

8   Leif Larsen and Gosia Sawicka, "Twitter Followers Available on the Open Market," CBC News, January 21, 2013.

9   Nicholas Confessore et al., "The Follower Factory," *New York Times*, January 27, 2018, nytimes.com/interactive/2018/01/27/technology/social-media-bots.html.

10 Sarah Perez, "FTC Settles with Devumi, a Company That Sold Fake Followers, for $2.5M," *TechCrunch*, October 22, 2019, techcrunch.com/2019/10/22/ftc -settles-with-devumi-a-company-that-sold-fake-followers-for-2-5m/.

11 Megan McCluskey, "Elon Musk Wants to Rid Twitter of 'Spam Bots.' Nearly Half His Followers Are Fake," *Time*, April 28, 2022, time.com /6171726/elon-musk-fake-followers.

12 Laurie Sullivan, "Google Found to Have Highest Number of Fake Reviews," MediaPost, October 28, 2021, mediapost.com/publications /article/368189/google-found-to-have-highest-number-of-fake-review.html.

13 Kathryn Dean, "Google's Negligence on Fake Reviews Is Yet Another Reason to Take Action Against Big Tech," *Toronto Star*, June 7, 2021, thestar.com/opinion/contributors/2021/06/07/googles-negligence-on-fake -reviews-is-yet-another-reason-to-take-action-against-big-tech.html.

14 Sophia Harris, "Bell Says Positive Employee-Planted Reviews Will Stop, but Critics Unsure," CBC, November 28, 2014, cbc.ca/news/business /bell-says-positive-employee-planted-reviews-will-stop-but-critics -unsure-1.2852809.

15 "Croatian Wikipedia Disinformation Assessment-2021," Wikimedia, accessed November 8, 2022, meta.wikimedia.org/wiki/Croatian _Wikipedia_Disinformation_Assessment-2021.

16 Rachel Cheung, "A Bored Chinese Housewife Spent Years Falsifying Russian History on Wikipedia," *Vice*, July 13, 2022, vice.com/en/article /pkgbwm/chinese-woman-fake-russian-history-wikipedia.

17 "Croatian Wikipedia Disinformation Assessment-2021."

18 Soroush Vosoughi, Deb Roy, and Sinan Aral, "The Spread of True and False News Online," *Science* 359, no. 6380 (March 9, 2018): 1146–51, doi .org/10.1126/science.aap9559.

19 Ben Nimmo and Mike Torrey, *Taking Down Coordinated Inauthentic Behavior from Russia and China* (Menlo Park, CA: Meta, 2022), politico .eu/wp-content/uploads/2022/09/27/NEAR-FINAL-DRAFT-CIB-Report -ChinaRussia-Sept-2022.pdf.

20 Muyi Xiao, Paul Mozur, and Gray Beltran, "Buying Influence: How China Manipulates Facebook and Twitter," *New York Times*, December 20, 2021, nytimes.com/interactive/2021/12/20/technology/china-facebook-twitter -influence-manipulation.html.

21 Nick Fielding and Ian Cobain, "Revealed: US Spy Operation That Manipulates Social Media," *Guardian*, March 17, 2011, theguardian.com /technology/2011/mar/17/us-spy-operation-social-networks.

22 John Markoff, "Automated Pro-Trump Bots Overwhelmed Pro-Clinton Messages, Researchers Say," *New York Times*, November 17, 2016, nytimes .com/2016/11/18/technology/automated-pro-trump-bots-overwhelmed -pro-clinton-messages-researchers-say.html.

23 Jacinda Santora, "Key Influencer Marketing Statistics to Drive Your Strategy in 2023," *Influencer Marketing Hub*, January 11, 2023, influencermarketinghub.com/influencer-marketing-statistics/.

24 "Are You a Social Media Influencer? Here's What You Need to Know," Canada Revenue Agency, March 2, 2022, canada.ca/en/revenue-agency /news/newsroom/tax-tips/tax-tips-2022/are-you-a-social-media-influencer -heres-what-you-need-to-know.html.

25 Ella Alexander, "Move Over Coachella, There's a New Festival That All the Models Will Attend in 2017," *Harper's Bazaar*, January 5, 2017, harpersbazaar.com/uk/culture/culture-news/news/a39192/what-is-fyre -festival-bahamas/ (page discontinued).

26 Nick Bilton, "Exclusive: The Leaked Fyre Festival Pitch Deck Is Beyond Parody," *Vanity Fair*, May 1, 2017, vanityfair.com/news/2017/05/fyre -festival-pitch-deck.

27 Gwen Aviles, "Kendall Jenner to Pay $90,000 Settlement for Promoting Fyre Festival," NBC News, May 21, 2020, nbcnews.com/pop-culture/pop -culture-news/kendall-jenner-pay-90-000-settlement-promoting-fyre -festival-n1212011.

28 Sara Koonar, interview with the author, November 10, 2022.

29 "FIFA World Cup Qatar 2022," NeoReach, n.d., neoreach.com/case
    -studies/fifa/.

30 *Influencer Ad Disclosure on Social Media: A Report into Influencers' Rate of
    Compliance of Ad Disclosure on Instagram* (London: Advertising Standards
    Authority, 2021), asa.org.uk/static/dd740667-6fe0-4fa7
    -80de3e4598417912/Influencer-Monitoring-Report-March2021.pdf.

31 "How TRIBE's Mike Bloomberg Partnership Influenced Political Ad
    Policy Change in Just 7 Days," Tribe, 2020, tribegroup.co/blog
    /mike-bloomberg-partnership-influences-political-ad-policy-change.

32 Stephanie Lai, "Campaigns Pay Influencers to Carry Their Messages,
    Skirting Political Ad Rules," *New York Times*, November 2, 2022, nytimes
    .com/2022/11/02/us/elections/influencers-political-ads-tiktok-instagram.html

33 "NextGen America Launches Hot Girls Vote Campaign Targeting Massive
    Youth Voting Bloc," NextGen America, accessed November 11, 2022,
    nextgenamerica.org/press/nextgen-america-launches-hot-girls-vote
    -campaign-targeting-massive-youth-voting-bloc/.

34 Isaac Stanley-Becker, "Pro-Trump Youth Group Enlists Teens in Secretive
    Campaign Likened to a 'Troll Farm,' Prompting Rebuke by Facebook and
    Twitter," *Washington Post*, September 15, 2020, washingtonpost.com
    /politics/turning-point-teens-disinformation-trump/2020/09/15/c84091ae
    -f20a-11ea-b796-2dd09962649c_story.html..

35 "Influencer Media," *Turning Point USA*, accessed November 11, 2022,
    tpusa.com/influencermedia.

36 Stephanie Levitz, "Liberals Pin Their Hopes on Social Media Influencers
    to Help Sway Voters," *Toronto Star*, June 4, 2021, thestar.com/politics
    /federal/2021/06/04/liberals-pin-their-hopes-on-social-media-influencers
    -to-help-sway-voters.html.

37 Taylor Lorenz, "To Fight Vaccine Lies, Authorities Recruit an 'Influencer
    Army,'" *New York Times*, August 1, 2021, nytimes.com/2021/08/01
    /technology/vaccine-lies-influencer-army.html.

38 "Video Featuring Social Media Influencers — CEO Appearance:
    Supplementary Estimates (B) 2019–20," Elections Canada, October 18,
    2022, elections.ca/content.aspx?section=abo&dir=comp/mar1220
    &document=influcam&lang=e.

39 Bill Curry, "Elections Canada Cancels Influencer Campaign After
    Discovering Partisan Comments," *Globe and Mail*, June 20, 2019,
    theglobeandmail.com/politics/article-elections-canada-cancels-influencer
    -campaign-after-discovering/.

40 Mary Charleson, "Influencer Marketing Versus Journalist Influence," Five-Minute Marketing, October 4, 2018, fiveminutemarketing.com/2018/10/influencer-marketing-versus-journalist-influence/.

11 FIGHTING BACK

1 Allan Thompson, interview with the author, November 15, 2022.
2 Thompson, interview with the author.
3 Tara Haelle, "Press Release Reporting Is Irresponsible — Especially in a Pandemic," Association of Health Care Journalists, August 6, 2020, healthjournalism.org/blog/2020/08/press-release-reporting-is-irresponsible-especially-in-a-pandemic/.
4 Cision Ltd., "2021 Global State of the Media," 2021, 4.
5 David Barstow, "Behind TV Analysts, Pentagon's Hidden Hand," *New York Times*, April 20, 2008, sec. U.S., nytimes.com/2008/04/20/us/20generals.html.
6 Pugliese, interview with the author.
7 Harvey Cashore et al., "Seatbelts on School Buses Could Have Prevented Thousands of Injuries, Numerous Deaths," CBC, October 14, 2018, cbc.ca/news/canada/school-bus-seatbelts-1.4826500.
8 "'Error' in Data Allowing Children to Bodycheck," CBC News, January 14, 2003, cbc.ca/news/canada/error-in-data-allowing-children-to-bodycheck-1.387854.
9 Duncan McCue, *Decolonizing Journalism: A Guide to Reporting in Indigenous Communities* (Toronto: Oxford University Press, 2022), 7–9.
10 Truth and Reconciliation Commission of Canada, *Canada's Residential Schools: The Final Report of the Truth and Reconciliation Commission of Canada*, vol. 6, *Reconciliation* (Montreal: McGill-Queen's University Press, 2015), 194, publications.gc.ca/collections/collection_2015/trc/IR4-9-6-2015-eng.pdf.
11 McCue, *Decolonizing Journalism*, x.
12 Paul Samyn, "An Apology for Marginalizing People of Colour; and a Promise to Atone for Our Past," *Winnipeg Free Press*, July 3, 2020, winnipegfreepress.com/featured/2020/07/03/an-apology-for-marginalizing-people-of-colour-and-a-promise-to-atone-for-our-past.
13 *Canadian Newsroom Diversity Survey* (Toronto: Canadian Association of Journalists, 2022), caj.ca/wp-content/uploads/Canadian-Newsroom-Diversity-Survey-2022.pdf.
14 "Calls to Action," Canadian Association of Black Journalists, January 28, 2020, cabj.news/calls-to-action.

15 Duncan McCue, "On Reconciliation and the Canadian Media," Reporting in Indigenous Communities, December 18, 2020, riic.ca/on-reconciliation-and-the-canadian-media/.

16 Jon Horler, "Investigation: Canadian News Media Dominated by Corporate Lobbyists," Ricochet, December 2, 2021, ricochet.media/en/3821/investigation-canadian-news-media-is-dominated-by-corporate-lobbyists.

17 Jack Nagler, "Who Are Those Commentators, Anyway?," CBC, February 17, 2021, cbc.radio-canada.ca/en/ombudsman/reviews/Who_Are_Those_Commentators_Anyway.

18 Jesse Brown, interview with the author, November 16, 2022.

19 Daniel Okrent, "Weapons of Mass Destruction? Or Mass Distraction?" *New York Times*, May 30, 2004, nytimes.com/2004/05/30/weekinreview/the-public-editor-weapons-of-mass-destruction-or-mass-distraction.html.

20 Privy Council Office, "Commission of Inquiry into the Actions of Canadian Officials in Relation to Maher Arar," Library and Archives Canada, 2006, epe.lac-bac.gc.ca/100/200/301/pco-bcp/commissions-ef/oconnor2006-eng/oconnor2006-eng.htm.

21 John Pilger, *Tell Me No Lies: Investigative Journalism and Its Triumphs* (London: Jonathan Cape, 2004), xv.

22 "Correction: Russia-Ukraine-War Story," AP News, November 16, 2022, apnews.com/article/russia-ukraine-war-zelenskyy-kherson-9202c032cf3a5c22761ee71b52ff9d52.

23 Malachy Browne, interview with the author, November 16, 2022.

24 Malachy Browne, David Botti, and Haley Willis, "Satellite Images Show Bodies Lay in Bucha for Weeks, Despite Russian Claims," *New York Times*, April 4, 2022, nytimes.com/2022/04/04/world/europe/bucha-ukraine-bodies.html.

25 Evan Hill et al., "Video: Gaza's Deadly Night: How Israeli Airstrikes Killed 44 People," *New York Times*, June 24, 2021, nytimes.com/video/world/middleeast/100000007787471/israel-airstrikes-gaza.html.

26 "About Us," The Narwhal, n.d., thenarwhal.ca/about-us/.

27 Thompson, interview with the author.

28 Emma Gilchrist, "Opinion: Canada Should Be Supporting Journalism's Future, Not Its Past," *Globe and Mail*, March 2, 2021, theglobeandmail.com/opinion/article-canada-should-be-supporting-journalisms-future-not-its-past/.

Index

Index

Index page

Index

Index

Tribe, 190
  See also public relations industry
Trucking Information Service, 22
  See also Bernays, Edward
Trudeau, Justin, 71–76, 79, 179, 193
Trump, Donald
  election polls, 162
  election talking points, 191
  fact-checking and, 180
  indictment, 66
  Kellyanne Conway and, 166
  lying, 69–70
  Michael Cohen and, 173
  statement about four
    congresswomen, 179
  unproven Covid-19 remedies, 145
  use of bots during election, 185
Trust Me, I'm Lying (Holiday), 19
  See also public relations industry
Truth and Reconciliation Commission,
  202, 204
Turner, John, 81
  See also *Winnipeg Free Press*
Turner, Stansfield. *See* CIA
Turning Point USA, 191
  See also public relations industry
Tyee, 212

Ukraine war with Russia, 4, 14, 119–20,
  192, 200, 209–10
Uniroyal Chemical Company, 122–23
United Fruit Company. *See* Bernays,
  Edward
United Mine Workers. *See* Ludlow
  Massacre
universities supported by DND, 114
University of Manitoba, 130, 132
University of Maryland, 144–45
University of Toronto, 40
University of Victoria Environmental
  Law Centre, 152
U.S. Army Chemical Corps, 138

U.S. Gypsum. *See* asbestos
USA Today, 89

Vance, Jonathan, 109, 111, 117–18
Vanity Fair, 187, 190
Veldhuis, Nils. *See* Fraser Institute
video news releases (VNRs). *See* Center
  for Media and Democracy
Vietnam Council on Foreign Relations,
  134
  See also CIA
Vietnam War, 13, 39, 113, 120, 122–24
Vioxx. *See* Food and Drug
  Administration
Volkswagen, 28

Wagner, Wendy, 148–49, 157
Walker, Michael, 48–49
Wall Street Journal, 2, 8
Washington Post, 21, 69, 83, 120–21,
  135, 140, 191
Wasilow, Sherry, 124–25
Watson, Paul. *See* Cold War
Wet'suwet'en, 101
White House Council on
  Environmental Quality, 150
Wikileaks, 112–13, 123
Wikipedia, 20, 182–83
Williams, Commander R.J. *See* CIA
Williamson, John. *See* Canadian
  Taxpayers Federation
Wilson, Michael, 79–82
Wilson-Raybould, Jody, 72–74
Winnipeg Free Press
  apology for colonial and racist past,
    202–3
  Brian Pallister stories, 78–79
  chemical spraying story, 138
  Michael Wilson story, 80–81
  Otto Lang story, 11–12
  Patrik Mathews story, 109
  Peter Nygard story, 38

About the Author

Photo by Michelle Rosner

BORN IN WINNIPEG, CECIL ROSNER has been a journalist for more than four decades, concentrating primarily on reporting and supervising investigative journalism projects. He has taught the principles of investigative work across the country and internationally and is the author of the definitive history of the genre in Canada — *Behind the Headlines: A History of Investigative Journalism in Canada*, published by Oxford University Press. His first job in journalism was with the *Winnipeg Free Press*, and his last full-time position was as executive producer of *The Fifth Estate*, CBC's flagship investigative journalism program. That capped a career of nearly thirty-two years with the public broadcaster. His journalism has won many awards, including Michener, Gemini, and New York and Columbus Film Festival prizes. In 2019 he was given a lifetime achievement award by the Radio Television Digital News Association. He is currently an adjunct professor at the University of Winnipeg.